Touring the
Shenandoah Valley Backroads

Other Titles in John F. Blair's *Touring the Backroads*® Series

Touring the Backroads of North Carolina's Lower Coast by Daniel W. Barefoot
Touring the Backroads of North Carolina's Upper Coast by Daniel W. Barefoot
Touring the Carolinas' Civil War Sites by Clint Johnson
Touring the East Tennessee Backroads by Carolyn Sakowski
Touring the Middle Tennessee Backroads by Robert Brandt
Touring North Carolina's Revolutionary War Sites by Daniel W. Barefoot
Touring South Carolina's Revolutionary War Sites by Daniel W. Barefoot
Touring Virginia and West Virginia's Civil War Sites Clint Johnson
Touring the Western North Carolina Backroads by Carolyn Sakowski

Second Edition

Touring the
Shenandoah Valley Backroads

Andrea Sutcliffe

JOHN F. BLAIR
PUBLISHER
Winston-Salem, North Carolina

JOHN F. BLAIR
P U B L I S H E R
1406 Plaza Drive
Winston-Salem, North Carolina 27103
www.blairpub.com

Manufactured in the United States of America

Images on front cover—
Top: Route 691, atop Great North Mountain near Jerome, Virginia
Middle left: Field near Hidden Valley Recreation Area, Bath County, Virginia
Middle right: Covered bridge between Orkney Springs and Fulks Run, Virginia
Bottom: Sunflowers near Martinsburg, West Virginia

Library of Congress Cataloging-in-Publication Data

Sutcliffe, Andrea.
    Touring the Shenandoah Valley backroads / by Andrea Sutcliffe. — 2nd ed.
        p. cm.
    Includes bibliographical references and index.
    ISBN-13: 978-0-89587-386-6 (alk. paper)
    ISBN-10: 0-89587-386-9 (alk. paper)
    ISBN 978-0-89587-393-4
    1. Shenandoah River Valley (Va. and W. Va.)--Tours. 2. Automobile travel—Shenandoah River Valley (Va. and W. Va.)—Guidebooks. I. Title.
    F232.S5S88 2010
    917.55'90444—dc22
                        2010025516

DESIGN BY DEBRA LONG HAMPTON

To the memory of my father, Edward A. Johnson,
whose idea of a good backroad was one
with grass growing down the middle

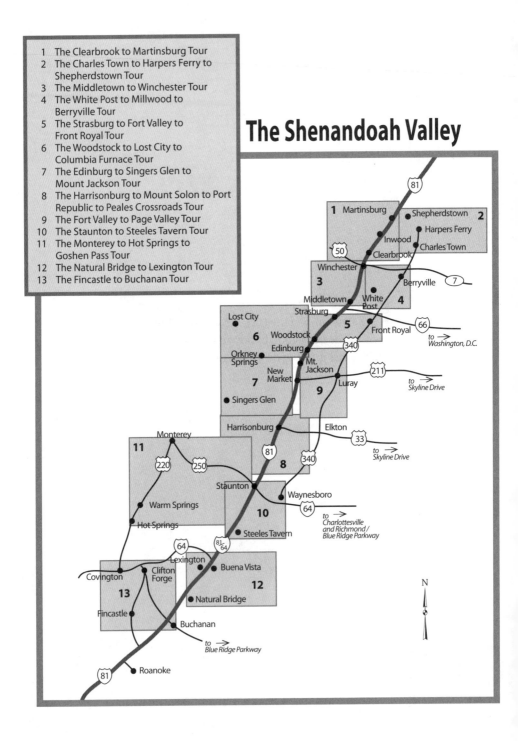

The Shenandoah Valley

Contents

Preface

The Shenandoah Valley has changed a bit since the first edition of this book was published in 1999. On the plus side, many more historic structures have been saved and restored, both as public places and as private homes. Several new museums have opened—most notably the beautiful Museum of the Shenandoah Valley in Winchester. On the minus side, several historic buildings have been lost forever, a result of fire, termites, neglect, or development. A growing population has brought increased prosperity to some of the larger towns. The downside is that many farm fields now sprout suburban-style homes instead of soybeans and corn.

The good news is that the Valley's backroads remain scenic and lightly traveled. From Harpers Ferry to Roanoke, the routes in this book offer travelers an easy way to exit Interstate 81 and transport themselves back to a slower pace of life. Many of the tours in this book go for miles without passing a single billboard, cell-phone tower, fast-food place, or gas station (be forewarned). Instead, they take backroads wanderers through lush forests, over rolling green hills and fields, around apple and peach orchards, across sparkling rivers and streams, past stunning mountain and valley vistas, and into towns and villages that have retained their old look and feel. In these places, the fascinating stories of the Shenandoah Valley's history wait to be discovered.

The Shenandoah Valley, long a hunting ground for Native Americans, was first settled by European immigrants in the 1730s, when English, German, Swiss, and Scotch-Irish families came into the Valley seeking fertile farmland and religious freedom.

In the 1750s, Valley settlers endured the horrors of the vicious random attacks that characterized the French and Indian War. During that same period, George Washington launched his military and political career in Winchester. Twenty years later, Valley men volunteered in great numbers to fight in the American Revolution. Several became well-known generals in the Continental Army. After the Revolution, the Virginia inventor James Rumsey helped lead the coming transportation revolution when he tested what some say was the first operating steamboat in America, and perhaps the world, on the Potomac River in Shepherdstown in 1787.

By the 1800s, the Valley's agricultural richness proved important in meeting the growing nation's food needs. One of its sons, Cyrus McCormick, invented the Virginia reaper, the machine that sparked a worldwide revolution in agriculture.

In 1862 and 1864, the Civil War came to the Shenandoah Valley, with several crucial battles fought here, many led by Valley hero Stonewall Jackson. "The Burning" by Union forces in 1864—the aim of which was to destroy the "Breadbasket of the Confederacy"—was a disaster of major proportions for the people in the central part of the Valley.

In the decades after the war, most of the Valley enjoyed an economic boom, leading to the construction of numerous mineral springs resorts in the mountain areas. It was then that the Shenandoah Valley became a popular summer getaway for East Coast city-dwellers.

For a while in the late 1800s and early 1900s, industry took hold in several places, often to the detriment of the Valley's natural resources. Today, the forests and rivers have recovered considerably, and industrial development in the Valley is limited mainly to light manufacturing.

As in the other volumes in this series, the goal of this book is to bring history to life for backroads travelers by pointing out significant places and events along the way. The past rests here in layers, many of which are visible if you look closely enough. In some spots, with just a little imagination, you can mentally transport yourself back in time 100 years or more.

In every tour, you'll see homes, churches, and buildings that date to the 1700s and 1800s. Most are still in use. Many log homes have long been covered with clapboard siding or stucco (or worse, asbestos shingles), but their limestone foundations reveal the antiquity of their construction. The placement of chimneys in many of these old homes gives a clue to the ancestry of their builders: end chimneys were preferred by the British, while central chimneys were the style of the Germans. On these backroads, you'll see countless old mills, barns, and outbuildings—especially old stone or log springhouses and smokehouses. As long as these structures are preserved by caring owners, we will not forget that people once got by—not really that long ago—without refrigerators and supermarkets.

Now for a word about the research. In some locales, historical records were quite good. Historian John W. Wayland, who wrote many books on the area in the first half of the 20th century, and Samuel Kercheval, who in the early 1800s established himself as the Valley's first historian, provided a good base for my initial research. At the local level, recorded histories have been produced largely through the efforts of area citizens working alone or with historical societies to capture the stories of the past. Some of those accounts appear to be more complete and accurate than others. Sometimes, it was difficult to determine which account of a historical event was the correct one. In those cases, I tried to find additional information and then make a judgment call. More times than I cared to, however, I had to add caveats like "According to local legend" and "So the story goes." My overall purpose was to create a general guide describing points of interest and local lore for travelers, not an academic history.

I routed the tours with history in mind, while also considering the scenic beauty of the drive and the time required to stay within the limits of a day trip. I could not include every town and historic site in the Shenandoah Valley and so had to make some hard choices. Often, if a historic building or site was too far off a tour's main route, or could not be seen from the road, I chose to leave it out. If you are interested in a more detailed history of any part of the Valley, please refer to the bibliography for suggested books, or contact one of the many county historical societies and museums listed in the appendix.

My father, a tireless backroads traveler, was well known in our family for saying, "Never go back the way you came." In designing these tours, I followed his advice. Most take the form of a circle that ends not far from where it began. But if your mind is agile enough to reverse directions, you may want to try, perhaps on another day, going back the way you came. I can guarantee that you will experience a totally different view and see things you missed the first time.

Known by various names over the centuries—the Indian Trail, the Indian Road, the (Great) Wagon Road, the (Great) Philadelphia Wagon Road, the (Great) Valley Road, the Valley Turnpike, the Valley Pike—today's U.S. 11 (or Route 11, as the locals call it) forms the backbone of the Shenandoah Valley. This road is one of the most historic routes in America. You'll encounter it often on these tours, as it passes through or near most of the Valley's major towns and cities. In the early 1700s, the Valley's first settlers used the Indian Trail to make their way here from Pennsylvania. For a century, the road was the best way for tens of thousands of settlers heading west to reach the Cumberland Gap. For many years in the 1800s, it was considered the South's best "highway." After large stretches were macadamized (meaning surfaced with broken bits of rock, not paved with asphalt) by the 1840s, the Valley Turnpike gave farmers and businesses a (relatively) quick and easy way to move their products to markets in Philadelphia and Baltimore. During the Civil War, though, it became an artery of war, a trail of tragedy and devastation. In 1926, as cars and trucks replaced horses and wagons, the Valley Pike became part of the major north-south federal road named U.S. 11, which still stretches today from the Canadian border in upstate New York all the way down to New Orleans.

Interstate 81, which was built to replace U.S. 11 as a major highway in the 1960s, runs parallel to U.S. 11 throughout the Valley. And so, for the traveler's convenience, Interstate 81 is the jumping-off point for all the tours in this book. They are arranged geographically from north to south, for a total distance on I-81 of about 200 miles from Martinsburg, West Virginia, to just north of Roanoke,

Virginia. Many of the tours end near the start of the next one, which will allow you to connect two or more tours in an area if you have the time and the inclination. Most roads are paved and well-maintained U.S., state, and county roads. In a few instances, the tours include short stretches of gravel roads, but you won't need a four-wheel-drive vehicle for any of them except perhaps on snowy winter days.

Driving instructions appear in italics. To give an idea of distances to turns and tour stops, mileages are given in tenths of a mile. Please keep in mind that these are approximate and that odometer readings vary from car to car.

Many of the museums and historic attractions mentioned are staffed by volunteers and have limited hours of operation. Some are closed during the winter months. For those reasons, it's a good idea to call ahead to confirm opening and closing times. Addresses and phone numbers are listed in the appendix. The Shenandoah Valley Travel Association and local visitor centers will be happy to provide information about food, lodging, outdoor activities, and commercial attractions (such as the many beautiful caverns in the area), which are not covered in this book.

Most people visit the Shenandoah Valley in the summer or early fall. But touring these backroads in winter or spring has its rewards. In the late fall and winter, when the leaves are off the trees, you'll be able to see old homes and buildings that are hidden at other times of the year. In early spring, the forests are dappled with the delicate white flowers of dogwood trees. By May and June, the pink blooms of mountain laurel and rhododendron add bursts of color to the green forests. Whenever you visit, you'll be surprised at the scenic mountain landscapes and the unspoiled wilderness that can be found not far from Philadelphia, Washington, D.C., Baltimore, Richmond, and Norfolk.

I could not have written this book without the help of staff members, librarians, and volunteers at the following places: the Shenandoah County Library, the Rockingham County Library, the Harrisonburg–Rockingham County Historical Society, the Society of Port Republic Preservationists, the Rockbridge Public Library, the Roanoke Public Library, the Augusta County Public Library, the Handley Library in Winchester, the Martinsburg Public Library, the James Madison University Library, the Rockbridge Historical Society, the Strasburg Museum, the Jefferson County Museum, the Bath Historical Society, and the Library of Congress. Thanks also go to Carolyn Sakowski at John F. Blair, Publisher, for giving me the chance to revise this book. I also must thank my dear friend, Lynn McFadden, who accompanied me on many of these tours as I re-drove them in 2009; her unflagging enthusiasm for the project and her willingness to drive a stretch of road more than once to get the directions right were much appreciated. Finally, thanks to my husband, Ed Sutcliffe, who cheerfully helped me in many ways. His love, support, and good humor held fast no matter how many times I asked him to turn around to double-check a sign or pull over to take a picture.

Touring the
Shenandoah Valley Backroads

The Clearbrook to Martinsburg Tour

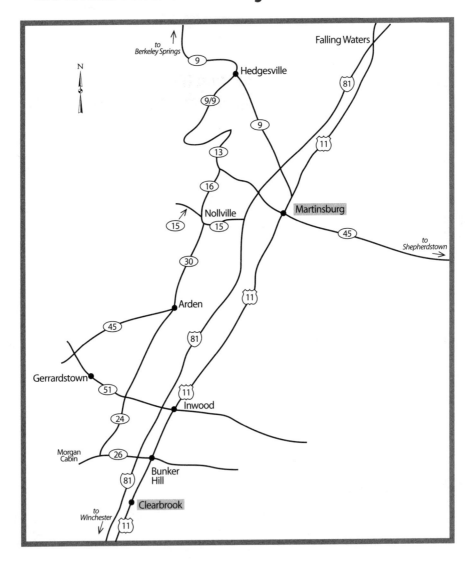

TOUR **1**
The Clearbrook to Martinsburg Tour

This tour begins north of Winchester on U.S. 11 in an area of early Quaker settlement. It passes a Civil War battle site at Stephenson and stops to visit a 1700s Quaker stone church, Hopewell Meeting, near Clearbrook, once the center of a thriving woolen industry in this area. From there, it crosses into West Virginia and heads west, passing another early settlement, Bunker Hill. It pauses at the restored log cabin of one of the area's first settlers and then winds through picturesque apple- and peach-orchard country along Apple Pie Ridge, visiting the historic towns of Gerrardstown and Hedgesville before entering the final stop on the tour, Martinsburg. Martinsburg is full of historic homes and buildings, many dating back to the time of its founding during the Revolutionary War.

If you can spend more than a day in this area, consider combining this tour with the next one, which begins in Shepherdstown, just 7 miles east of Martinsburg.

Total mileage: Approximately 52 miles

To begin the tour, take Exit 317 off I-81 just north of Winchester. Turn right on U.S. 11 North, known in this neck of the woods as the Martinsburg Pike. In about 1.5 miles, you'll enter the village of **Stephenson,** *where a Civil War battle took place on June 15, 1863 (when the community was known as Stephenson's Depot, a stop on the Winchester and Potomac Railroad). In 0.5 mile, look on the right side of the road at the intersection of Stephenson Road, just past a Methodist church, for a large stone historical marker.* It describes how Confederate general Edward "Allegheny Ed" Johnson's troops, in a dawn attack, surprised Union general Robert H. Milroy's men, who were retreating from Winchester. The Southerners were able to capture the Union wagon train and take 2,300 prisoners. Johnson's army then moved on to Pennsylvania, where it was defeated two weeks later in the Battle of Gettysburg. There are several Civil War Trails markers in this area, including one for Stephenson Depot and one for the Third Battle of Winchester.

A stone monument near the historical marker commemorates the loss of 13

Hopewell Meeting

Confederate artillery soldiers from the First Maryland Battery by quoting General Robert E. Lee: "I regard this as the Thermopylae of my campaign." Lee was referring to a battle in which the ancient Greeks, with a small but courageous force, were able to use their knowledge of the area's terrain to delay an enemy advance and give the larger force time to regroup.

Continue 1.3 miles to the community of **Clearbrook**. *As you approach the town, look for a convenience store on the left. Turn left just after the store on to Route 672 (Hopewell Road). Drive about 1 mile (you'll pass over I-81). A sign on the left at Waverly Road reads "Waverly Farm Jerseys." Just beyond the farm sign, turn left into the next driveway.* It leads to a beautiful old two-story limestone building known as Hopewell Meeting, built by early Quaker settlers in 1759.

Alexander Ross came to Pennsylvania from Ireland as an indentured servant around 1693. (Many immigrants paid for their ocean passage by agreeing to a period of servitude to the person who sponsored their journey.) Ten years later, when Ross was about 21, he gained his freedom. For many years he worked as a carpenter. But when the colony of Virginia began to encourage settlement in the Shenandoah Valley in the early 1730s, Ross, a devout Quaker, and Morgan Bryan, an Irish Presbyterian, applied for a land grant. Between 1730 and 1732, they were granted 120,000 acres in the northern Valley. Ultimately, they brought 70 families from around Chester, Pennsylvania, to settle in this area. Ross kept a 2,400-acre tract for himself and built

Defining the Shenandoah Valley

Although definitions vary, the Shenandoah Valley today is generally considered to run from the West Virginia counties of Berkeley and Jefferson, where the Shenandoah River joins the Potomac River at Harpers Ferry, to points south of Lexington, Virginia. It is all part of the larger Valley of Virginia, which stretches from the Potomac River to the eastern part of Tennessee. Strictly speaking, however, the Valley—as defined by the Shenandoah River and its affluents—is an area that extends from Harpers Ferry to south of Staunton.

Because the Shenandoah River runs south to north, Valley residents have long referred to the northern part of the Valley as the "lower Valley" and the southern part as the "upper Valley." Geographically, it may make sense, but it can get confusing. If you hear a long-time resident say he's heading "up the Valley," he's probably going south, not north.

a home. (Bryan's granddaughter, Rebecca Bryan, who was born here in 1739, later married Daniel Boone.)

Quaker settlements in the area grew throughout the 1700s. By around 1800, the Quakers had established 17 meetings, or churches, in the Shenandoah Valley and neighboring Hampshire County, now part of West Virginia.

Hopewell Meeting still has an active Quaker congregation. It is said to be the oldest religious structure in continuous use in the Shenandoah Valley. Hopewell Meeting had its beginnings as a log structure built not long after settlers arrived in 1734. About three years after a fire destroyed it in 1757, settlers built the eastern part of the current structure. It was enlarged between 1788 and 1794 and at one time had a partition down the middle to allow for services by both Orthodox and original Quakers. A large portion of the southern wall is original to the 1759 structure.

You passed the road to Alexander Ross's home, Waverly, before turning into Hopewell. From the meeting house, look south down the hill past the cemetery to see Waverly's dark rooftop and brick chimney. Ross built this house, using limestone from the property, between 1734 and 1748. His descendants sold it and the surrounding 500 acres in 1826 to George Fayette Washington, a great-nephew of the president (he was the grandson of Charles Washington, who was George Washington's youngest brother). It is believed that George Fayette Washington gave the house its current name. The home stayed in the Washington family until 1923. During the Civil War, both Union and Confederate troops camped on the grounds.

As the years passed, the number of Quakers in the Valley gradually diminished. Some people moved away because of their opposition to both war and slavery (many were persecuted for their pro-Union stance during the Civil War). Others—including Dolley Todd Payne, who became Mrs. James Madison—married outside the faith and were no longer allowed to be members of the church.

To continue the tour, retrace your route back to U.S. 11 and turn left. For more than 200 years, Clearbrook was a spinning and weaving center. One of the oldest mills in the area, and the last to shut down, in 1971, was the Clearbrook Woolen Company. It moved here in 1930, after a fire destroyed its predecessor, the Brucetown Woolen Mill (formerly known as the Pine Grove Woolen Factory and the Jobe Woolen Mill). The woolen industry here and elsewhere in the United States declined by the mid-1900s because of cheaper foreign wool and the advent of synthetic fabrics.

Continue north on U.S. 11 for 3.1 miles

Guns at Hopewell Meeting

In the 1700s, the surrounding mountains were home to many species of wild animals. As Valley historian John Wayland noted, "In the early days Friends {Quakers} going to or from Hopewell were occasionally chased by wolves, and the men carried their rifles to the meeting house and stacked them in a corner. They were there for defense against the wolves, not the Indians. The latter were not hostile to the Friends."

Although most Shenandoah Valley residents lived in constant fear of Indian attack in the 1750s and 1760s, the Indians respected the Quakers and left them alone. The Quakers had gained a reputation in Pennsylvania for treating Indians fairly, even offering to pay for the land they settled. The Indians were said to appreciate this gesture but weren't sure how to handle it, since the concept of private property was foreign to them.

Edgewood Manor

to the West Virginia state line. From here, it is another 2.8 miles to an old red-brick man-sion on the left, Edgewood Manor, in **Bunker Hill**. Edgewood Manor was completed in 1839 by General Elisha Boyd for his son, John Boyd. It is a private home today. This is the same General Boyd who built the mansion known as Boydville in Martinsburg (described later in this tour). Boyd operated two mills, a brick plant, and a cooper's shop at Edgewood in the 1820s.

Bunker Hill was the scene of several skirmishes during the Civil War. John Boyd's son, John Jr., was captured at Edgewood by Union soldiers, charged with being a spy, and sentenced to hang. Stonewall Jackson once camped for three weeks on the home's lawn. The tall monument at Edgewood's entrance drive commemorates Confederate general James Johnston Pettigrew of North Carolina, who was wounded at Falling Waters, north of Martinsburg, while retreating from Gettysburg. Pettigrew died at Edgewood before he could reach Winchester for medical treatment.

From Edgewood, drive another 0.2 mile on U.S. 11 into Bunker Hill. Turn right on to Route 26 (just past the Bunker Hill Presbyterian Church), which passes through the Mill Creek Historic District. As many as 10 mills operated in this area from the 1730s to the 1900s.

Less than 1 mile down Route 26 is an old stone building that was once the Bunker Hill

Old Bunker Hill Flour Mill

Flour Mill. The mill was built around 1800 on the site of an earlier mill dating to the 1730s. Its waterwheel and race can still be seen on the right side.

Turn around at the mill and drive back to U.S. 11. Cross U.S. 11 and continue west on Route 26. Just down the road on the right is a restored woolen mill that houses Bunker Hill Antiques. Just past the antique shop is Christ Episcopal Church, established in 1740 by Morgan Morgan (see below), Dr. John Briscoe, and Jacob Hite. It is thought to be one of the oldest churches in the Valley. Built in 1851, the present structure is the third church on this site. Several settlers, including Morgan Morgan, are buried in its cemetery.

Continue down Route 26 for 2.3 miles to the stop sign at the intersection with Route 24 (Godmiller road). Stay straight past the stop sign. In 0.5 mile, on the left you will see a clapboard-covered cabin with a West Virginia historical marker. This is Morgan Cabin, a 1976 reconstruction that used many of the original logs of a cabin built by Morgan Morgan. A Welsh immigrant who came here from Pennsylvania in 1728, Morgan initially erected a crude cabin for his family near this spot. About four years later, he completed the larger cabin on this site. It is thought to be the first settler's house in what is now West Virginia. The clapboard exterior was added in 1994 to protect the original logs.

Morgan's sons and grandsons fought in the Revolutionary War. His grandson

Morgan Cabin

Zackquill Morgan House

James was an army chaplain who was killed execution-style at this cabin by British Tories, who cruelly forced his wife and children to watch.

The old stone-and-clapboard house across and down the road was built in 1761 by Zackquill Morgan, one of Morgan Morgan's sons and the founder of Morgantown, West Virginia.

Turn around at Morgan Cabin and go back down Route 26 to the stop sign at Route 24 (Godmiller Road). Turn left. This lovely stretch of rolling road takes you past thousands of acres of apple and peach orchards. Great North Mountain is to the left.

In 2.4 miles, you'll see a large apple storage building on the left near an intersection. At the stop sign, turn left on to Route 51. (Note that it may not be marked as such. West Virginia backroads often lack road signs, so look for the landmarks mentioned here.) You'll pass Mountain Ridge Intermediate School on the right just after the turn. Route 51 was one of the early roads for settlers heading west.

After 0.5 mile, you'll pass a lovely old clapboard-faced home on the left. This is Marshy Dell, a two-story log home built by an Irish immigrant, Gilbert McKown, who came to Virginia via York, Pennsylvania, in 1774. McKown fought in the Revolutionary War and witnessed Cornwallis's surrender at Yorktown. The original house was half the size of the one you see today; in 1810, McKown and his son built an addition that doubled the home's size, making it one of the largest log homes in the county. He added the siding later. At some point, McKown brought his father, Andrew, to Virginia from Ireland. The elder McKown was a stone mason, and he built his own house—the small stone dwelling near the main house—in the Irish style.

During the Civil War, both Confederate and Union soldiers made themselves at home on the McKown farm, camping in the back yard and helping themselves to livestock and farm products. This bit of history comes to us from the diaries of Gilbert McKown's wife, Sarah, who kept a daily journal of life at the farm for 39 years; her accounts, which have been transcribed and published, are available in some libraries and from the Berkeley County Historical Society.

*Proceed into the charming village of **Gerrardstown**.* Laid out by the Reverend David Gerrard in 1784, Gerrardstown is noted for being home to the first Baptist church

Marshy Dell

west of the Blue Ridge. The village seems locked in the 19th century. Many of its original homes are still occupied, including the lovely stone house on the right in the heart of the village.

At the small general store on the left, turn left on to Dominion Road and go several hundred feet to see the Hays-Gerrard House, on the left near the historic marker. One of the state's oldest stone houses, it was built by John Hays, who came to this area with a group of Baptists in 1744. It was later the home of David Gerrard, the town's founder and Baptist minister whose father, John, was the first Baptist minister west of the Blue Ridge. Upstairs, the house features an "Indian closet"—a place for people to hide during Indian attacks, which were common in the area in the mid-1700s.

Return to Route 51 and turn left. A picturesque old brick home, Prospect Hill, is on the left after 0.5 mile; it's a little hard to see the house from the road. Built between 1792 and 1802 by William Wilson, this Federal-style private home is the centerpiece of a working farm. Wilson made his money selling supplies to settlers moving west. On the property are the remains of a log home built in the mid-1700s by the Kelly family. In the mid-1750s, the last Indians came through nearby Mills Gap and murdered the Kelly family at their cabin here. The story goes that George Washington, then a young British Army colonel charged with building forts during the French and Indian War, sent troops here to protect area residents.

Continue north on Route 51 until it intersects Route 45. Turn right on Route 45 East, toward Martinsburg. Here, near the middle of the intersection, a stone marker notes that the John Mills Tavern stood at this spot on Mills Gap in 1769. There is a parking area on the right, just after you start to turn, where you can pull over to view the valley below. Because of the profuse vegetation here, the views are better from late fall to early spring.

After 4.2 miles, you'll come to a stop sign. Ignore the signs to stay on Route 45 East and instead go straight to the second stop sign and the intersection with Route 30. Again, note that the road may not be marked. Turn left on to Route 30 (Arden Nollville Road). You will pass many interesting old homes and rolling hills covered with apple and peach orchards as far as the eye can see—a gorgeous sight in the spring when the

Buffalo near Martinsburg

trees are in bloom. In 0.7 mile, look to the left when you see signs for a fruit farm and farm market; you may see buffalo in the field along the road.

After 1.7 miles, you'll see, on the left behind trees, a white house with a large stone chimney. Known as the Pendleton House, it was constructed in 1775 by Philip Pendleton and is thought to be one of the largest log structures ever built in Berkeley County. The original logs have long been covered with stucco. This treatment, fairly common in the Valley in the 1800s, not only preserved the log structure but helped insulate the house and give it a more "modern" look.

About 1.2 miles past the Pendleton House, turn left at the stop sign on to Route 15; it may not be marked as such. In less than 0.5 mile, the road passes a farm complex on the left called Bella Vista, also known as the Frederick Seibert House. This home, built in 1807, has beautifully maintained grounds. On a pond near the road are several old stone buildings that once housed a distillery and tavern.

Just past Bella Vista, turn right on to Route 16 (Thatcher Road). Route 16 ends at a stop sign after 2.2 miles. Turn left. In less than 1 mile, the road passes an old white frame church. Veer to the left to stay on this road, which will take you up and then down Great North Mountain through a thick forest. As the road ends its descent, look for the sign that says, "1-lane bridge ahead." Turn right on to Route 9/9 (Cannon Hill Road), just before the bridge. You can pull over to the left side of the road before Back Creek

Pendleton House

Bella Vista

to take a look at this unusual bridge. It is interesting because it was built with rail-road rails. This Great North Mountain gap was named for John Park, who obtained a grant from Lord Fairfax in 1756 for property located nearby.

Route 9/9 will take you to the old settlement of **Hedgesville***, less than 4 miles away, where it meets Route 9, Hedgesville's main street. Turn right.* (If you turn left here and drive 1.4 miles, you'll see the old Snodgrass Tavern, said to have been visited by George Washington and his stepdaughter, Patsy, on their way to visit the mineral water baths in Berkeley Springs in 1769. The old tavern, which dates to the 1740s, is on the right past a concrete bridge.)

Hedgesville sits on the edge of a well-traveled gap of Great North Mountain. Many old homes line its shaded streets. The town was founded in 1830, but settlers lived in the area for nearly 100 years before that. This was the site of Fort Hedges, one of the many stockade forts built along the mountains during the French and Indian War. The picture-pretty Mount Zion Episcopal Church, built in 1817 on land donated by Josiah Hedges, is on the left side of Route 9 after the turn.

Continue on Route 9 East for about 5 miles to the city of **Martinsburg***.* The road quickly changes from a sleepy country backroad to a busy industrial and commercial highway. The L. Norman Dillon Farm Museum is located on the right at the traffic light where Route 9 meets Ridge Road. The emphasis of this private

Mount Zion Episcopal Church

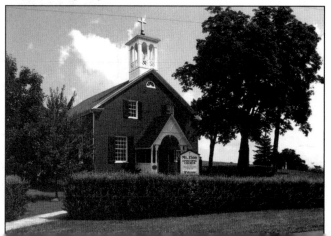

Berkeley Springs Side Trip

The historic town of Berkeley Springs is a 20-minute drive west of Hedgesville on Route 9. Its mineral waters, historians say, were well known to Indian tribes from as far away as the Great Lakes and the Carolinas. George Washington first visited the springs on a surveying expedition in 1748. The spot later became a favorite retreat of his for many years; he even bought land here. Originally called Bath, the town's days as a springs resort began in the late 1700s. They continue to this day at Berkeley Springs State Park, which invites visitors to "take the baths."

Ten miles south of Berkeley Springs is Cacapon State Park. The park offers picnic areas, golf, fishing, hiking, tennis, volleyball, swimming, and nature programs.

museum is on farm equipment and farming techniques of the 1800s and 1900s. L. Norman Dillon, a lifelong farmer, began the museum to preserve the area's agricultural heritage. It is open on weekend afternoons from April through October (see more information in the appendix).

Martinsburg is the county seat of Berkeley County, which has more than 100 properties listed on the National Register of Historic Places. The county was formed from Frederick County in 1772 and is named for Lord Norborne Berkeley, Baron de Botetourt, who was Virginia's colonial governor from 1768 to 1770. Berkeley asked the British government to give him the job so he could pay off heavy gambling debts. But he quit after two years because he disagreed with England's policy of imposing taxes on the colonists. The Virginia colonists liked him so

DOWNTOWN MARTINSBURG

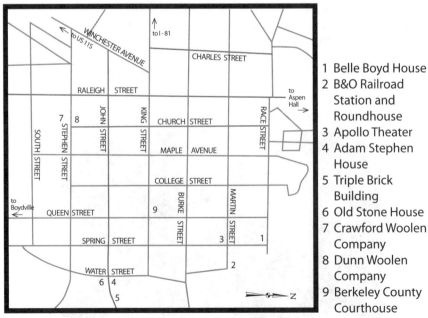

1 Belle Boyd House
2 B&O Railroad Station and Roundhouse
3 Apollo Theater
4 Adam Stephen House
5 Triple Brick Building
6 Old Stone House
7 Crawford Woolen Company
8 Dunn Woolen Company
9 Berkeley County Courthouse

much that they named two counties after him (this one and Botetourt County in the southern Shenandoah Valley). They also erected a statue in his honor in Williamsburg, Virginia.

Continue straight through several more intersections, following the signs for Route 9 East and U.S. 11 South. As you enter the older section of Martinsburg, you'll see an old brick firehouse—the Westphal Hose Company—straight ahead. Stay straight. The road curves to the left at the next light and becomes West Queen Street. Go under the railroad bridge and turn right at the next traffic light on to Race Street; drive just 0.1 mile, or three short blocks. Turn right on Boyd Street. At the end of this residential street, you'll come to the grounds of Aspen Hall, once an inn but now a private home. Aspen Hall is one of the oldest and loveliest large homes in Berkeley County. Edward Beeson II, a prosperous Quaker and influential Martinsburg citizen, began building the first section of this Georgian-style mansion around 1750 (or 1771 or 1776, depending on the source). It took years to finish. Another smaller house on the property, which is still standing, was built around 1754 by John Mendenhall, one of Beeson's relatives by marriage. It was later known as Fort Mendenhall, when it was probably surrounded by a stockade to protect citizens from Indian attack. Part of the fort's blockhouse, made of limestone, is still visible. George Washington not only housed troops here during the French and Indian War, but he reportedly attended a wedding in the house in 1761.

Return to Race Street, turn left, and cross Queen Street. The old red-brick house on the right at the next corner is the Belle Boyd House. Now the home of the Berkeley County Historical Society, this 1853 Greek Revival house was the childhood home of Civil War spy Belle Boyd. It became the home of the historical society after it was saved from demolition in 1992, when its owner at that time wanted to make room for a parking lot.

As described in The Strasburg to Fort Valley to Front Royal Tour (page 96), Belle Boyd began her covert career when, at the age of 16, she shot a Union soldier in her parents' home at 500 South Queen Street here in Martinsburg; that house no longer stands. The headstrong Belle had a few childhood adventures while living in this house on Race Street as well, including an episode in which she rode her pony into the house, miffed that her father wouldn't let her attend a dinner party. Not surprisingly, Belle became an actress after the Civil War.

The Belle Boyd House contains a museum with 11 rooms of displays devoted

The Belle Boyd House

to Berkeley County's history. The museum offers exhibits about early Indian settlements, the Civil War in this part of the Shenandoah Valley, Belle Boyd, and other topics of local interest. The society's genealogy and history library contains copies of county records and early newspapers. The Belle Boyd House is also home to the Ben Boyd Bookstore, which sells books, historical society publications, and history-related memorabilia. The house is open daily except Sundays and Wednesdays year-round.

Drive past the Belle Boyd House, continuing on Race Street as it curves to the right into a large parking area facing several old railroad buildings. These structures, which include a 16-sided roundhouse, were once part of a busy passenger and freight center for the Baltimore and Ohio (B&O) Railroad. The B&O was the nation's first common-carrier railway; it began laying track near Baltimore in 1829. Taking on an incredibly difficult technological and engineering challenge, the pioneering B&O stretched from Baltimore across Maryland and Virginia, then up and over the Appalachians, finally reaching its goal of the Ohio River at Wheeling in 1852.

The first B&O trains were running between here and Harpers Ferry by 1842. Today, Amtrak trains serve commuters and other passengers from a new station carefully designed to look as if it has always been here. The station is a stop on Amtrak's *Capitol Limited,* which runs daily between Washington, D.C., and Chicago. The new station is attached to the 150-year-old B&O hotel and station house, which now houses a bookstore and a visitor and Amtrak information center. Restoration work on the old B&O buildings began in 1999 and will continue for years.

During the Civil War, Martinsburg was important to both sides because of the railroad and its strategic location near the Potomac River. The town changed hands dozens of times during the war. In May 1861, to prevent the Union from using the railroad to transport troops and supplies, General Stonewall Jackson carried out a daring plan to capture railroad cars and locomotives. Two groups of Confederate forces—one in Cherry Run, West Virginia (about 15 miles north of Martinsburg), and the other at Point of Rocks, Maryland—blocked train traffic on the 44-mile stretch and took 56 locomotives and more than 300 freight cars. Jackson then gave orders to put four of the lighter-weight locomotives on the rail line to Winchester.

B&O shops

There, he ordered them fitted with broad tires, hooked to teams of 40 horses each, and dragged south along the graveled Valley Pike for 40 miles to Strasburg to be put to military use.

The following month, Jackson, fearing approaching Union forces, decided to destroy the railroad. First he blew up the 800-foot railroad bridge at Harpers Ferry, which, along with the destruction of several other bridges to the west, effectively put the railroad out of business. A few days later, Jackson received orders to burn everything at the B&O's Martinsburg depot—railcars, locomotives, shops, and machinery. He wrote to his wife that he was saddened to have to do it but that he had no choice but to obey orders. Jackson later sent ten of the burned locomotives to Strasburg, again pulled by teams of horses along the Valley Pike for what must have been a very slow trip.

After much rebuilding in the late 1860s, the railroads became important to Martinsburg once more, making possible its growth as a packing and distribution center for the region's apple orchards. In 1885, another rail line, this one from Pennsylvania, was extended south to Martinsburg, making the town a major rail junction and sparking a period of rapid industrial growth.

Although the buildings you see here today were built after the Civil War, they are important both historically and architecturally. The West Roundhouse was constructed using an early cast-iron framing system and is the oldest fully covered roundhouse in the United States. (Sadly, the East Roundhouse was destroyed by fire in 1990.)

Two of the shop buildings are also among the B&O's few remaining significant structures. The shops were the backdrop for the Great Railway Strike of 1877, in which a striking worker was killed, setting off a nationwide protest against low wages.

The CSX railroad, the modern owner of the B&O, operated these shops until 1985. In 1999, a public group, the Berkeley County Roundhouse Authority, bought the property and began raising funds for restoration. In 2001, the American Society of Civil Engineers designated the complex as a Historic Civil Engineering Landmark.

Martinsburg has long been a crossroads. Around 1713, its location on the north-south Indian trail (which has been known at different times as the Great Philadelphia Wagon Road, the Valley Turnpike, and today's U.S. 11) made it a stopover for Tuscarora Indians heading north after they were driven out of the Carolinas. By the 1730s, British, Scotch-Irish, and German settlers began arriving in the area from eastern Virginia and Pennsylvania.

From the railroad station parking lot, turn right on Martin Street. Go to the end of the block and turn left on Spring Street. The Apollo Theater, on the corner of Martin and Spring Streets, has been used as a vaudeville, concert, and movie theater since 1913. It now operates as a community theater.

Drive three blocks to John Street and turn left. Continue past the stop sign at Water Street and drive across the railroad tracks to the park-like area on the left. Park in the grassy area and walk up the paved drive to two restored historic buildings—the Adam Stephen House and the Triple Brick Building.

This area is the original part of town, built along the banks of Tuscarora Creek. Adam Stephen built the lovely limestone house that bears his name between 1771 and 1789. Abandoned for many years, the house was donated to the city in 1959, and a major restoration effort was completed in the 1990s. The house is furnished as it might have been in the late 1700s to early 1800s.

Adjacent to the Adam Stephen House is the Triple Brick Building, so called because it once housed three apartments. It was built in 1874 by a later owner of the Adam Stephen House as temporary housing for railroad workers. Now a museum, its exhibits include local fossils, artifacts of early Indian and colonial life, military uniforms, early surveying equipment, railroad items, and quilts. (Contact the Berkeley County Historical Society, listed in the appendix, for hours of operation for both properties.)

Adam Stephen, a surgeon from Scotland, laid out the town in the years before the Revolution. He had first settled in Fredericksburg, Virginia, in 1748. He came to this area as a colonel in the French and Indian War and later bought property here. As was the custom, he wanted to name the town after himself, but he worried it would be confused with the Shenandoah Valley town of Stephensburg (since renamed Stephens City), south of Winchester. Instead, he named it after his friend Thomas Bryan Martin, who was a colonel and a nephew of Lord Fairfax. (In 1758, Thomas Martin and George Washington were Frederick County's representatives in the Virginia House of Burgesses.) In the Revolutionary War, Adam Stephen served as a major general under Washington in the battles at Trenton, Princeton, Chadds Ford, and Brandywine. But his military career came to an end at the Battle of Germantown, which the British won. Among other things, Stephen was accused of being drunk

Triple Brick Building

during the battle. In foggy conditions, he mistook fellow general Anthony Wayne's troops for Redcoats and ordered his men to fire on them. In the confusion that resulted, the troops made a "crazed retreat." Washington replaced his old comrade with the Marquis de Lafayette.

At the Virginia Constitutional Convention in 1788, Stephen was an outspoken supporter of ratification of the United States Constitution. He died in Martinsburg in 1791. His tomb lies beneath the monument honoring him, which is on the grounds of an old home called Boydville, located at 601 South Queen Street, three blocks south of the Berkeley County Courthouse. Boydville was built by General Elisha Boyd in 1812 on land he bought from Adam Stephen.

From the Adam Stephen House, turn around and drive back to John Street. Go one block to Water Street and turn left. On the left corner is the Old Stone House. One of the city's earliest residences, it was probably built in 1727.

Drive one block to East Stephen Street, turn right, and drive five blocks. Near the intersection with Church Street, the old brick buildings you see were the main buildings of what was once a complex of woolen mills.

In the 1890s, William Henry Crawford came to this area from New York and established several mills. One was the Crawford Woolen Company (later known as the Berkeley Woolen Company), and another was the Martinsburg Worsted and

Porte Crayon:
Early Valley Journalist

A famous writer and illustrator of the mid-1800s, David Hunter Strother was born in Martinsburg in 1816 and later lived at Norborne Hall, a large 1813 house located at 396 West Race Street, at one time the town's poorhouse. Strother, who also had a home in Berkeley Springs, wrote and illustrated popular travel articles, often about the Shenandoah Valley, for *Harper's New Monthly Magazine* and other national publications under the pen name of Porte Crayon. *Harper's* hired him to cover John Brown's trial in 1859. He later joined the Union Army, serving in the topographical corps, where he put his knowledge of Virginia geography to practical use. After the war, he published *Personal Recollections of the War by a Virginian*. Strother later served as U.S. consul general in Mexico from 1879 to 1885.

Cassimere Company (later known as the Dunn Woolen Company).

Crawford built an elegant home at 505 South Queen Street, a private residence today. He apparently lived beyond his means; he filed for bankruptcy protection in 1912. Two years later, he died of cirrhosis of the liver at the age of 47, having lost everything. The woolen mills were taken over by new owners and were operated until the late 1940s and early 1950s. During the first half of the 20th century, they provided wool blankets for the military in both world wars and upholstery fabric for the major automakers.

From 1985 until 2000, these structures were home to the Blue Ridge Outlet Center, a popular shopping mall. Today they are used by various Berkeley County offices and by the West Virginia University Extension Service.

Continue to the stop sign at Raleigh Street and turn right. Drive two blocks to King Street and turn right. Drive to the traffic light at Queen Street and turn left. At this intersection, the Martinsburg Public Library is on your right, and the yellow-domed Berkeley County Courthouse is on your left. The courthouse was completed in 1856 on the site of an earlier courthouse. Belle Boyd was held here after one of her many arrests for spying for the Confederacy. Across the street on the right side of the intersection at 208 South Queen Street is the Admiral Boarman House. It was built about 1802 and is one of the oldest brick homes in Martinsburg.

Martinsburg's downtown has been called "a little encyclopedia of small-town architecture from the late 18th to mid-20th century" by the *Washington Post*. The city has designated seven historic districts. A walking tour guide is available at the Martinsburg–Berkeley County Visitor Center, located at 115 North Queen Street.

The downtown area has several interesting shops, restaurants, buildings, and churches. For a taste of times past, don't miss the old-fashioned soda fountain at Patterson's Drug Store, located at 134 South Queen Street.

The tour ends in Martinsburg. Follow the signs from the downtown area to I-81. If you'd like to continue exploring the area, Route 9 East will take you to Shepherdstown and then to Harpers Ferry, while Route 45 East will lead you to Charles Town. For more about these three historic towns, see the next tour.

Old Stone House

Berkeley County Courthouse

Civil War Side Trip

U.S. 11 North continues to Hagerstown, Maryland, and the nearby Antietam Battlefield. On the way to the battlefield, about 6 miles north of Martinsburg near the intersection of Route 11/4, 0.1 mile east of U.S. 11, is Falling Waters. This is the site of what is said to be the first Civil War battle to take place in the Shenandoah Valley. On July 1, 1861, the Confederates fought a brief battle—lasting perhaps 45 minutes—led by a relatively unknown officer, Thomas J. "Stonewall" Jackson.

Two years later, on July 13, 1863, Confederate troops retreating from Gettysburg crossed the Potomac River here.

The Charles Town to Harpers Ferry to Shepherdstown Tour

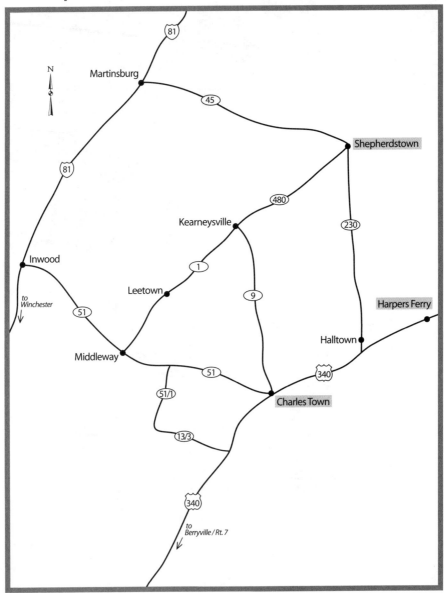

TOUR 2

The Charles Town to Harpers Ferry to Shepherdstown Tour

This tour covers the northern end of the Shenandoah Valley, visiting the historic towns of Charles Town, Harpers Ferry, and Shepherdstown in West Virginia's Jefferson County. This area was Washington country for many years—the first president and many members of his family bought land and built homes here. As president, George Washington was instrumental in establishing a federal armory at Harpers Ferry, which decades later became the scene of a pivotal event that foreshadowed the Civil War.

The tour begins off I-81 at Inwood and passes through Middleway, Charles Town, Harpers Ferry, Halltown, Shepherdstown, Kearneysville, and Leetown before returning to I-81 at Inwood. Most of Harpers Ferry is a National Historical Park, and several interesting museums are housed in the town's restored buildings. The National Park Service suggests allowing three hours to see everything; if you plan to hike along the scenic C&O Canal, expect to spend most of a day. Harpers Ferry has many shops, restaurants, and even a few places to stay. The historic neighborhoods, museums, shops, and restaurants of Shepherdstown and Charles Town are also inviting, so you may want to split this tour over two days, in case you're tempted to spend much of your time out of the car.

Total mileage: Approximately 60 miles

To begin the tour, take Exit 5 off I-81 south of Martinsburg. Turn on to Route 51 East at the stop sign at the end of the ramp. Follow Route 51 as it turns right at a traffic light, then turns left at the next traffic light. Continue straight on Route 51. In less than 4 miles, you'll cross a bridge over Opequon Creek. This creek forms the boundary between Berkeley and Jefferson Counties, the two West Virginia counties in the Shenandoah Valley.

On the right just across the bridge is the entrance to Priest Field, owned by the Catholic Church. There were few Catholic settlers in the Valley—most were Quakers, Lutherans, Mennonites, Baptists, and Episcopalians. The story of how the Catholic Church came to own property in Middleway, West Virginia, is one of the Valley's enduring legends, with many variations.

The tale begins around 1794 with a Lutheran settler of Dutch descent named Adam Livingston. In those days, the road you are traveling was a main east-west route. The village of **Middleway** (originally called Smithfield) had developed around Smith Tavern, a popular stop for travelers. One evening, Adam Livingston took one of those travelers into his home. The man became ill later that night and, fearing the worst, asked his host to call for a priest. Livingston refused, saying that no priest lived nearby, and that even if one did, he certainly wouldn't invite him into his home. The stranger died that night and was buried quickly and without ceremony.

Not long after, a string of bizarre events began. One account says that horses were heard running around the house at night, that flaming logs left the fireplace and danced about the kitchen, and that Livingston's farm animals died, his barn burned, and his money vanished. But the strangest occurrence of all was the sound of scissors clipping away day and night—scissors that left small holes in all the clothes, linens, and rugs in the house. Visitors claimed they left the house with holes in their clothes. For many years the town was known as Wizard Clip because of the mysterious snipping that went on there.

In desperation, Livingston traveled to Shepherdstown, where a priest, Father Dennis Cahill, listened to his story and was persuaded to come to Middleway. The priest said Mass in the house, and the strange occurrences stopped soon afterward. Amazed and grateful, Livingston converted to Catholicism. In 1802, he deeded 34 acres of his property to the Catholic Church on the condition that a chapel be built there.

Livingston later moved to Pennsylvania, selling all his land except for the field along Opequon Creek that he had offered to the church. It wasn't until many years after his death that the Catholic Church built the small frame structure that became known as Priest's Field Chapel. In 1978, the church established a retreat and conference center here. In 1984, it erected a monument to Adam Livingston on the grounds.

Continue straight on Route 51 East (Middleway Road) for almost 4 miles past the bridge. Look for a West Virginia state historical marker for Cedar Lawn on the right side of the road and prepare to turn right just beyond it, on to Route 51/1 (Earle Road), although it may not be marked as such. After 0.8 mile on this road, you'll pass Richwood Hall, an old brick mansion dating from the 1820s. One-half mile past Richwood Hall, you'll see Cedar Lawn on the right. This handsome old home is across the street from (and is part of) O'Sullivan Farms, the state's largest and oldest thoroughbred horse farm. Here, horses are bred, raised, and trained for racing at the nearby Charles Town racetrack.

The home was part of the Harewood estate, which included some 3,800 acres originally owned by Samuel Washington, President George Washington's younger brother. The first house built on the property was a log-and-plank house named Berry Hill. It was built by Samuel's son, Thornton, in 1780. Thornton's son, John Thornton Augustine Washington, built Cedar Lawn around 1825.

In 1848, one of John's 13 children—Benjamin Franklin Washington—caught gold-rush fever. A local lawyer, Benjamin organized an expedition of 80 Jefferson County citizens who hoped to get rich quick in California. No fortunes were made,

but Benjamin stayed on and later became the first editor of the *San Francisco Examiner.*

Harewood, the house built by Samuel Washington around 1770, is not on this tour. It is on the right a short distance up Route 51, past where you turned on to Earle Road. Harewood was the location of Dolley Payne Todd's wedding to future president James Madison in 1794. By that time, Harewood had passed to Samuel's son, George Steptoe Washington, who was married to Dolley's sister, Lucy. Both women were dismissed from the Quaker faith for marrying "out of meeting." George Washington was a frequent visitor at this home. A direct descendant of Samuel Washington still lives in Harewood.

George Washington became familiar with this part of the Shenandoah Valley while he was a young man surveying for Lord Fairfax in the late 1740s. His first land purchase, in 1750 at the age of 18, consisted of several hundred acres of fertile farmland near Bullskin Run, located a short distance southwest of Cedar Lawn near Summit Point. Within two years, he acquired 2,315 acres in the region. He encouraged his older half-brother, Lawrence, who owned Mount Vernon at the time, to buy land in this area. Lawrence purchased several thousand acres before dying of tuberculosis a few years later, at which time the land passed to his brothers.

To see two more Washington family homes, continue until the road ends at a stop sign. Even though it may not be marked as such, the intersecting road is Route 13 (Summit Point Road). Turn right. After 0.4 mile, turn left on to Route 13/3 (Huyett Road). In 0.7 mile, you'll pass the buildings of the Claymont Court Society for Continuing Education on the left. Just past the school are Blakeley (on the right side of the road) and Claymont Court (up the hill via a long driveway on the left).

Why Virginia Split

West Virginia was created when Virginia's westernmost counties refused to join the Confederacy with the rest of Virginia in 1861. Residents of the trans-Allegheny area (and even the Shenandoah Valley) had long believed that their political and economic interests were not fairly represented in Richmond, where the state assembly was controlled by well-to-do plantation owners, lawyers, and businessmen on the east side of the Blue Ridge. There were few large farms west of the Blue Ridge and relatively few slave owners.

West Virginia became a state, on the Union side, in 1863. Probably because of their strategic value to the North, the counties of Berkeley and Jefferson were also made part of the new state, even though many, if not most, of their residents sided with the Confederate cause. For years after the war, the story goes, many residents of Jefferson County continued to insist they lived in Virginia, not West Virginia.

Blakeley

Blakeley, which is partly surrounded by a grove of old oak trees, was built around 1820 by John Augustine Washington II, a grandson of George Washington's brother John Augustine Washington. It is said that John built a more modest house here than he might have, since he was in line to inherit Mount Vernon. That estate on the Potomac River south of Washington, D.C., came into his possession in 1829, after the death of his uncle, Bushrod Washington, who had inherited it upon George Washington's death in 1799.

Across the road from Blakeley (in the distance) is Claymont Court, a large home built by Bushrod Corbin Washington around 1820. This other grandson of John Augustine Washington was active in local politics and represented the county in the Virginia Assembly. At present, Claymont Court is owned by a private educational organization, which holds retreats and conferences here.

Continue past Claymont Court on Huyett Road until you reach a stop sign. Turn right, then make an immediate left on to U.S. 340 North. After about 3 miles on U.S. 340, take the exit marked "North 340/West 51/Charles Town/Harpers Ferry." At the end of the ramp, turn left, following the signs for Route 51 West. This road becomes East Washington Street, Charles Town's main street.

Charles Town is worth a stop for its excellent Jefferson County Museum and for a walk or drive around its downtown area and peaceful tree-lined neighborhoods. The town was laid out on 80 acres by Charles Washington, brother of the president, who inherited the property from their brother Lawrence. Charles gave

The Blakeley–Mount Vernon Connection

George Washington inherited Mount Vernon from his brother Lawrence because Lawrence's children did not survive childhood. When George died without fathering children, Mount Vernon (upon Martha Washington's death) went to a nephew, Bushrod Washington, a United States Supreme Court justice who was the eldest son of John Augustine Washington (another brother of the president). Bushrod also died without children and thus Mount Vernon was passed along to his nephew, John Augustine II, builder of Blakeley. One of John's two sons, John Augustine Washington III, was born at Blakely in 1821 and died during the Civil War while serving as aide-de-camp to General Robert E. Lee.

Claymont Court

the main street his family name and christened the four major cross streets after himself and his brothers—Samuel, George, and Lawrence. He probably named Mildred Street for his wife, although the name may have honored a sister who died in infancy. This was a Washington family town if there ever was one. The cemetery at the Zion Episcopal Church (on Congress Street between Mildred and Church Streets) "may hold the largest number of Washington family descendants in the United States—more than 70—including some twenty who were born at Mount Vernon," according to the Charles Town walking tour guide.

Today, Charles Town is probably best known for its year-round horse races at the large racetrack you'll pass on your way to the downtown area. Except for the Civil War years, horse racing has been a favorite pastime here since the town's founding. After the war, horse racing returned to Charles Town, but all bets were off, thanks to West Virginia's ban on gambling. It wasn't until 1933 that betting on horse races became legal again.

After you pass the racetrack, look on the left for the gray-brick home at 417 East Washington Street; it now operates as a bed-and-breakfast. Built in 1839 by a Dr. Stribling, the home was used as a headquarters by Union general Philip Sheridan. He and General Grant met here to make plans for dealing with Confederate general Stonewall Jackson in the Shenandoah Valley.

After the traffic light at Mildred Street, turn left on to South Samuel Street. The house on the left corner as you turned, at 201 East Washington Street, is the Tate-Fairfax-Muse House. It was built in 1800 and leased in 1803 to Ferdinando Fairfax, who inherited the Fairfax family fortune. George and Martha Washington were his godparents.

Continue for three blocks on South Samuel Street to Hunter Street. On the left corner, at 515 South Samuel Street, is the Gibson-Todd House. A red-brick Victorian house stands here, next to the site of John Brown's execution in 1859. (The story of John Brown is told later in this tour.) The gallows stood just north of the house, in the yard to the left.

Continue down South Samuel Street to Mason Street. Turn right. (This becomes Beckwith Street.) Go to the stop sign at South George Street and turn left. Then make an immediate right on to Blakeley Street; drive to the end. The large white house on a hill at the

The site of John Brown's hanging

end of the street (at the intersection with Mordington Avenue) is Happy Retreat. It was built by Charles Washington—George's youngest brother—who moved here with his wife, Mildred Berry, from Fredericksburg, Virginia, around 1780. Using logs, he built two single-story log structures, separated by a breezeway. In 1837, a later owner added second floors to the original buildings and built the center section. The house has been greatly enlarged over the past 200 years and was privately owned until recently. A local group is planning to acquire and develop the property as the Charles Washington Happy Retreat Historical State Park.

Turn around and go back down Blakeley Street to the stop sign at South George. Turn left on to South George and go to Academy Street. The first house on the right, at 311 South George, is the Bishop House. It was built in 1896 by Jonathan Peale Bishop, whose son, John, was a writer and a friend of F. Scott Fitzgerald, who often visited him here.

Continue down South George Street. The house at 216 South George, a red-brick Victorian, is the Washington House Inn. It was built in 1899 by descendants of Samuel and John Augustine Washington, two of the president's brothers.

Continue down South George Street to the traffic light at North Washington Street. Across South Washington Street, the Jefferson County Courthouse is on the right, and the visitor center is in the middle of the block on the left. *To continue the tour, turn left.* The visitor center offers a walking-tour pamphlet of Charles Town describing 33 historic sites.

The impressive Jefferson County Courthouse, still in use, was built in 1836 to replace an 1803 structure. Jefferson County, named for Thomas Jefferson, was created in 1801. The courthouse was reduced to a shell after suffering heavy Confederate attacks during the Civil War; it has undergone significant restoration and renovation since.

The courthouse was the setting for two of only three treason trials to take place in the United States prior to the 1940s. The more famous was the trial of John Brown in October 1859. The other was in 1922 and involved three men whose actions while leading striking coal miners in Logan County, West Virginia, led to treason and murder charges.

The trial of John Brown in 1759 (see the story of his famous Harpers Ferry raid later in this tour) lasted only three days, and the jury returned a guilty verdict after less than an hour of deliberation. The trial was covered by newspapers all over the

Charles Town visitor center

country and drew many spectators, including John Wilkes Booth, who assassinated President Lincoln six years later. Brown was sentenced to hang at a gallows constructed on a nearby field (now the grounds of the Gibson-Todd House, described earlier in this tour). To help keep order during the hanging, some 1,500 troops, including a cadet corps from Virginia Military Institute (V.M.I.), were called in. One of the corps commandants was a professor, Major Thomas J. Jackson, later known as "Stonewall."

Turn right on to East Washington Street and drive one block to Samuel Street. At 200 East Washington Street is the Jefferson County Library. The Jefferson County Museum is in the back of the library building, with an entrance around the corner on Samuel Street. Open Tuesdays through Saturdays from mid-March to mid-December, the museum describes the history of the county from early Indian times through

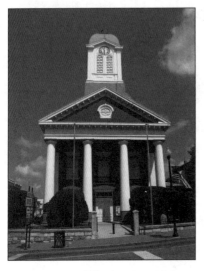

Jefferson County Courthouse

World War II. It contains attractive displays on daily life in the 1700s and 1800s, as well as exhibits on the Washington family, the Civil War, and John Brown's raid. One of the museum's most popular items is the metal frame of the cot that Brown, who was wounded in the raid, rested on during his trial.

Next door to the library is the Charles Town Presbyterian Church. This church was used as a hospital by both sides during the Civil War.

The building on the northwest corner of East Washington and Samuel Streets, across from the museum and library, was once the home of Andrew Hunter, one of the two state prosecutors in the Brown trial.

Like most of the Shenandoah Valley, Charles Town and the surrounding area suffered terrible damage during the Civil War. One of the several skirmishes in the region took place near Summit Point, about 7 miles west of here.

It was near that same spot in 1755 that General Braddock's troops camped on their way to fight at Fort Duquesne, near what is now Pittsburgh, during the French and Indian War. Three young captains who later distinguished themselves in the American Revolution were with Braddock at his defeat at Fort Duquesne. All three—Charles Lee, Horatio Gates, and Adam Stephen (who founded Martinsburg)—were British-born, all were wounded in that battle, and all later sided with the colonists during the Revolution. In a strange twist of fate, all three were promoted to major gen-

Harpers Ferry and the Civil Rights Movement

John Brown's failed attempt to cause a slave uprising made Harpers Ferry a symbol of the fight for racial justice and equality. During the Civil War, the town became a refuge for runaway slaves. After the war, missionaries from New England established Storer College here, an integrated institution with the goal of educating former slaves. In Harpers Ferry in 1906, W.E.B. DuBois and several others held the first United States meeting of the Niagara Movement, a civil-rights group formed to draw public attention to the racial injustices that continued in the years after the war. The members of that organization went on to establish the National Association for the Advancement of Colored People (NAACP) in 1909.

eral, two were subsequently court-martialed, and all ended up living near Charles Town after the war. Their stories—and their famous toast to one another—are related later in this tour.

The next stop is **Harpers Ferry**. *To get there, turn around and head back down Washington Street the way you came into town. You are on U.S. 340 North; follow the signs for Harpers Ferry past several shopping centers, then follow the signs to the Harpers Ferry National Historical Park entrance, which is on the right at a traffic light. If you want to drive through the town (be aware that no parking is available), turn left instead of right at the park entrance traffic light, following the signs for Bolivar and Harpers Ferry.*

To park at Harpers Ferry National Historical Park, you'll pay a small per-car entry fee, which includes parking, transportation to and from the town, and entry into all the museums. Shuttle buses run every few minutes up and down the 2-mile scenic road into the historic area.

The historic sections of Harpers Ferry have been carefully restored by the National Park Service and are worth at least a two-hour stop. You could easily spend a day or more seeing everything recommended in the National Park Service brochure, which you can pick up at the visitor center. If you enjoy hiking, you can walk the C&O Canal Towpath, which runs along the Potomac River, or part of the Appalachian Trail, which runs through here. The national headquarters of the Appalachian Trail Conference is in Harpers Ferry.

Harpers Ferry sits perched below a cliff at the confluence of the Potomac and Shenandoah Rivers, one of the prettiest settings in the Valley. In 1783, before there was a town here, Thomas Jefferson passed through the area on his way to serve in the Continental Congress in Philadelphia. He later wrote about the site in his only book, *Notes on the State of Virginia*: "The passage of the Patowmac through the Blue Ridge is perhaps one of the most stupendous scenes in nature. You stand on a very high point of land. On your right up comes the Shenandoah, having ranged along the foot of the mountain an [sic] hundred miles to seek a vent. On your left

Harpers Ferry from Potomac River bridge

approaches the Patowmac, in quest of a passage also. In the moment of their junction they rush together against the mountain, rend it asunder, and pass off to sea. . . . This scene is worth a voyage across the Atlantic."

If you are willing to walk a steep but paved path up from town, you can view this scene from the place he did, at a point above the Shenandoah River called Jefferson Rock. The view, although beautiful, may not seem quite as dramatic to modern eyes as it did to Jefferson's. In fact, John Quincy Adams, who came here in the early 1800s, wrote that he thought Jefferson had overstated the scene.

Harpers Ferry was settled in the early 1730s by a man from Pennsylvania, Peter Stephens, who operated a ferry service here. In 1747, a Philadelphia millwright named Robert Harper passed through the area on his way to Winchester to build a meeting house for a Quaker congregation. He recognized the business potential of the site and ended up buying land, building a gristmill, and taking over the ferry service.

Harper House, which Harper completed in 1782, is one of the oldest surviving buildings in town. Harper died that same year and never lived in the house. It served as the town tavern until 1803; among its guests were George Washington and Thomas Jefferson. Harper House stands near the beginning of the walkway to Jefferson Rock.

In 1794, the federal government authorized that several armories be built to manufacture and store guns and ammunition. At the time, the young nation was concerned about a possible future conflict with Britain. President Washington, remembering the area from his days as a surveyor, selected Harpers Ferry as the site for one of the armories, since it offered ready access to all the necessary resources for gunmaking: reliable water power, a source of iron ore, and abundant timber for making the charcoal to power furnaces and forges. Construction began in 1799. By the mid-1800s, more than 10,000 muskets, rifles, and pistols were being made here each year.

In 1803, Meriwether Lewis came to Harpers Ferry to buy weapons and supplies for his famous expedition to the western part of the continent.

The town continued to grow as many other types of businesses were drawn by

Jefferson Rock

Harper House

a good supply of water power and various transportation options. By the 1830s, the town had stagecoach service, toll roads, the Chesapeake and Ohio Canal, and the Baltimore and Ohio Railroad. By the late 1850s, the armory shops alone employed about 400 people.

Harpers Ferry made national headlines on October 16, 1859, when John Brown—an ardent abolitionist—and his 21-man "army of liberation" entered the federal armory area, took several hostages, and occupied the armory's fire-engine house, now referred to as "John Brown's Fort." Brown's goal was to capture the thousands of weapons stored in the armory and launch a slave revolt that he hoped would result in the abolition of slavery in the United States. But his plan was deeply flawed. A day and a half later, the "fort" was stormed by 90 U.S. marines sent from the Washington Navy Yard under the command of Colonel Robert E. Lee. Brown was wounded in the attack and arrested; two of his sons died in the siege. Brown was tried and hanged in Charles Town that December. Historians believe that his actions drew increased attention to the issue of racial inequality and moved the country closer to civil war.

The Civil War destroyed Harpers Ferry. The town changed hands eight times over the course of the war, and both sides participated in the raids and destruction that occurred. In September 1862, General Stonewall Jackson, following General Lee's orders (for a change, the story goes), carried out the first invasion of the North here, resulting in the surrender of 12,500 Union soldiers—the largest Confederate capture of the war. The site of that battle, now known as Schoolhouse Ridge Battlefield, is located above the town. The battlefield was turned over to the National Park Service in 1998 by the Civil War Trust and is now part of Harpers Ferry National Historical Park. In 1864, Harpers Ferry served as the base for General Philip Sheridan's campaign of destruction in the Shenandoah Valley—known locally as "The Burning."

Because of the destruction, most Harpers Ferry citizens moved away during the war and never came back. The town's strategic location on the two rivers, a great advantage for business and industry, also proved to be its greatest long-term problem. Severe flooding periodically destroyed buildings and discouraged rebuilding and resettlement. The National Park Service took over the lower section of the town in 1944 and began restoring the buildings to their 1860 appearance.

Leave Harpers Ferry the way you came in; turn left from the visitor center parking lot on to U.S. 340, as if you were heading back to Charles Town. Continue south for 1.6 miles and take the Route 230 North exit, to the right. This road soon enters Halltown on its way to Shepherdstown.

Halltown is a reminder of the once-thriving paper industry in the Harpers Ferry area. A paperboard factory dominates the town, which was named for John H. Hall, an inventor. Hall owned a rifle factory in Harpers Ferry and developed the idea of using interchangeable parts, which allowed for machine production of rifles.

Turn right at the stop sign to stay on Route 230 through Halltown. The housing developments that will soon come into view have transformed the rural feel of this area.

West of Halltown (but not on this tour) is another Washington family home, Beallair, a private residence today. Thomas Beall of Georgetown built the stone portion of the house sometime in the late 1700s on land owned by his father. Beall's daughter married George Corbin Washington, a grand-nephew of the president. Their son, Lewis William Washington, moved into the house in 1840.

Lewis Washington was literally dragged into John Brown's raid at Harpers Ferry. Brown wanted a hostage with a well-known name. He sent a band of men to take Lewis Washington and two family heirlooms that had been gifts to George Washington: a sword from Frederick the Great of Prussia and a pistol from Lafayette of France. Brown was probably aware of these relics because John Cook, Brown's advance man, had been living in Harpers Ferry for a year or so and somehow learned about them. Brown's men broke into Beallair late on the night of October 16 and awakened Colonel Washington, who turned over the heirlooms and was taken by the raiders (along with a few of his slaves) to Harpers Ferry. Brown is said to have worn the sword during his siege. Colonel Washington was shaken but unhurt.

The Halltown area was also home to William Darke, who lived at Duffields. Darke fought with Braddock at Fort Duquesne during the French and Indian War. He served as a general during the American Revolution and was a delegate to the Virginia Constitutional Convention in 1788. One day, according to local lore, he and James Stephenson of Martinsburg decided to settle a score by having a duel. Stephenson, a small man, came ready to fight with a small, slim rapier. Darke, who was tall and beefy, arrived carrying a very large sword. The onlookers began to chuckle at the contrast in sizes, and their laughter was soon shared by the would-be duelists. They called off the fight and reportedly became fast friends.

Continue north for 6 miles past Halltown until you reach a stop sign where another road merges with Route 230. Continue north for 2 miles to Shepherdstown. Follow Route 230 North as it turns right on to Princess Street, then go two blocks and turn left on German Street at the stop sign. German Street is the town's main street.

Old Shepherdstown bank building

Shepherdstown is one of the Valley's oldest European settlements. Some historians believe there were settlers in this area by 1717. Around 1730, people began to come here from Pennsylvania in search of fertile farmland. They crossed the Potomac about a mile south at Pack Horse Ford, one of the few places the river could be forded without benefit of a bridge or ferry. Thomas Shepherd arrived in 1732, received a land grant of 222 acres, and laid out the town he called Mecklenburg. It was officially chartered in 1762.

Congressional records from 1790 indicate that George Washington considered this town as one of three possible sites along the Potomac for a new United States capital, which was being planned at the time. The Winchester newspaper actively promoted the site, arguing that its western location was at the geographic center of the new and growing nation.

In 1798, the citizens changed the name to Shepherd's Town to honor the community's founder. In the 1800s, this was a busy river port. With easy access to the C&O Canal, merchants and farmers could ship their wares east to Washington and west to Cumberland. Their main exports were flour and cement.

No Civil War engagements took place here, but several of the town's buildings served as makeshift hospitals for the many soldiers wounded in the Battle of Antietam, fought just a few miles away. Many soldiers were buried here.

Today, Shepherdstown is a small college town and vibrant arts community with well-preserved 18th- and 19th-century homes, churches, and buildings, many of which have been turned into galleries, shops, and restaurants. The Shepherdstown Visitor Center is located at 136½ East German Street.

Probably the most impressive building in town is McMurran Hall, at the corner of German and King Streets, now part of Shepherd University. It served as the Jefferson County Courthouse in the years that Shepherdstown was the county seat, between 1865 and 1871. Local citizens decided that the vacant building would be best used for educational purposes, and Shepherd College was created in 1872.

McMurran Hall,
Shepherd University

Thomas Shepherd's first house stood on this piece of land.

Across the street from McMurran Hall is the town library, housed in a quaint-looking 1800 building that originally served as the town's market house and later as the town hall, the jail, the courthouse, and the fire hall. In the 1760s, the town whipping post stood near here.

Several local hotels and taverns have had long histories. The Entler Hotel, at the corner of German and Princess Streets, dates back to 1793. It is now home to the Historic Shepherdstown Commission, which operates a museum that is open weekends from April through October. A section of the museum is devoted to the town's most famous resident, James Rumsey, and his inventions. Rumsey invented what many believe was the first successful steamboat, which he demonstrated on the Potomac River here in December 1787. A half-size-scale working model of his 1787 steamboat is housed in a carriage house in back of the museum.

Rumsey was born in Cecil County, Maryland, in 1743 and moved to what is now Berkeley Springs, West Virginia, in 1782. There, he ran an inn and a store and built summer cabins for the visitors to the mineral springs resort—including one for George Washington. It was there that Rumsey gave Washington a demonstration of a model of a self-propelled boat, an idea that intrigued Washington and led him to publicly endorse the inventor.

Washington had long been interested in making Virginia's rivers navigable. In 1785, he put Rumsey in charge of the Potowmack Navigation Company, which tried valiantly but unsuccessfully to build canals at several spots along the Potomac

Nearby Antietam—
The Worst Day of the Civil War

The Battle of Antietam—the bloodiest battle of the Civil War—took place in Maryland 10 miles from Harpers Ferry, just two days after General Stonewall Jackson's victory at Harpers Ferry. The South, outnumbered two to one, lost this battle. More than 23,000 men were killed or wounded there on a single day—September 17, 1862.

River. Rumsey quit in frustration after a year on the job.

Rumsey moved to Shepherdstown in 1785 to be closer to a navigable part of the Potomac. He spent the next two years developing a steam engine that could propel a boat using a jet of water. He soon became known around town as "Crazy Rumsey." On December 3, 1787, he loaded the craft with two tons of rock and eight of the town's ladies, then navigated up and down the river for two hours in front of an audience that included Revolutionary War generals Horatio Gates and William Darke. The site of his demonstration is commemorated on the bluff above the river at the end of Mill Street; turn right into the town park to view the river and see the James Rumsey Monument.

George Washington kept up with Rumsey's progress and provided support and encouragement. In the meantime, John Fitch, a silversmith from Connecticut, was experimenting in Philadelphia with a different kind of steam engine that powered paddles, which he demonstrated in Philadelphia in August 1787. He ran a commercial steamboat service in Philadelphia for several months in 1790, but a lack of investors forced him to abandon his efforts there.

In 1788, Rumsey gained financial backing for further steamboat work from the American Philosophical Society in Philadelphia, which in turn founded the Rumseian Society. Benjamin Franklin was this investment group's first president. The Rumseian Society sent Rumsey to England to obtain European patents and gain financial support.

Rumsey arrived in London in 1788 and spent the next four years building and promoting a 100-foot steamboat. During that time, he became acquainted with a young American art student, Robert Fulton. Just as things were going well for Rumsey, he suffered a fatal stroke while speaking to a London scientific society in December 1792. His rival, John Fitch, died in 1798. Coincidentally or not, Rumsey's London acquaintance, Robert Fulton, abandoned his failing career as an artist and turned to engineering around 1794. Fulton returned to the United States in December 1806, where a Boulton & Watt steam engine that he had ordered in

Left: *James Rumsey Monument*
Above: *Rumsey Steamboat Museum*

Entler Museum

England was waiting for him. Just months later, in August 1807, Fulton launched the *North River Steamboat*, better known as the *Clermont*, on the Hudson River in New York.

The Rumseian Society is still around. Based in Shepherdstown, it works to "set the record straight," according to its brochure, to see that Rumsey's contributions to steamboat navigation (and mill technology) are recognized. Their working replica of his first boat and steam engine is on display at the Rumsey Steamboat Museum, located behind the Entler Museum on East German Street. In a nice bit of payback, Rumseian Society members hauled their 1787 replica of Rumsey's steamboat from Shepherdstown to upstate New York in August 2007 to participate in Fulton steamboat bicentennial events. There, it successfully, if briefly, steamed up the Hudson River.

Also located behind the Entler Museum, facing Princess Street, is a charming stone building called "The Little House." It's a furnished scale model of a two-story house about 10 feet square. It was built by home economics students at Shepherd College in 1928.

"The Little House"

Prato Rio

In 2000, Shepherdstown made headlines worldwide when President Bill Clinton mediated the Israeli-Syrian peace talks at a local hotel.

To continue the tour, drive west on German Street and turn left on Route 480 South (Duke Street), following the signs toward Kearneysville. In less than 1 mile, you'll pass Morgan's Grove Park, on the left after the traffic light. It is here that Hugh Stephenson assembled a company of riflemen (some 93 Berkeley County volunteers) on July 16, 1775, to begin their famous Beeline March to Cambridge, Massachusetts, where—along with another company formed by Daniel Morgan in neighboring Frederick County—they became the first Southern units to join General Washington's troops. The men made the 600-mile journey in less than a month, and Washington reportedly met them with tears of gratitude. The two Virginia companies must have created quite a stir in New England, dressed in buckskins, coonskin hats, and moccasins. Later, Morgan spent the horrible winter with Washington at Valley Forge.

In 1825, two of the surviving riflemen fulfilled a pledge made by the group 50 years earlier to meet on the silver anniversary of their departure. An early family named Morgan—unrelated to the soldier Daniel Morgan—owned property nearby, hence the name of the park.

Farms in the Shenandoah Valley provided large amounts of food and provisions to the Continental forces; in 1781 alone, some 200,000 pounds of flour, 10,000 bushels of wheat, and 500,000 pounds of beef were shipped out. Arms and ammunition were also produced in the Valley to supply the troops, as well as hemp, which was used to make ropes and sail material for naval ships.

Continue on Route 480 South for nearly 4 miles to the traffic light in Kearneysville. Stay straight through the light, crossing Route 9. The road is now marked Route 1, heading toward Leetown.

A state historical marker at the intersection in **Kearneysville** notes that the house of Revolutionary War general Horatio Gates—Traveler's Rest—is 0.5 mile southwest. The house, built around 1773, still stands off Route 1, a short distance down Bower Road. It is privately owned. Although Gates is credited with leading the Continental Army to victory at the Battle of Saratoga, he charged when he should have retreated at the Battle of Camden in South Carolina, an action that led to his court-martial and suspension. He regained his command in 1782, later retired to his home here, and stayed until 1790, when he moved to New York.

In about 3 miles, you'll reach **Leetown**. After entering the town, you'll see a state historical marker titled "The Bower." It says that General Adam Stephen, who founded Martinsburg, lived here from 1754 until 1772, when he moved to Martinsburg. The mansion now on the property was built by Stephen's grandson, Adam Stephen Dandridge, in 1805. The Dandridge family still owns the house, which is located west of Leetown.

Continue 1 mile to a state historical marker on the right. This marker commemorates Prato Rio, General Charles Lee's home. The village that grew up here later became known as Leetown in General Lee's honor. The limestone house, still occupied today, is down a driveway just past the historical marker. This property first belonged to early Shenandoah Valley settler Jost Hite; he called the log cabin he built here "Hopewell." Hite's son sold this 3,000-acre plantation to Lee.

Lee was born in Wales and came to America in 1756 as an officer in the British army. (He was not related to the famous Lee family of Virginia.) He quit his commission and joined the American forces after the Battle of Lexington in 1775, the year after he bought this house and its surrounding acreage. Lee's fellow Revolutionary War general Horatio Gates told him about the property and encouraged him to buy it.

Lee retired here a bitter man, having been court-martialed and suspended from the Continental Army after retreating at the Battle of Monmouth in 1778. Washington, upon hearing of Lee's order to retreat, came to Monmouth and took over command, saving the day for the Americans. When Washington reprimanded Lee, Lee exploded with an angry response; he later had a blow-up with Congress. Some historians think his retreat was intended to embarrass Washington. They trace Lee's resentment of Washington to the time when Washington was named to command the Continental Army; Lee believed he was much better qualified for the job.

Lee lived a hermit-like life after his dismissal, sharing his house (which was unusual in that it had no interior walls) with his beloved dogs (he never married). Local lore goes that after the war, Washington wrote him a letter stating that he was coming through the area and would like to see Lee as a friend once more. When Washington arrived, the house was empty, and a sign on the door read, "No meat cook'd here today."

Lee's few friends in the area included General Horatio Gates and General Adam Stephen (see more about Stephen in The Clearbrook to Martinsburg Tour), both of whom had also lost their commands in the Continental Army. The story goes that the three old soldiers would gather at Prato Rio and toast each other as follows: "To Major General Charles Lee, who was cashiered from the Continental Army because, when he should have advanced, he retreated; to Major General Horatio Gates, who was cashiered because, when he should have retreated, he advanced; and to Major General Adam Stephen, who was cashiered because, when he might have advanced or retreated, he did neither."

The story of Gates's demise is interesting. He had been commissioned as a brigadier general and as the adjutant general of the Continental Army shortly after it was formed in 1775. He was placed in command just in time for the victorious Battle of Saratoga, which he tried to claim credit for, even though the battle was won by the field commanders, including Benedict Arnold and Daniel Morgan. (It's said that Arnold referred to Gates as "Granny Gates.") Gates's dismissal from command came after his embarrassing defeat at the Battle of Camden in South Carolina, in 1780. Congress voted to hold a board of inquiry (a precursor to court-martial) to look into Gates's actions during the battle, but the board never met, thanks to Gates's strong opposition. Gates returned to Washington's staff headquarters in Newburgh, New York, but was not given another command.

Charles Lee did not live to see the formal end of the Revolution. He traveled to Philadelphia in 1782 and died shortly after. His will specified that he not "be buried in any church or churchyard, or within a mile of any Presbyterian or Anabaptist meeting house. For since I have resided in this country I have kept so much bad company when living that I do not choose to continue it when dead." Against his wishes, he was buried with full military honors in Philadelphia's Christ Church graveyard.

Continue about 3.2 miles to the intersection with Route 51, where the tour ends. Turn right on to Route 51 West at the stop sign. In 4.8 miles, turn right on U.S. 11 North at the traffic light, then go a short distance and turn left at the next traffic light back on to Route 51 West, which will take you to the I-81 exit at Inwood, where you began.

The Middletown to Winchester Tour

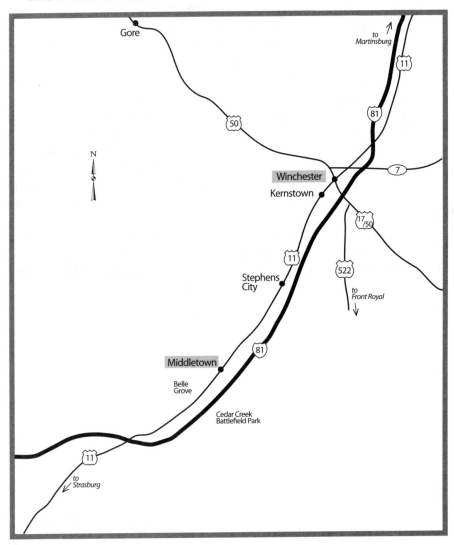

TOUR **3**
The Middletown to Winchester Tour

This tour begins in Middletown, just north of Strasburg, at Belle Grove Plantation and the surrounding Civil War battlefield of Cedar Creek. Passing the old Wayside Inn, it heads north on the Old Valley Pike (U.S. 11) toward Winchester, passing through the early Opequon-area settlements around Stephens City and Kernstown. Many Civil War engagements took place along this road and in the Winchester area.

The tour ends in Winchester, with a walking tour of the historic district and directions to the Museum of the Shenandoah Valley and Glen Burnie Historic House and Gardens. Winchester was once home to President George Washington, polar explorer Richard E. Byrd, novelist Willa Cather, country-western singer Patsy Cline, and actor Dan Ackroyd.

Total mileage: Approximately 20 miles

To begin the tour, take Exit 298 off I-81 and turn on to U.S. 11 North toward Winchester. In 2 miles, you'll see signs on the left for Belle Grove.

Belle Grove is an impressive limestone mansion built in 1797 by a descendant of the Shenandoah Valley's early pioneer settler, Jost Hite. The home and grounds are open daily for tours from April through October and on weekends at other times of year. In 1864, the Battle of Cedar Creek was fought all around this house; the Cedar Creek Battlefield Park is a short distance north on U.S. 11 past Belle Grove's entrance. The two sites form a combined national historical park.

Jost Hite came to the Shenandoah Valley from Pennsylvania in 1731 or 1732. He brought with him 16 families, including his five sons and three daughters and their families. One Hite son-in-law was Jacob Bowman, whose many descendants live in the Valley today. Bowman later wrote of their hardships: "[S]everal of the families who first removed and settled there were put to such hardships and difficulties as are scarcely to be conceived[,] being obliged to live in the waggons [sic] till they could build some small huts to shelter themselves from the inclemency of the weather."

Belle Grove

Hite, whose German name was Hans Yost Heydt, was born in Kraichgau, Germany (southeast of Heidelberg). He first settled in Kingston, New York, in 1711. Around 1716, he moved to Pennsylvania, and some 15 years later secured two land grants in the Shenandoah Valley totaling 140,000 acres. He built a home north of here, which will be described later in this tour.

Hite was one of the first of thousands of immigrants to follow the Indian Trail—later known as the Great Wagon Road, the Valley Turnpike or Valley Pike, and U.S. Route 11—from Pennsylvania into the Shenandoah Valley and beyond, in search of cheap and fertile land.

The royal colony of Virginia encouraged these early settlers, offering generous grants of land with few strings attached, except the requirement that a family establish a home on the land within two years. The colony even eliminated the requirement of mandatory Church of England attendance, which gave the Quakers, Mennonites, and Lutherans in Pennsylvania further incentive to come here. But the colony's motives were largely self-serving. Virginians on the eastern side of the Blue Ridge viewed the Shenandoah Valley as a buffer zone—a place where increased settlement would help keep the Indians on the far side of the mountains.

Belle Grove has been restored to its appearance in the early 1800s. This grand home was built by Major Isaac Hite, Jr., one of Jost Hite's grandsons and a Revolutionary War officer whose first wife was Nelly Madison, the sister of President James Madison. It is said that James Madison and his bride, Dolley, spent the night in an earlier house on this property after their marriage at Harewood near Charles Town in 1794.

After learning of his brother-in-law's plans to build Belle Grove, Madison wrote to his friend Thomas Jefferson for design advice. Although no written record exists to indicate any response from Jefferson, the structure's emphasis on symmetry and a few other touches have led some to believe that Jefferson offered ideas for the house.

Belle Grove's exterior was built using limestone quarried from the property. The front portion of the house features "dressed" limestone—limestone blocks that were chiseled smoothed to form a flat surface, which was considered more attractive in those days. Because it cost more, the dressed stone blocks were used only on the front of the house. This extra work must have impressed early visitors, but, ironically, the stones look more like today's plain old concrete blocks.

Isaac Hite attended the College of William and Mary, where he was the first person to be taken into the academic honor society Phi Beta Kappa by its charter members in 1776. Not long after, he left school to participate in the Revolutionary War. Later, he became an astute farmer and businessman, operating a distillery, a quarry, gristmills, sawmills, and a general store.

Nelly Madison Hite died in 1802, leaving Hite with two children. He remarried and had 10 more children. He enlarged the house to accommodate them all. Interestingly, after the second Mrs. Hite died in 1851, none of the children wanted Belle Grove, so it was sold.

By the fall of 1864, General Philip Sheridan was using the house as Union field headquarters. One of the South's most promising young men, Major General Stephen Ramseur, was mortally wounded in the Battle of Cedar Creek nearby and taken to Belle Grove, where he died the day after the battle. Several Union soldiers who had been his classmates at West Point sat with him at his bedside, including, the tradition goes, Major General George A. Custer.

From 1900 until the 1930s, Belle Grove was operated as an inn. A frequent guest was a botanist from New York, Frances Welles Hunnewell, who bought the house and began to restore and furnish it. He died in 1964 and deeded the property to the National Trust for Historic Preservation.

Continue a short distance north of Belle Grove on U.S. 11 to Cedar Creek Battlefield. This Civil War battlefield is managed by a private nonprofit foundation that purchased 158 acres here in 1989—land that had been zoned as an industrial park. The foundation added a visitor center (open daily from April through October) in 1996, and purchased another 150 acres in 2000, saving much of the battlefield area from development. Easily seen from U.S. 11 is the Heater House, a log farmhouse covered by white clapboard that survived the battle and is being restored by the foundation. Living history events are held here each October.

The Battle of Cedar Creek began as a surprise attack on 30,000 sleeping Union troops by some 17,000 Confederates led by Lieutenant General Jubal Early before dawn on October 19, 1864. The Union had won important victories the previous month at Winchester and Fisher's Hill, and "The Burning" of the Valley—a devastating attempt to cut off food and supplies to the Confederate troops in eastern Virginia—had begun that fall. Early's men drove the Federal troops past Belle Grove and through Middletown, where Early stopped to regroup.

In the meantime, General Sheridan, who had been in Winchester when the attack began, rode his horse down the Valley Pike (inspiring the poem "Sheridan's Ride") and organized a successful Union counterattack. This battle marked the end of the Confederates' military power in the Valley and helped ensure President Lincoln's reelection just three weeks later. Interestingly, two future presidents fought in this battle on the Union side: Colonel Rutherford B. Hayes and Major William McKinley.

Wayside Inn

Continue 1 mile up the road to **Middletown.** This town was called Senseney Town, after its founder, when it was chartered in 1796. The current name reflects the fact that the community is halfway between Stephens City and Strasburg.

You will pass the Wayside Theater, one of a dwindling number of small-town summer stock theaters left on the East Coast. It occupies a 1940s building that was once the town's movie house.

The stretch of U.S. 11 around Middletown saw a great deal of Civil War action, as noted by the numerous state historical markers between here and Winchester. The marker in front of the Wayside Inn cites the spot as the place where General Stonewall Jackson's army, on May 24, 1862, attacked General Banks's forces, which were retreating from Strasburg.

The original portion of the Wayside Inn, built in 1797, was known as Wilkenson's Tavern. By the mid-1800s, it was Larrick's Hotel and served as a stagecoach inn and relay station. In the early 1900s, it was enlarged and began catering to tourists traveling by automobile; it calls itself "America's First Motor Inn."

Continue north on U.S. 11. Just north of Middletown is the campus of Lord Fairfax Community College. The historical marker in front of the school notes during the Battle of Cedar Creek, General Early stopped his advance here on the morning of October 19, 1864, and was pushed back by General Sheridan later that day.

Continue 1 mile farther up the road to another historical marker. It marks the place where the Union army stood when General Sheridan rejoined it during the Battle of Cedar Creek, thereby halting the Union retreat.

Continue driving north on U.S. 11 for 3 miles. Just before U.S. 11 enters Stephens City, look for a handsome old stone farmhouse on the left. The stone section of LaGrange was built around 1790 by Vance Bush; a later owner was a physician named McLeod.

Stephens City, which narrowly escaped being burned during the Civil War, captures a bit of mid-20th-century history as the location of the Family Drive-In Theater—one of the few remaining outdoor movie theaters on the East Coast.

Stephens City is the second-oldest town in Frederick County and one of the most intact. Many of its original log homes, most now covered by clapboard, are still standing. The Newtown History Center, located in the red-brick house next to the single traffic light in town is open most days from June through November. It offers visitors a look into the town's history, as well as a map and description of many of the old properties—some dating back to the late 1700s—that can be viewed during a self-guided walking tour.

Stephens City was founded by Lewis Stephens, the son of Peter Stephens, who was from Heidelberg, Germany, and one of Jost Hite's original settlers. Although Peter Stephens came here in the early 1730s, Stephensburg wasn't chartered until 1758. Around the time of the Revolutionary War, the settlement became known as Newtown, apparently because it was the newest town on the Great Wagon Road at the time. The name stuck for decades to come.

Around the time of the California gold rush, the town became well known for its 13 wagon-making shops. The wagons, called Newtown wagons, were praised for their sturdiness. The coming of the railroad after the Civil War put an end to that business.

About 1 mile out of Stephens City, U.S. 11 dips as it approaches Opequon Creek. After you pass the sign for this creek, turn left on to Route 649 (Springdale Road). On the left just a short distance from the intersection, you will see the old Springdale Flour Mill. Built in 1788, it replaced an earlier mill that stood on the same spot. Operating under a string of owners until 1970, its machinery is still intact. The first mill here was built around 1738 by Jost Hite, the Valley pioneer mentioned at the beginning of this tour.

In 1772, Jost Hite's son John sold the mill to David Brown, who rebuilt and enlarged it. There are two houses associated with the mill property. A frame house on the left side of Springdale Road just before the mill has at its core a two-room log house dating to the mid-17th century; some say this log building was Jost Hite's first house in this area. The handsome stone house across the road from the mill was built in the latter part of the 19th century. Unfortunately, its interior was destroyed by fire in 1932.

Directly across U.S. 11 from the mill complex is a handsome limestone house known as Springdale. According to a datestone in the south gable end of the house,

Springdale Flour Mill

Springdale

it was built by John Hite in 1753. The ruins of Jost Hite's 1730s stone house remain in the yard. John Hite was a county justice, militia colonel, and a close friend of George Washington, who is said to have visited him here. During the Civil War, Springdale is thought to have served for a time as the headquarters of William Dwight, one of Sheridan's generals.

*About 1 mile past Springdale, U.S. Route 11 passes under I-81. **Kernstown** is about 1.5 miles north. Turn left at the traffic light at Route 706 (Opequon Church Lane).* Just a block away is the home of one of the first religious congregations in the Shenandoah Valley—the Opequon Presbyterian Church. It was formed by some of Jost Hite's settlers in 1736. Today, an 1897 building stands on the site of two earlier churches. The cemetery contains a headstone for a man named Wilson, who died in 1742. It is the oldest known gravesite in the Shenandoah Valley. Across from the church are signs and maps explaining the Second Battle of Kernstown.

Kernstown is best known for the two Civil War battles that took place here. The First Battle of Kernstown—considered to be Stonewall Jackson's only military defeat—was fought on March 23, 1862, as Jackson's men attacked General James Shields, hoping to regain control of the Valley. Unfortunately for the Confederates, Jackson relied on Colonel Turner Ashby's reports of the Union troop numbers, which were greatly underestimated. But the battle achieved one of Jackson's goals: to keep 35,000 Union soldiers engaged in the Valley, away from Richmond.

The Second Battle of Kernstown was fought in the fields surrounding the Opequon Church on July 24, 1864. General George Crook, whose 12,000 Union troops were near Winchester, believed that the Confederates were leaving the Valley. General Jubal Early, whose 17,000 men were south of Winchester, decided to advance on Crook's forces and soon realized their smaller numbers. A bloody battle ensued, with the loss of 600 Confederate soldiers and nearly 1,200 Union troops. Crook's forces retreated back to Winchester.

During the Civil War, the road that is now U.S. 11, which was one of the few macadamized roads in the region, was operated as a toll road. One of the Valley's most enduring tales describes how, in 1864, a young tollkeeper on a stretch of the road south of Winchester lowered her barrier to collect tolls from General Sheridan and his Union troops. The general and his staff paid up, but they told her she'd have to collect from the government for everyone else. After the war was over, she did.

Continue straight on U.S. Route 11 (now called Valley Avenue) past the Ward Plaza shopping center; you will pass through several traffic lights as you wind through a busy commercial part of **Winchester.** You'll soon enter a residential area of older homes. Shortly, you'll see the huge front lawn of Handley High School on the left. The high school's beautiful main building was built in the early 1900s from funds left to the city by Pennsylvania judge and philanthropist John Handley (read more about Judge Handley later in this tour). The First Battle of Winchester took place on May 25, 1862, on Bowers Hill, behind the school, as well as on South Kent Street. This engagement occurred in the middle of Stonewall Jackson's famous Valley Campaign; here, his forces chased Union general Banks's army out of Winchester.

Continue past the high school on U.S. 11, turning right at the traffic light. On the right as you turn is the restored

The Three Battles of Winchester

Winchester was the site of three major Civil War battles. Its terrain was flat and not easily defended. When attacked by one side, the other side evacuated. This occurred an estimated 72 times in all. One historian called the town "basically indefensible."

The First Battle of Winchester occurred on May 25, 1862. Stonewall Jackson chased out General Banks's forces, already on the run after their defeat a few days earlier in Front Royal. The battle took place on Bowers Hill, behind present-day Handley High School, and on Camp Hill, on what is now South Kent Street.

The Second Battle of Winchester took place June 13 through June 15, 1863. General Richard Ewell, on his way to Gettysburg, found General Milroy's troops occupying Winchester. Ewell struck from two sides (the northwest and the northeast), forcing the Union troops into retreat. Action took place at Star Fort, West Fort, and Stephenson Depot, north of town.

The Third Battle of Winchester occurred on September 19, 1864, when General Philip Sheridan drove General Jubal Early's forces from what is now Route 7 down the Valley Pike to Fisher's Hill, south of Strasburg. He defeated the Confederates once more a few days later.

Triangle Diner, a landmark in Winchester since 1948. It was prefabricated by the leading diner manufacturer Jerry O'Mahony and shipped to Winchester in pieces by rail from New Jersey. O'Mahony built more than 2,000 diners from 1917 to 1952, but this is one of the few still remaining. The country-western singer Patsy Cline, who attended Handley High School, worked here "slinging hash." She also worked at the soda fountain at Gaunt's Drug Store next door. The store's walls hold many pictures of Cline.

Turn left at the busy intersection at Pleasant Valley Avenue and follow the city's bright yellow and red tourism signs to the Winchester Visitor Center, which is on the right after you turn, just past Shenandoah University's Byrd School of Business building.

On the visitor center grounds are three historic buildings. Abram's Delight Museum, a lovely old 1754 stone structure, is the oldest house in Winchester. Around 1729, Abraham Hollingsworth built a log cabin here, close to a small Shawnee Indian village of 100 or so people. The legend goes that he bought more than 500 acres of land around the Shawnee Springs from the Indians in exchange for a cow, a calf, and a piece of red cloth.

The Indians remained in the area until 1754, when they headed west to the

Handley High School *Abram's Delight*

Ohio Valley to join other tribes siding with the French, who were fighting the British over territorial claims. That same year, Hollingsworth's son, Isaac, built the first portion of the stone house that stands here today. His father's statement that the spot was "a delight to behold" was the inspiration for the home's name. According to the Virginia Landmarks Register, the stonemason of record for Abram's Delight was Simon Taylor, who also worked as a stonemason at Springdale, the Hite home mentioned earlier.

Next to Abram's Delight is a typical Valley log cabin, dating to 1780. It was moved to this site from nearby Cork Street in the 1960s. The third building on the visitor center grounds is the Hollingsworth Mill, built in 1833. It houses the local historical society, which features an interesting exhibit of area artifacts.

Winchester was the first town established in the Shenandoah Valley, and it claims to be the first English-speaking community west of the Blue Ridge. It was settled largely by Germans and Scotch-Irish who came to Virginia from Pennsylvania.

DOWNTOWN WINCHESTER

1 Rouss City Hall
2 Old Court House Civil War Museum
3 Old Post Office Building
4 Handley Library
5 Logan House
6 McGuire House
7 Alexander Tidball House
8 Daniel Morgan House
9 Ambler Hill
10 Christ Episcopal Church/Lord Fairfax tomb
11 Rouss Fire Hall
12 George Washington's Office Museum
13 Red Lion Tavern
14 First Presbyterian Church
15 Godfrey Miller House
P Parking

Patsy Cline, Winchester Native

Patsy Cline was a well-loved country-western singer who died tragically in a plane crash in 1963, just as her career was taking off. Born Virginia Patterson Hensley in Winchester in 1932, she lived in the house at 608 South Kent Street from ages 16 to 21. When she married Charlie Dick in 1957, she lived in the house at 720 South Kent Street. She also attended Handley High School.

Patsy began singing at area clubs and dance halls in the 1950s. One of her biggest hits, "Crazy," was written for her by Willie Nelson. She was the first woman to be elected into the Country Music Hall of Fame and the first woman to become a member of the Grand Ole Opry. A local group is working to restore the house at 608 South Kent Street so it can be opened to visitors for tours and special events; the group also has long-term plans to establish a Patsy Cline Museum in Winchester.

Patsy Cline is buried at Shenandoah Memorial Park, about 4 miles south of town on Route 522 South. *To visit her grave, follow the signs to Route 50 East from downtown Winchester or from I-81, Exit 313. Turn on to Route 522 South, toward Front Royal. Enter the cemetery at the north gate and take the first right to the bench on the left, near Omps Funeral Chapel.*

Patsy Cline's house

Gaunt's Drug Store

A typical Valley log cabin next to Abram's Delight

Its founder, Englishman James Wood, worked as a surveyor for Orange County, Virginia, in the 1730s. In those days, Orange County stretched into this part of the Shenandoah Valley. While surveying here, Wood obtained a grant for some 1,300 acres from Royal Governor Gooch of Virginia. Around 1738, he built a log-and-stone home he called Glen Burnie near the site of today's Glen Burnie, described later in this tour. He began laying out the town in 1744—but only after having to accede to Lord Fairfax's claim that his original grant was illegal.

Wood's town lay-out had twenty-six lots centering on Loudoun Street, which was created by rerouting the Philadelphia

Wagon Road (today's U.S. 11) through the town. The first structure, in 1744, was a primitive courthouse, on the site of the present-day Old Court House Civil War Museum. By the early 1750s, there were about sixty "rather poorly built" houses, according to Moravian missionaries who had passed through the town.

Frederick County was formed from Orange County in 1738. Its name honors Frederick, Prince of Wales. The town was first known as Frederick Town; the name was changed to Winchester early on, both to honor Wood's English birthplace and to avoid confusion with nearby Frederick, Maryland.

Lord Fairfax officially held title to all the lands in the Northern Neck proprietary, which extended well into the Shenandoah Valley. Any settlers who had received land grants from the colonial government before Lord Fairfax's arrival were required to reapply for their land and pay annual "quit rents." Jost Hite resented Fairfax's demands and began a court battle that wasn't resolved for more than 40 years, after both men were dead. The Hite family won in the end.

Probably because of a request by Lord Fairfax, who also owned land in the area of the town, Winchester was officially chartered in 1752, with 88 additional lots. Wood named many of the streets—Washington, Amherst, Loudoun, and Boscawen—after French and Indian War heroes. Lord Fairfax named his streets after places in London—Leicester, Piccadilly, and Cork. Wood later became a colonel in the militia, the first clerk of the court of Frederick County, and the person who launched George Washington's political career.

During the Civil War, three major battles were fought in Winchester. For most of the war, the town was under Union control. Its proximity to Washington, D.C., its value as a supplier of food and supplies to the Confederacy, its railroads, and its location on the Valley Pike made Winchester strategically important.

After recovering from the devastating effects of the war, Winchester began to grow at a rapid rate, largely due to the success of its apple, wheat, and woolen industries. Today, apples are still important to the local economy, which is also supported by light manufacturing and a growing educational institution—Shenandoah University, formerly Shenandoah Conservatory of Music, which moved here from Dayton, Virginia, in 1960. (See The Edinburg to Singers Glen Tour, page 124, for its early history). The city is well known in the mid-Atlantic region for its Shenandoah Apple Blossom Festival, an event held every May since 1924.

To continue on to Old Town Winchester, turn right out of the visitor center park-

Poor Prince Fred

The British writer Thomas Carlyle said that the following epigram, written in 1751 on the occasion of the death of Prince Frederick—for whom Frederick County was named—was an accurate expression of England's feelings about the man:

Here lies Prince Fred
Who was alive and is dead;
Had it been his Father,
I had much rather;
Had it been his brother,
Sooner than any other;
Had it been his sister,
There's no one would have missed her;
Had it been his whole generation,
Best of all for the Nation;
But since it's only Fred,
There's no more to be said.

ing lot back on to Pleasant Valley Road and continue for about 1 mile to the traffic light, where you'll turn left on to Cork Street. (You'll see red and yellow tourism signs pointing the way.) Mount Hebron, the large cemetery on the corner, contains four separate cemeteries. To visit the cemeteries, turn right at the next intersection, which is Kent Street. Many early Valley settlers, including Revolutionary War hero Daniel Morgan and 2,576 Confederate soldiers are buried here.

Continue down Cork Street to Cameron Street and turn right. Park on the street or in the Court Square public garage one block down on the right. A bronze statue in front of the Judicial Center on Cameron Street honors Admiral Richard E. Byrd, a pioneer naval aviator and polar explorer who was born in Winchester at 326 West Amherst Street (the house no longer stands).

Although some 200 homes in and around Winchester were destroyed during the Civil War, many interesting old homes and buildings remain. The following abbreviated walking tour covers a few in the historic downtown area.

The impressive building across Cameron Street from the Judicial Center is the Rouss City Hall, built in 1900 and named for the mid-1800s Winchester merchant Charles Baltzell Rouss. After serving in the Confederate Army during the

Rouss City Hall

Richard E. Byrd statue

Traffic Congestion, 1700s-style

By the late 1780s, Winchester had established itself as a major trade center. According to one early estimate, some 132,000 barrels of flour were sent from Winchester to Alexandria each year. The traffic between the two towns became so heavy that merchants petitioned the Virginia Assembly for new roads and for additional ferries across the Shenandoah River, especially where the Winchester-Alexandria Road (what is now Route 7) crossed. They claimed congestion was so bad that wagons often had to wait two or three days before they could get across the river.

Civil War, Rouss moved to New York City. He claimed he intended "to fight Yan-kees with brains instead of bullets." There he opened a general merchandise store on Broadway that grew into a multi-store empire. When the economy crashed in the 1870s, he started over with auction houses. He built a mercantile building at 549-555 Broadway that was considered huge for its era. It still stands today with the name "Charles Broadway Rouss" carved in stone across the front. (Rouss had changed his middle name to Broadway.) He was worth nearly $10 million when he died in 1899. Rouss remembered Winchester with several generous financial gifts, one of which paid for almost half of the new city hall. He also left money to fund the fire department, a waterworks, and the iron fence around Mount Hebron Cemetery. Although he died in New York City, he is buried in a huge mausoleum in Mount Hebron cemetery.

To begin the walking tour from the parking garage, walk across Cameron Street, turn right, walk to just past the city hall, and turn left on to Rouss Avenue. A large sign with a map of the town and its landmarks will greet you. Continue straight to Lou-doun Street, which is traffic-free and is known locally as the Loudoun Street Mall. Turn right. A few steps away is the Frederick County Courthouse. Built in 1840 in the Greek Revival style, this grand old brick structure was considered by some to be one of the prettiest courthouses in the state. No longer a courthouse, the building has been turned into the Old Court House Civil War Museum, a fitting role since it was used as a prison and hospital during the conflict. More than 3,000 artifacts are on display.

From the Old Court House Museum, continue walking down the Loudoun Street Mall. With numerous restaurants, outdoor cafes, and shops, this mall can be a lively place, especially at lunchtime. Although many historic buildings here have been restored and are well maintained, others have been modernized beyond recognition. A portion of the building at 119-129 North Loudoun Street was once the Taylor Hotel, whose guests included Henry Clay, Daniel Webster, and Stone-wall Jackson. Built in 1846 on the site of an old tavern, it served as both Union and Confederate headquarters, depending on which side controlled Winchester at the time. One story goes that the hotel changed hands four times in one day. It was here that Stonewall Jackson promoted Turner Ashby to the rank of general, a

Old Court House Civil War Museum

title he held for only 10 days until his death near Harrisonburg in June 1862. In the early 1900s, the hotel closed, and a variety store occupied the building for most of the 20th century. Plans to renovate the building for commercial use are underway.

Continue down to the end of the Loudoun Street Mall and turn left at Piccadilly Street. Just across Indian Alley, at 25 West Piccadilly, a business occupies a beautiful old painted brick house with extensive ironwork. It was built in 1845 by a local attorney, Philip William. Local legend says that the ironwork was taken down and buried during the Civil War so it wouldn't be confiscated and melted down for ammunition. George S. Patton, the grandfather of the World War II general of the same name, was wounded during the Third Battle of Winchester and brought to this house, which belonged to his cousin. He died here.

The stone house at 35 West Piccadilly was built in 1797 by George Reed, a coppersmith whose shop was next door. It is typical of stone buildings in early Winchester, featuring two stories with two rooms on each level. As in most houses like this one, the dormers were added later.

Directly across the street is the Old Post Office Building, an Italian Renaissance Revival structure that now houses a bank.

Continue to Braddock Street. You can't miss the large red apple sitting on the front lawn of a large white Greek Revival house across Braddock Street. Some 20 painted apples the size of this original one can be found all over Winchester, created by local artists. The house, which was built in 1850 by tobacco merchant Lloyd Logan, is now a gift shop. It was once headquarters for Union generals Milroy and Sheridan. The town was outraged when Milroy moved in and literally threw the Logan family out on the street. From 1874 to 1909, the structure housed the Episcopal Female Institute. The large front porch is a 20th-century addition.

The impressive building across the street, at the intersection of Piccadilly and Braddock, is the Handley Library. This Beaux-Arts–style building was built between 1908 and 1913 from funds left to Winchester by a man who never lived here. He was Judge John Handley of Scranton, Pennsylvania, who first visited friends here in 1869 and grew to love the town. Handley made a fortune in coal investments. When he died in 1895, he left the city a bequest, which grew to nearly $2 million, to be used to build and maintain a public library and a high school, among other worthy projects. Judge Handley was buried, at his request, in Mount Hebron Cemetery.

Left: *Original apple in front of Logan House;* below: *Another Winchester painted apple*

The library was designed by two New York architects, J. Stewart Barney and Henry Otis Chapman. It has a large copper dome (with a stained glass dome inside) and coupled columns on either side of the entrance porch. The design was intended to represent a book, with the rotunda serving as the spine and the two side wings as the opened pages.

As the library grew, the problem arose of how to expand the building. Hard as it is to believe, one consultant advised tearing down this structure and starting anew. Instead, a wing was added in 1979, and it fit in so well with the original design that the library won an award from the American Institute of Architects.

Walk up North Braddock Street one block. Past the rear of the library, look for a historical marker across the street at the corner of Fairfax Lane. It states that George

Handley Library

George Washington's Early Years in the Shenandoah Valley

George Washington first came to the wilderness that was the Shenandoah Valley in 1748 as a boy of 16, when he accompanied a surveying party. A year later, he began working for Lord Fairfax as a paid surveyor for His Lordship's huge landholdings west of the Blue Ridge.

By 1752, Washington decided to pursue a military career as a member of the Virginia Regiment. Ambitious from the start, in 1753 he asked Robert Dinwiddie, Virginia's royal lieutenant governor, to select him to deliver a letter of protest from King George II to the French in the Ohio Valley. At the time, the Ohio Valley was claimed by both the French and the British. During his journey, Washington experienced several months of harrowing adventures and close calls. Although his mission failed, he still hoped for a promotion to colonel in the regular British army. When it didn't come ("provincials" like Washington could not receive commissions higher than captain), he quit and returned to Mount Vernon to become a planter.

By 1755, he was back in the British army, this time as an unofficial aide to General Braddock during the disastrous defeat at Fort Duquesne. After that, the British abandoned their interest in the area west of Virginia. As a result, the Virginia Assembly decided to create its own army to defend its western lands. It named 22-year-old Washington "the Colonel of the Virginia Regiment and Commander in Chief of all Virginia Forces." He was put in charge of building small forts along Virginia's long Allegheny border in an attempt to protect settlers from French and Indian attack. He used Winchester as his base of operations for several years because it was the only town in the backcountry and was strategically located to boot.

The task seemed impossible from the start, but Washington gained valuable experience in dealing with day-to-day problems, such as managing shortages of funds and troops and reporting to incompetent British authorities. Many historians believe that the hard times Washington experienced during his early years in Winchester prepared him for his leadership role in the American Revolution. And it was in Winchester in 1758 that Washington, age 26, was elected to his first political office—Frederick County representative to the Virginia House of Burgesses in Williamsburg. In 1761, one of the bills he presumably introduced prohibited hogs from roaming free on Winchester's streets. (For a detailed account of Washington's time in the Shenandoah Valley, see *The Planting of New Virginia* by Warren R. Hofstra.)

Washington once owned this lot (designated as lot 77). He bought it in 1753 while living in Winchester as a young man. The blacksmith shop that once stood on the site served nearby Fort Loudoun, one of many forts that Washington was charged with building in the 1750s to protect Valley settlers from Indian attacks. Fort Loudoun was quite large, with barracks for as many as 450 men, although no more than about 200 were ever quartered here. (Nothing remains of the fort, but a historic marker marks the site at 419 North Loudoun Street, at the intersection with Peyton Street). Washington purchased about 1,000 acres of land in the Winchester area. Lot 77 (mentioned above) and lot 16 in the downtown area were mentioned in his will, the only area properties he still owned at the time of his death in 1799.

Continue walking two and a half blocks up North Braddock Street. The house at 415 North Braddock Street is now a museum known as Stonewall Jackson's

Stonewall Jackson's Headquarters

Headquarters, operated by the Winchester-Frederick County Historical Society. General Jackson lived and worked here between November 1861 and March 1862. A charming Gothic Revival structure with diamond-pane windows, the house was built in 1854 and sold two years later to Lewis T. Moore. A colonel with the Fourth Virginia Volunteers, Moore was injured in the First Battle of Manassas. While he was hospitalized, he learned that Jackson needed a headquarters in Winchester and offered the general the use of his home. Jackson used the home's parlor as his office; it is furnished today much like it was when he was here. In a letter to his wife at the time, Jackson commented on the beautiful gilded wallpaper in the parlor. More than 100 years later, the wallpaper was faithfully reproduced and rehung, a gift from actress Mary Tyler Moore, a great-granddaughter of Colonel Moore. Open daily from April through October, the house contains many Jackson mementos and artifacts, including his prayer book and the chair and desk he used here.

Turn around and walk back down North Braddock Street, passing the library and the big red apple. Turn right on Amherst Street to see several private homes. The house across Amherst Street on the corner at 103 North Braddock is known as the McGuire House. It dates to around 1790. This was the boyhood home of Stonewall Jackson's personal physician during the Civil War, Dr. Hunter Holmes McGuire. Dr. McGuire also served as the medical director of the Army of Northern Virginia.

At 123 North Amherst is the Beall House, built by schoolteacher Eli Beall in 1820.

At 138 North Amherst is the Alexander Tidball House, built around 1835. Tidball was a prominent attorney in Winchester.

As you walk along the streets in this neighborhood, look at some of the chimneys on homes and buildings. Many lean markedly northward. This occurred because the mortar on the south side of the chimney dried and expanded faster than that on the north side.

Cross North Washington Street into the next block. At 223 North Amherst is Ambler Hill, a yellow clapboard house of frame peg construction built by local merchant John Norton in 1786. The house took its name from the man Norton's widow married after Norton's death in 1797. Over the years, it has housed a boardinghouse and two schools.

At 226 North Amherst Street is the Daniel Morgan House, the southeastern portion of which was built by George Flowerdew Norton around 1786. The house was purchased and enlarged by Daniel Morgan for his daughter in 1800. Morgan died here in 1802. (For more about this fascinating Revolutionary War hero and U.S. congressman, see The White Post to Millwood to Berryville Tour, pages 70-71.) In the late 1800s and early 1900s, this house was owned by two sisters who ran a school on the grounds. Two of their students were Harry F. Byrd, the future Virginia governor and U.S. senator, and his brother, the explorer Richard E. Byrd, mentioned earlier.

Return to the corner of Amherst and Washington Streets and turn right on Washington. Walk one block and turn left on West Boscawen Street. The large church on the corner is Christ Episcopal Church, built in 1829; a church has occupied this site since 1752. The tomb of Lord Fairfax is in the courtyard on the right side of the church.

The large house diagonally across the intersection at 5 South Washington Street is called The Gables; it was built in 1899 for the Baker family, of baking chocolate fame. The Baechter family came to Winchester from Germany around 1755, and several members became town merchants. William H. Baker (the Anglicized version of Baechter) founded Baker Chocolate in New York; he also served as president of the Shenandoah Valley Bank and as vice president of the Virginia

The Gables

Rouss Fire Hall

Woolen Company, once an important Winchester industry.

Farther down the block on West Boscawen Street are several buildings that look much as they did in the 1800s. The stone building at 143 West Boscawen was built by a tanner. The house at 125 West Boscawen is an early log home that was later covered with clapboards. Built between 1806 and 1815, it was once a hatter's shop. On the corner is the Rouss Fire Hall, built in 1896 with funds from Charles Broadway Rouss, mentioned earlier.

From the fire hall, turn right on to North Braddock Street and walk two blocks to Cork Street. The dark brown log-and-stone cabin at the corner of Braddock and Cork Streets is George Washington's Office, now a museum. The log portion of this circa 1748 structure is thought to have been used by young Colonel Washington in 1755 and 1756, when he was put in charge of building a series of forts along a 300-mile stretch of western frontier. From here he is said to have directed the construction of Fort Loudoun, mentioned earlier. The museum is open daily from April through October.

To complete the downtown walking tour, go left past Washington's office and continue down Cork Street across Indian Alley to South Loudoun Street. The stone structure on the corner diagonally across the street was once the Red Lion Tavern, built around 1783 by one of Daniel Morgan's Revolutionary War riflemen, Peter Lauck.

Turn left on South Loudoun Street, which will put you at the south end of the Loudoun Street Mall. The lovely old stone house at 28 South Loudoun dates to 1785 and was bought in 1850 by merchant Godfrey Miller. *This completes the walking tour. Continue up the mall and turn right on Boscawen Street, then walk down to Cameron Street to your car.*

Not part of this driving tour, but a must-see for readers who wish to learn the full story of the Shenandoah Valley, is the Museum of the Shenandoah Valley, a beautiful 50,000-square-foot building (designed by the architect Michael Graves)

George
Washington's
Office Museum

The former Red Lion Tavern

that opened in 2005 on the grounds of Glen Burnie. To see the museum as well as Glen Burnie and its gardens, you should allow half a day.

To get to the museum from the Court Square parking garage, turn right on to Cameron Street (the one-way street in front of the garage) and go to the first intersection, which is Piccadilly Street. Turn left and drive to North Braddock Street. Turn left again. Go two blocks and turn right on to Boscawen Street, which will turn into Amherst Street (U.S. 50) in a few blocks. On the way, at 530 Amherst Street, you will pass a lovely gold-painted brick structure called the Hexagon House, built in the early 1870s. It is the only hexagonal, or six-sided, 19th-century house in Virginia. Today it is home to Preservation of Historic Winchester, Inc.

After you pass a group of professional offices on the right, look to the left for signs pointing to a left-hand turn into the museum.

In addition to a large gallery explaining the history and prehistory of the Shenandoah Valley through artifacts, maps, exhibits, decorative arts, dioramas, and multimedia presentations, the Museum of the Shenandoah Valley has three other galleries. The Julian Wood Glass, Jr., Gallery contains an impressive collection

Hexagon House

of paintings, furniture, and decorative objects from the 18th and 19th centuries. The R. Lee Taylor Gallery features a fascinating collection of miniature houses and rooms, created over the past century by more than 75 artisans. Another gallery contains changing exhibitions.

Glen Burnie was the home of the James Wood family and its descendants for nearly 200 years, from the 1790s to 1992. Winchester founder James Wood built a log-and-stone house on this site around 1738; his son Robert built the original part of the current Glen Burnie between 1794 and 1798. The house is elegantly furnished with historically valuable paintings and fine antiques, including some rare Shenandoah Valley pieces. Most were collected by the last descendant to live in the house, Julian Wood Glass, Jr. He left the property to a foundation to be run as a house museum. The six acres of beautifully designed gardens surrounding the house are reason enough to visit here. The house and the gardens are open from

Museum of the Shenandoah Valley

March through November; the Museum of the Shenandoah Valley is open year-round.

Robert Wood's brother, James Wood, Jr., was born in 1741 in an earlier structure on the grounds of Glen Burnie. James was only 19 years old when he became his father's deputy clerk of court for Frederick County. Between 1766 and 1775, he represented Frederick County in the Virginia House of Burgesses. He was also an Indian fighter and a Revolutionary War general. In 1796, he was elected governor of Virginia. He went on to serve three terms.

The tour ends here. *To return to I-81, drive back to the downtown area and follow the I-81 signs on Cameron Street. (Cameron Street is also U.S. 11. As it continues north, it passes several Civil War historical markers before eventually connecting with I-81 a few miles north of the city, and where The Clearbrook to Martinsburg Tour begins.)*

Willa Cather's Birthplace

Novelist Willa Cather was born near Gore, 13 miles west of Winchester on U.S. 50, in 1873. She spent her early childhood in the home of her maternal grandmother. Known as Willow Shade, the house still stands on U.S. 50, its location noted by a historical marker. Cather moved with her parents to Nebraska when she was nine years old.

In 1923, she won the Pulitzer Prize for her novel *One of Ours*. Only her last book—*Sapphira and the Slave Girl*— dealt with the Gore area. That novel drew on the many tales her grandmother once told her.

The White Post to Millwood to Berryville Tour

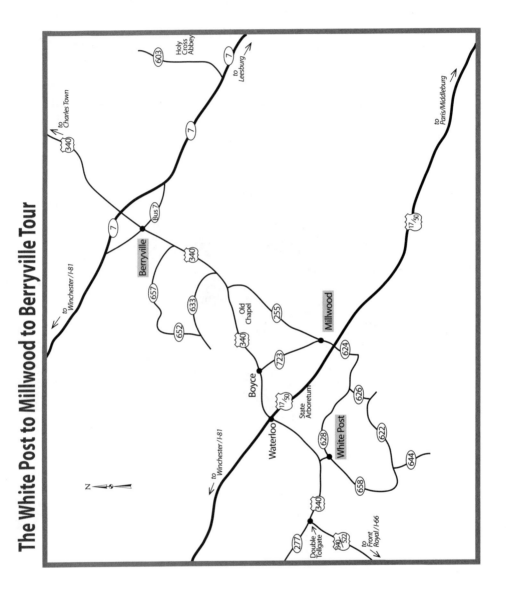

TOUR 4

The White Post to Millwood to Berryville Tour

This tour covers Clarke County, on the northeastern edge of the Shenandoah Valley. This area was settled by immigrants and landed gentry alike, the most famous of the latter being the largest Valley landowner ever, Lord Fairfax. Other famous families who built homes and estates here—including the Washingtons, the Carters, the Byrds, and the Burwells—were attracted by the area's pleasant climate and fertile soil.

The tour starts in the village of White Post, where the young George Washington worked for Lord Fairfax as a surveyor. It continues down a Virginia Byway to the 1800s railroad town of Boyce and the 1700s settlement of Millwood. Along the way, it pauses for a visit to the State Arboretum of Virginia. It ends at the county seat of Berryville—originally called Battletown, not because of any military battles there but because of its rough-and-tumble reputation in the 1700s.

Total mileage: Approximately 65 miles

*The tour begins in the historic hamlet of **White Post**. There are two ways to reach White Post, depending on the direction you're coming from. **From the Baltimore–Washington, D.C., area,** take Exit 6 off I-66 and follow the sign toward Winchester, which will put you on U.S. 340 North. In about 7.5 miles, turn right at the traffic light at Double Tollgate to stay on U.S. 340 North to White Post and Boyce. **From I-81,** take Exit 307 (marked "Stephens City to Route 340"), then drive east, following the sign marked "To U.S. 340." You are now on Route 277 (Fairfax Pike). In 4.5 miles, you'll come to a traffic light at the U.S. 340 intersection at Double Tollgate. Continue straight through the light toward White Post. The road is now U.S. 340 North.*

In 1.7 miles, turn right on to Route 628 (Berry's Ferry Road) just before a barbecue restaurant.

Clarke County was formed from Frederick County in 1836. It was named to honor George Rogers Clark, the Revolutionary War hero who (at his own expense) led 175 soldiers to help secure the Old Northwest Territories—what are now Kentucky, Ohio, Indiana, Illinois, and Missouri—for the United States. The reason for the county's spelling of Clarke with an *e* is unknown. It may well be a simple mistake by some clerk almost two centuries ago.

This area was settled mostly by well-to-do English and Americans of English descent. Families like the Carters, the Burwells, the Randolphs, and the Byrds began coming here in the 1780s and early 1800s from the Tidewater area of eastern Virginia. For them, the main attractions were a better climate and plenty of fertile farmland on which to grow wheat, by that time a more profitable crop than tobacco.

Much of this tour takes place within the 30-square-mile Greenway Historic District, a designation of the National Register of Historic Places. Rolling pastures, horse farms, and countless old homes and farm buildings are set against the backdrop of the Blue Ridge mountains. Many of the side roads remain unpaved, preserving the look and feel of earlier times.

The county's most famous early resident was probably Thomas, the sixth Baron Fairfax of Cameron. He had inherited from his mother (the daughter of Lord Culpeper) the lands known as the Northern Neck Proprietary—some 5 million acres that stretched from the Rapidan River in southeastern Virginia to most of northern Virginia, including parts of the Shenandoah Valley. For a small fee—10 shillings per 100 acres, plus office costs—and an annual rent, he granted settlers parcels of land.

Lord Fairfax first came to America to check on his landholdings in 1736, when he was 53 years old. After a year, he returned to England, leaving his cousin, William Fairfax, in charge of his land business. Lord Fairfax returned to Virginia in 1747. For a while, he lived with William Fairfax in the family mansion, Belvoir, on the Potomac River near Mount Vernon. (William's daughter, Anne, married Lawrence Washington, George's elder half-brother and builder of Mount Vernon.)

By the late 1740s, most of the remaining Fairfax lands were located west of the Blue Ridge, so Lord Fairfax moved his land-office operations from Belvoir to property near what came to be called White Post. Here, he built a complex of buildings, including a modest cabin (no longer standing) and several other structures. He called this rather primitive estate Greenway Court, after his mother's estate in Kent, England. Built around 1760, the land office—a single-story stone structure with only two rooms—and two smaller original outbuildings still stand, but they remain in private hands. Efforts are underway to restore them.

Lord Fairfax held that any land grants awarded by the colony of Virginia for his property before he arrived in America were illegal. He became involved in lengthy

The Most English County in the Valley

Most Virginia Tidewater families who came to the Clarke County area in the late 1700s were landed gentry who brought with them the traditional English pastimes of horse racing and fox hunting, activities that remain popular here and in neighboring counties. In fact, the area was well known as a horse-breeding center between 1785 and 1842, a reputation that continues here today.

Sir Archie, considered a founding sire of American distance racehorses, was born around 1807 to a mare belonging to Captain Archie Cary Randolph, who lived at Carter Hall, near Millwood.

legal squabbles with the Virginia colonial authorities—and in particular with Jost Hite, one of the Valley's original settlers.

Some historians say that Lord Fairfax's intention was not to take away settlers' lands but rather to clarify ownership and boundaries—and also to be able to collect annual rents. Others say that he was determined to exert control and didn't want to miss out on any potential source of income; even in those days, English lords were short of cash. The lawsuit involving the Hite family went on for years and was finally resolved after both Jost Hite and Lord Fairfax were dead. The Virginia assembly ultimately abolished the system of "quit rents" entirely.

The story goes that Lord Fairfax never married because his fiancée jilted him for a wealthier suitor just before their wedding. He apparently never overcame his distrust of women after that painful episode.

Although Lord Fairfax entertained frequently, he did not live ostentatiously. He had planned to build a mansion on the Greenway Court property but never got around to it. He became involved in local political affairs but tried to remain neutral throughout the Revolution, even though he was a Loyalist. He lived to be 88 years old and was buried in Winchester, where his tomb can be visited today (see The Middletown to Winchester Tour, page 57).

It was in 1749 that Lord Fairfax hired his cousin's Mount Vernon neighbor, the 17-year-old George Washington, to help survey the western boundary of his holdings. Unable to afford college because of the death of his father a few years earlier, Washington needed a paying job. He could not have realized at the time that this assignment would give him a knowledge of the Allegheny wilderness that would lead to his first military appointment a few years later.

For several years, Washington worked out of Greenway Court, where he is said to have used Lord Fairfax's library to further his education. Legend has it that in 1750, Lord Fairfax directed Washington to erect the now-famous white post near the Ashby Gap–Winchester Road (also called the Old Dutch Trail, today's U.S. 340) to mark the way to Greenway Court. Unless it has been knocked down again by a motorist surprised by its placement in the middle of the intersection, you can't miss seeing this post; it stands where Routes 628 and 658 meet.

The village of White Post is a Virginia Landmarks Register Historic District. Its churches and more than 20 old homes from various eras are set on lush green lawns and shaded by huge old trees. A short distance north on Route 658 is Bishop Meade Memorial Episcopal Church, built in 1875 and named for the third Episcopal bishop of Virginia, a local resident. Its architectural style is called high-style Gothic Revival. After the

The "white post"

Bishop Meade Memorial Episcopal Church

War of 1812, Meade led a revival of the Episcopal Church in Virginia.

Continue straight past the white post on Route 628. The second house on the right is a one-and-a-half-story clapboard (over log) home with two stone chimneys. This is Meadea, built in the 1780s. One of the oldest homes in Clarke County, it is typical of early homesteads in the area.

Return to the white post and turn left to go south on Route 658. On the right after 0.6 mile, you'll see a brick Greek Revival house called Mesilla. It's set back from the road behind a stand of trees. Mesilla was built between 1830 and 1850 and remains a private residence.

About 0.5 mile past Mesilla, also on the right, is an old stone house known as the Porter's Office of Greenway Court; it is also a private residence. The surviving buildings of Lord Fairfax's Greenway Court are located southwest of here, on private property off Route 644, and are not visible from the road.

Route 658 turns sharply to the left about 0.5 mile past the Porter's Office and is marked Sugar Hill Road. Continue for 2.3 miles. Just past a gentle curve in the road, turn left on to Route 622 (Borden's Spring Road), which is an unpaved Virginia Byway. After 0.1 mile, look to the left for the first set of stone gate posts at the entry to the beautiful rolling estate known as Federal Hill; continue a short distance to the second set. Built

Meadea

by Samuel Baker in the early 1800s, this structure was home to three generations of his family. The mansion sits high on a hill well back from the road, facing the Blue Ridge Mountains. It remains a working farm today.

The Bakers and their neighbors at nearby Guilford (located on Route 644 just beyond the turnoff to Route 622) were related by marriage. Guilford was built between 1812 and 1820 by the family of James Madison Hite, who was a son of Isaac Hite (who owned Belle Grove, near Middletown) and a nephew of President Madison. Guilford was later the home of the Ashby family.

Continue on Route 622 past where it intersects Route 627 (Montana Hall Road). Stay straight. From here, drive another 0.5 mile to the intersection with Route 626 (Nelson Road) and turn left. In another 0.7 mile, stay straight through the Route 628 intersection—don't turn left. In less than 1 mile, you'll see a driveway on the right and a sign pointing to Long Branch. A state historical marker describing Long Branch is located nearby.

If you are here on a Wednesday through Sunday afternoon between April 1 and October 31, you may want to consider touring Long Branch. It's one of the few great old homes in the area open to the public for tours. Even if you decide not to take the tour, go up the long driveway to see the house and its extensive grounds and horse farm. The estate occupies a magnificent setting, with wonderful views of the Blue Ridge in the distance.

Robert Carter Burwell, originally of Carter's Grove on the James River in the Tidewater area, began building Long Branch around 1810. Burwell inherited the

Long Branch

Horses at Long Branch

land from his grandfather, Robert Burwell, who inherited it from Robert "King" Carter, the wealthy agent for Lord Culpeper and later for Lord Fairfax. Robert Carter Burwell obtained design help from America's first professional architect, Benjamin Henry Latrobe, although no records survive to document Latrobe's specific contributions. Burwell died in 1813, before the house was finished.

Long Branch was bought in 1842 by a Burwell descendant, Hugh Mortimer Nelson, who remodeled it in the Greek Revival style. Nelson died in the Civil War, but the estate remained in his family well into the 20th century.

By 1986, the house had begun to deteriorate. Harry Z. Isaacs, a Baltimore textile executive, bought Long Branch and restored the property in less than three years. He had received a cancer diagnosis shortly after the purchase, so he moved quickly to complete the work. During that time, Isaacs traveled all over the world to find antique furnishings, fabrics, and wallpaper that were just right for the house. The results of his labors are impressive. He also transformed the surrounding 400 acres into a working horse farm. Before he died in 1990, he established a private nonprofit foundation to maintain the estate and open it for public tours, which are led by local volunteers.

Leaving Long Branch, turn right at the end of the driveway to continue in your original direction on Route 626. Go to the stop sign at Route 624 (Red Gate Road) and turn left. In about 0.5 mile, you'll come to Route 17/50 (John Mosby Highway), a four-lane divided highway. Turn left. In about 1 mile, you'll see a brown highway sign announcing the turnoff ahead on the left for the Orland E. White Arboretum, also known as the State Arboretum of Virginia at Blandy Experimental Farm, a research arm of the University of Virginia. Turn left into the arboretum.

The grounds of the arboretum make it a perfect place to stop for a picnic lunch. It's also a great place for walking along marked trails and learning about an enormous variety of trees and other plants. If time is short, you can take a three-mile loop driving tour around the property and catch a glimpse of a historic old home, Tuleyries, still a private residence. Maps showing self-guided trails and the loop driving tour are available at the information kiosk next to the arboretum parking lot.

Tuleyries was built around 1833 by Colonel Joseph Tuley, Jr., who was originally from New Jersey. Tuley and his father had made a fortune as tanners in Millwood. The locals thought the name for the house—which was derived from Tuley's own name but alluded to the French royal palace called Tuileries—was a bit much. Wryly,

An Amazing Collection of Plants

More than 5,000 species of plants are grown at the State Arboretum of Virginia, including the largest selection of boxwood cultivars in North America (the arboretum is headquarters of the American Boxwood Society). The arboretum also has representatives of more than half the world's pine species. Its ginkgo planting area contains more than 500 trees, one of the largest groves outside

State Arboretum of Virginia

China. Other planting areas feature maples, oaks, chestnuts, dogwoods, hollies, magnolias, roses, azaleas, irises, daylilies, herbs, and perennials. The arboretum's buildings date to around 1825 and were once slave quarters for the nearby Tuleyries estate. The grounds are open at no charge to the public year-round from dawn to dusk. Picnickers are welcome. Restrooms and a gift shop are located in the Quarters Building.

they suggested a better name might be "Hide Park."

Tuleyries was later owned by Upton L. Boyce before being bought by Graham F. Blandy, a New Yorker, in 1903. Upon his death in 1926, Blandy deeded the land to the University of Virginia, which uses the farm as an educational center.

Return to Route 17/50, turn left, drive 1.4 miles to the traffic light, and turn right on to U.S. 340 North at **Waterloo**. *After 1.5 miles, turn right at the yellow flashing traffic light on to Route 723 (East Main Street).* This will take you into the old part of **Boyce**, where you'll see a mix of restored and original buildings and Victorian homes. Once a thriving railroad town, the community was named for Colonel Upton L. Boyce, who owned Tuleyries. An attorney for the Norfolk and Western Railroad, Boyce is said to have helped bring the Shenandoah Valley Railroad through Clarke County in 1879. The station created the town, which was established in 1880.

Tuleyries

Antique shop in Boyce

The 1913 Boyce train station

Continue across the railroad tracks on Route 723. The 1913 Boyce train station, which served the Norfolk and Western Railway until passenger rail service ceased here in 1957, was larger and grander than stations at nearby larger towns, thanks to the wealth and pretensions of the local citizens. An example of vernacular Craftsman style, it was built across the tracks from the original 1880s station. It has been restored and is home to the Railway Mail Service Library, an archives and research center devoted to the study of transportation and mail distribution in the United States between 1862 and 1977.

The 1780 limestone Georgian house known as Saratoga—a National Historic Landmark—is just ahead on the right. Unfortunately, it is privately owned and is not visible from the road. It was built by Revolutionary War hero Daniel Morgan and named after the victory he helped secure at the Battle of Saratoga in New York.

An original American success story, Morgan was the son of Welsh immigrants to New Jersey. He made his way to Virginia in 1753, when he was just 17 years old. Having no prospects and no money, he took whatever work he could find—as a farm laborer, as manager of a sawmill, and as a wagon driver hired by Robert Burwell, one of the local gentry. Morgan was soon able to buy his own wagon, after which he found work hauling supplies for General Braddock during the French and Indian War.

Years later, as a captain of the local militia, Morgan wasted no time in responding to General George Washington's call for troops in 1775. He recruited 93 riflemen and took just 26 days to march them 600 miles to join Washington's forces at Cambridge, Massachusetts. By December 1775, Morgan was fighting under General Benedict Arnold's command during the assault on Quebec, where he was forced to surrender. He remained a prisoner of war there for five months. In 1777, he joined General Horatio Gates in the Battle of Saratoga.

Ill health forced Morgan to resign from the army in 1779, after which he began building his estate in Boyce. At that time, hundreds of Hessian prisoners of war were being held in the Winchester area. Local lore says that these German mercenaries for the British army were put to work as stonemasons and woodworkers for the many fine homes being built in the area. Some historians dispute that story, saying that the prisoners were not held in the area for the several years needed to construct such large homes. Nevertheless, more than 40 percent of those prisoners chose to remain in America once freed. They may well have offered their skills to area residents as paid workers.

Morgan was recalled to service in 1780 after the Continental Army (led by General Horatio Gates) was badly defeated at the Battle of Camden in South Carolina. Morgan won a surprise victory against a larger British force at Cowpens and was promoted to brigadier general.

After the war, he served a term in the U.S. Congress. He saw military action once more, in 1794, when he was sent to command troops to put down the Whiskey Rebellion in western Pennsylvania. He died in Winchester in 1802 at the home he bought for his daughter (see The Middletown to Winchester Tour, page 57).

Morgan's daughter inherited Saratoga. Her descendants later sold it to Nathaniel Burwell, son of Colonel Nathaniel Burwell of Carter Hall (visited later on this tour). General Robert E. Lee camped on its grounds during the Civil War. Saratoga remains a working farm today.

Directly across the road from Saratoga, you'll see an impressive-looking set of gates marked "Kentmere." The house called Kentmere was destroyed by fire in 2009. It was part of the Scaleby estate just up the road. The mansion at Scaleby—all 30,000 elegant square feet of it—was built between 1909 and 1911 by Mr. and Mrs. Henry Gilpin, of the famous New York railroad family. It was named for the family's ancestral seat, Scaleby Castle in Cumberland County, England.

Continue on Route 723 toward **Millwood,** *located about 1 mile ahead.* This portion of the road is lined on both sides with beautiful limestone walls. Several old frame houses front the narrow road as it enters town. Clark House, located on the right at 2014 Millwood Road, was built in 1842 and originally served as a tavern. During the Civil War, it was the location of a meeting to negotiate the surrender of Confederate colonel John Mosby.

The community of Millwood formed around a large mill completed in 1785 by Colonel Nathaniel Burwell (pronounced "Burl") and Daniel Morgan. The mill is just ahead on the right.

Burwell predicted, correctly, that wheat would be a profitable crop for the area in the years following the Revolutionary War, and that building a large mill to turn grain into flour would be even more profitable. Probably with the help of Hessian craftsmen, Morgan oversaw the construction of the limestone mill, which was worked around the clock during its heyday in the mid-1800s.

The Burwell-Morgan Mill is open to visitors Saturdays from 1 to 5 P.M. and Sundays noon to 5 P.M. from May through November. Saturdays are "grinding days," and visitors can watch the mill in operation. It has undergone three renovations since it

Burwell-Morgan Mill

ceased operation as a commercial mill in 1953. Now owned by the Clarke County Historical Association, it is well worth a stop. A video describing the mill and local history is shown, and local volunteers give tours and explain the operations. At one time, barrels of flour and cornmeal from this mill were taken to the Shenandoah River and floated on barges to Harpers Ferry, where they were loaded on canal boats for shipment to the ports of Georgetown and Alexandria.

Burwell was living at Carter's Grove in the Tidewater area at the time of the mill's construction and during its early days of operation. He built Brookside, the frame house across from the mill, in 1786 as a summer home and a place to live while he constructed his mansion, Carter Hall, nearby. The other frame house on the property was the miller's house. Located behind the mill, it dates to 1820.

Millwood has a real old-time feel about it and has several great shops to explore. Jackie Onassis is said to have shopped for antiques here in the early 1990s. Don't miss the old Locke Store, across the street from the mill. Located on the site of the first general store in Millwood, this early-1900s building is now home to a gourmet food and wine shop.

From the mill's parking lot, turn left, go past Locke Store, and make an immediate right on to Route 255 North (Meade Road). This road will take you past more old homes and antique shops.

*After 0.2 mile, you'll pass the entrance gates to Carter Hall, a stately stone Geor-*gian-style mansion that Colonel Nathaniel Burwell built in the 1790s. Today, it is headquarters for Project Hope, an international health education foundation. It is not open to the public.

Millwood antique shop

Burwell's grandfather was Robert "King" Carter, who built Carter's Grove (now owned by Colonial Williamsburg). Nathaniel Burwell inherited Carter's Grove when he was only five years old, after the death of his father. King Carter's 50,000 acres of land included what was called the Shenandoah Tract, here in Clarke County. After graduating from William and Mary, Nathaniel came here in the 1770s to manage the estate.

In 1862, General Stonewall Jackson set up temporary headquarters on the grounds of Carter Hall, refusing offers to use the house itself. Interestingly, according to the National Register of Historic Places application for Carter Hall, General Jackson's physician performed a cataract operation on George Burwell (Nathaniel's son) on the mansion's portico.

Burwell died in 1814. In his later years, he had invited Edmund Randolph to live with him at Carter Hall. Randolph was governor of Virginia from 1786 to 1788. He then served under George Washington as the first attorney general of the United States. He later was named secretary of state, after Thomas Jefferson resigned the position in 1794. Randolph died at Carter Hall in 1813.

A short distance down the road, on the left after you pass Carter Hall, is Christ Episcopal Church of Cunningham Parish, a Gothic stone structure dating to 1832. It was built under the direction of its rector, William Meade, who was then bishop of the Episcopal diocese of Virginia. The small frame building with the red door to the right of the church is Cunningham Chapel.

Continue down Route 255 for nearly 3 miles. Just as the road passes under a railroad bridge and veers left toward the intersection with busy U.S. 340, look to

Carter Hall

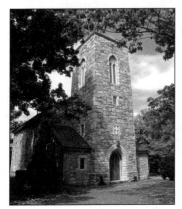

*Christ Episcopal Church
of Cunningham Parish*

your left. The small stone building (which has an unpaved driveway you can turn into) is known as Old Chapel. This is one of the earliest Episcopal churches west of the Blue Ridge. It was built in 1793 to replace a 1740s log church that was located nearby, thanks to a donation of land from Nathaniel Burwell.

Though the congregation later moved to the larger Christ Episcopal Church, the parish still holds a special annual service at Old Chapel. Many of the area's original citizens are buried in the chapel's well-maintained graveyard, including Nathaniel Burwell and Edmund Randolph.

From Old Chapel, continue a short distance on Route 255 to the intersection with U.S. 340 and turn right on to U.S. 340 North. On the left soon after the turn is a stone home, which is difficult to see from the road, called Chapel Hill. The oldest section of Chapel Hill was built around 1826 by Dr. Charles Byrd, who sold the house that year to Phillip Burwell. In the 20th century, it belonged to William "Wild Bill" Donovan, head of the OSS (today's CIA) during World War II. Donovan acquired his nickname during his Army service in World War I.

In another 0.5 mile, turn left on Route 633 (Annfield Road). Drive about 1.5 miles to Annfield, on the right. Annfield has been called one of the most beautiful mansions in Virginia. A prime example of Federal-style architecture, it is typical of the homes built by families who came here from the Tidewater area. Annfield was constructed in the 1790s by Matthew Page, who named it for his wife, Ann Randolph

Old Chapel

Meade Page. She was a sister of Bishop William Meade and a well-known early abolitionist.

Annfield was the birthplace of Mary Custis, Robert E. Lee's wife; her mother was a guest here in 1808. The home is built of limestone blocks and has a two-story pedimented portico, with each level supported by four white columns; a Chippendale railing encloses the upper porch.

The roads on this part of the tour are idyllic country byways with huge stands of old trees, miles of stone walls, brown-fenced horse farms, and rolling green fields. Every so often, an apple orchard comes into view.

Continue 0.8 mile to Route 652, a gravel road. Turn right. Go 1.4 miles to the stop sign at Route 657, turn right again, and go 2 miles to Avenel, on the left. Surrounded by a grove of large white oaks, Avenel was built by the Gold family in 1814. Mosby's Rangers skirmished with the Sixth New York Cavalry nearby in September 1864; at that time, the estate was known as Gold's Farm. The beautiful barn on the property was one of the few to escape Sheridan's burning of the Shenandoah Valley in 1864. In the 1930s, U.S. senator Harry Flood Byrd, Sr., bought the property. He later gave it to his son, Richard E. Byrd (whose uncle of the same name was the Arctic explorer).

Continue on Route 657 for about 1 mile until you reach U.S. 340. Turn left on to U.S. 340, which will take you into Berryville. Turn right at the traffic light on to West Main Street (Route 7 Business) to enter the downtown area. Prepare to turn left at the next intersection, on to Church Street. Park here to visit the museum and take a short walking tour.

Berryville began in the mid-1700s as a frontier settlement known as Battletown, so named because some of its early residents spent their evenings drinking and fighting at local taverns. According to records, one of the regular participants in these activities was the young Daniel Morgan. The hamlet formed at the intersection of the Winchester-Alexandria Road (today's Route 7 Business) and the road to Lord Fairfax's land office at Greenway Court (today's U.S. 340). It was renamed Berryville in 1798 for Benjamin Berry, who donated the land and helped develop the town site. When Clarke County was formed from Frederick County in 1836, Berryville became the county seat. More recently, it was home to the late United States senator Harry F. Byrd, Sr.

The Clarke County Courthouse is on Church Street. The complex includes the old red-brick courthouse, built in the Roman Revival style in 1838, and a more modern structure built in 1978.

At the top of Church Street above the courthouse complex is Grace Episcopal Church, built in 1852. General Robert E. Lee is said to have attended a service here on his way to Gettysburg.

Walk back to Main Street to see several other buildings of historic interest. Turn left on Main.

At 26 East Main is the building that once belonged to Coiner's Department Store, which operated here from 1896 to 1996. During that entire time, clerks used a pulley-operated cash carrier to transfer money back and forth to the cashier.

At 32 East Main Street is the Clarke County Historical Association Museum. For operating hours, call the number listed in the appendix. The museum features antiques and artifacts reflecting the area's history, including Lord Fairfax's money chest. It also houses an extensive archive of county history.

At 106 East Main is The Nook, thought to be the oldest home in Berryville. The central portion, of painted clapboard construction, was built in 1765 by Major Charles Smith, who came to the area from Prince William County after serving in the French and Indian War; he later served in the Revolutionary War and as high sheriff of Frederick County. He bought 20 acres of land here from his father-in-law,

DOWNTOWN WINCHESTER

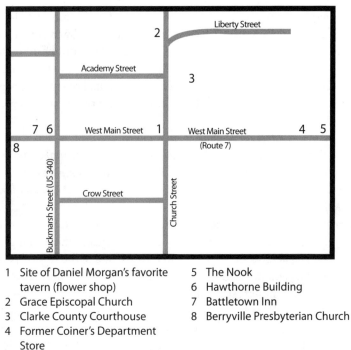

1 Site of Daniel Morgan's favorite tavern (flower shop)
2 Grace Episcopal Church
3 Clarke County Courthouse
4 Former Coiner's Department Store
5 The Nook
6 Hawthorne Building
7 Battletown Inn
8 Berryville Presbyterian Church

Clarke County Courthouse

Coiner's Department Store

John Hite. Smith positioned the house so that its corners matched the four points of the compass. His son later sold the property to Benjamin Berry. In the years following the Civil War, a woman named Harriot Hammond ran a girls' school in the house.

Turn around and walk west on Main Street.

On the corner with Church Street, at 2 West Main, a flower shop stands on the site of one of the old 1700s taverns whose regulars gave the town its early name of Battletown. The tavern at this location was supposedly a favorite of Daniel Morgan. Across the street on the corner (at 1, 3, and 5 East Main), the large white clapboard building with red trim was built as the Berryville Hotel in the late 1800s.

Historic Sites Just North of Berryville

The area north of Berryville, north of the intersection of U.S. 340 and Route 7, contains several historic sites.

Drive north on U.S. 340 from the Route 7 interchange. The fields along the road are where Generals Lee and Longstreet camped on their way to Gettysburg in June 1863. And in August 1864, Mosby's Rangers attacked General Philip Sheridan's 7-mile-long Union wagon train here, capturing 600 horses and mules and 200 prisoners.

Nearby on U.S. 340 not far from the intersection with U.S. 7, alongside the southbound lanes, is one of Virginia's more intriguing state historical markers. Titled "Buck Marsh," it notes that pioneer Joseph Hampton and his two sons lived near here in a hollow sycamore tree for several months in 1744.

About 3 miles north of the U.S. 7 interchange, on the northbound side of U.S. 340, is the beautiful old limestone house called Fairfield. It was built by Warner Washington, a cousin of George Washington, sometime before 1770. A sign at the entrance marks the spot, but the home is a private residence and is difficult to see from the highway.

Fairfield is said to be one of the finest Washington homes still standing. Its interior is similar to that of Kenmore in Fredericksburg, Virginia, the home of George Washington's sister. Some think that architect John Ariss designed both houses. Fairfield's wings and dormers were added in the 1900s.

Warner Washington's second wife was Hannah Fairfax, the daughter of William Fairfax of Belvoir and the sister of George William Fairfax, who sold Warner Washington 1,600 acres here soon after his marriage to Hannah in 1764. George and Martha Washington and Martha's daughter, Patsy, visited Fairfield in 1769 on their way to the resort now known as Berkeley Springs. The house remained in the Washington family until 1815.

The Nook   *Former Berryville Hotel*

At 100 West Main Street, across U.S. 340, is the Hawthorne Building, which has stood here since around 1820. Portions of the structure reportedly date to 1795.

Next door at 102 West Main is the Battlefield Inn, a Federal-style structure built around 1809, when it was known as the Sarah Stribling House. It is now a hotel and restaurant.

Berryville Presbyterian Church, at 123 West Main, was built around 1854 and is the oldest church still standing in town. It was used to house troops during the Civil War.

The tour ends in Berryville. **To reach the Washington, D.C., area,** *follow Route 7 Business (Main Street) to Route 7 and turn right (east). This will take you past Leesburg, into the Tysons Corner area of Northern Virginia, and to I-495, the Washington Beltway.* **To return to I-66,** *take U.S. 340 South to Front Royal.* **To return to I-81,** *take Route 7 Business West, which intersects Route 7 West; turn left to go toward Winchester.*

If you take Route 7 East toward Washington, you'll pass Audley Farm, one of several homes in this area once owned by the Washington family. The farm is visible at the intersection of Route 7 Business and Route 7; look directly across the highway before you turn right.

Audley was built by Warner Washington's son, Warner Washington II, around

Hawthorne Building

1795. Nelly Parke Custis Lewis, George and Martha Washington's granddaughter, and her husband, Major Lawrence Lewis, bought the house in 1825. But the couple never lived here, residing instead at Woodlawn, the house George Washington built for them near Mount Vernon in Alexandria. The Lewises' son, Lorenzo, inherited Audley from his father in 1839. Lorenzo and his wife lived here until he died in 1847. Nelly had moved to Audley to be with her son shortly after her husband's death; she lived here until she died in 1852. The house, privately owned, has been remodeled several times since the early 1800s. Today, Audley is a racehorse breeding farm.

Side Trip to Holy Cross Abbey

Holy Cross Abbey—well known in the Washington, D.C., area for its Christmas fruitcakes and other baked goods—is about 5 miles east of Berryville, past Audley Farm. *Take Route 7 East and turn left on Route 603 (Castlemans Road) just before the Shenandoah River bridge. The entrance to the abbey is 1 mile down Castlemans Road.*

The abbey is a monastery of the Cistercian Order of the Strict Observance (Trappists), which moved to the Shenandoah Valley from Rhode Island in 1950. The main part of the abbey is housed in a 1784 home once known as Cool Spring. In 1864, the grounds were the site of a Civil War battle between General Jubal Early's troops and units of the Union's West Virginia army; the Confederates won.

Holy Cross Abbey is supported largely by its bakery. Visitors are welcome at the abbey's chapel, gift shop, and information center seven days a week. Their website is www.hcava.org.

The Strasburg to Fort Valley to Front Royal Tour

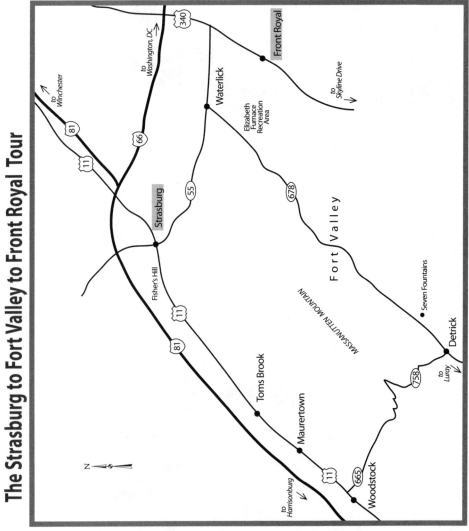

TOUR **5**

The Strasburg to Fort Valley to Front Royal Tour

This tour begins in Strasburg. Founded by the German immigrant Jacob Stover in 1749, it is best known today for its many antique shops, its famous pottery industry (which began in 1761), and nearby Civil War sites. The tour heads south down the Valley Pike (U.S. 11) to the northern edge of Woodstock. There it turns to climb Massanutten Mountain to the Woodstock Tower, which offers a bird's-eye view of the "Seven Bends" of the Shenandoah River (at least when the leaves are off the trees) and panoramic views to the east and west. The tour then descends into Fort Valley—called "The Fort" by locals—a sparsely populated and picturesque "valley within a valley" that has a timeless feel about it. It ends in Front Royal, known as Helltown during its wilder days in the 1700s. Front Royal saw much Civil War action and was the setting for the exploits of legendary Confederate spy Belle Boyd.

Several museums covering local history and the Civil War are included in this tour.

Total mileage: Approximately 50 miles

The tour begins in **Strasburg***. Take Exit 298 off I-81 and follow U.S. 11 South toward town for about 1 mile.* The Stonewall Jackson Museum at Hupp's Hill, on the right, may be open, but readers should be aware that it closed in 2010 and was put up for sale, along with Crystal Caverns. Visitors, however, are welcome to stroll the Civil War walking trails on the grounds, which contain the ruins of trenches and earthworks built by General Nathaniel Banks as protection for his Union troops against enemy fire. Banks's 8,000 soldiers camped at this spot in May 1862 to control access to the Valley Pike and the railroad through Manassas Gap.

Caught by surprise when General Stonewall Jackson attacked 1,000 of his men in nearby Front Royal on May 23, Banks quickly left Strasburg and headed up the Valley Pike toward Winchester. The next day, Jackson's troops engaged some of Banks's men at Cedar Creek, resulting in a Union defeat. On May 25, Banks and Jackson had another encounter—now known as the First Battle of Winchester— which the Confederates also won.

Hupp House

About 0.5 mile past Hupp's Hill, also on the right, is the Hupp House (also called the Hupp Homestead and the Frontier Fort), built around 1755. Its size is deceiving. It looks like a snug one-story house from the road, but the house is two-and-a half stories tall when seen from the back. It was probably built by Peter Hupp, one of the earliest German settlers in the area. It is thought he came to the Valley by way of Pennsylvania in the 1730s.

Like so many of the 18th-century limestone structures in the Valley, the Hupp House served as a fort to protect its inhabitants and their neighbors from Indian attacks during the French and Indian War in the mid-1700s. A spring ran into the cellar of the house, which meant that residents didn't have to venture outside for water during dangerous times. In later years, the spring also provided a steady supply of water for a distillery that occupied the stone building north of the homestead.

George F. Hupp, a later owner, accumulated about a thousand acres in this area during the 1800s. A paymaster during the War of 1812, he was later a farmer who owned or had an interest in several of the county's iron furnaces. He became a wealthy man; the 1850 census listed the value of his cash and real estate holdings at $113,000, a fortune at the time.

Today, both buildings are private homes. The lush grounds include a creek and a pond. Interestingly, a later Hupp House owner, Bruce Hupp, had a business raising watercress in the stream behind the house in the early 1930s. He and two cousins first opened Crystal Caverns to the public in 1922.

Later generations of Hupps lived in the Classical Revival–style brick home—known as the Hupp Mansion—across the street. This house was originally a stone structure but was enlarged several times over the years. During the Civil War, General Stonewall Jackson used the mansion as his headquarters in 1862; General Philip Sheridan used it as a residence in 1864. Some sources say that Union generals Banks and Shields also used it as their headquarters.

Continue into town on U.S. 11, now called Massanutten Street. After passing under a railroad bridge, you'll begin to see a few of the town's many antique shops—Strasburg calls itself the "Antique Capital of Virginia." The largest, the Strasburg

Colonial Inn

Antique Emporium, is on the left as you approach the traffic light at the intersection with King Street, the town's main street. The building it occupies was once the Strasburg Textile Mill, which made silk casket linings (and silk parachutes during World War II). The mill operated from the early 1900s until 1977.

The Colonial Inn, which was once the Spengler Hotel, is the painted brick building on King Street (Route 55) at the intersection with Massanutten Street (U.S. 11). It is thought to have been built in the early 1800s by a relative of Anthony Spengler, an early citizen. It most likely served as an inn and stagecoach stop. John Wayland, the prominent Valley historian, noted that much of the area's history took place in front of this inn: "Here the Blue and Gray passed and repassed from 1861 to 1865." One story goes that a tired Stonewall Jackson once reviewed his troops from a chair on the sidewalk in front of the inn.

Turn left at the intersection and go 0.2 mile to the Strasburg Museum, housed in the old train station on the right. This museum, open daily from May through October, contains extensive exhibits of interesting artifacts and relics that reflect everyday life in the Strasburg area from the 1700s into the 1940s. A room within the museum offers a large display and description of the town's famous pottery. In fact, the museum building originally housed the Strasburg Steam Pottery Company. After the pottery company closed its doors, the building was turned into the Southern Railway depot, which operated here from 1913 until the 1960s.

Strasburg Museum

Strasburg was well known by the 1830s and 1840s for its many pottery shops, which originally produced salt-glazed crocks of blue and gray for everyday use. Strasburg potters later specialized in fancy ware featuring multicolored glazes of green, cream, and brown. From 1809 until the end of the 19th century, at least 10 potters had shops in town, and it gained the nickname "Pot Town." The most noted were the Bell brothers—Samuel and Solomon—and their descendants, who produced high-quality stoneware from 1834 to 1908. All old Strasburg pottery is highly valuable, but pieces marked with the Bell name are particularly treasured today. After the Civil War, the demand for pottery declined once cheaper glass jars became plentiful, and most of the pottery shops had disappeared by the early 1900s. The craft has not been forgotten, however. The Shenandoah Potters Guild carries on the town's tradition today.

Strasburg was once a key railroad center. Another depot in town served both the B&O Railroad and the Southern Railroad. During the Civil War, Stonewall Jackson called Strasburg the "fountainhead of rail traffic for the South." From Strasburg, he sent captured enemy locomotives and railroad cars to points south to aid the war effort. Those engines and cars—their wheels fitted with broad tires—had been seized in Martinsburg, West Virginia, and dragged by teams of horses up the Valley Pike to Strasburg. The operation must have been an amazing thing to watch. In those days, the Valley Pike was macadamized, which simply meant that the road surface was covered with crushed stone, not paved in asphalt as it is today.

Strasburg, one of the oldest towns in the Valley, has an interesting history dating back to the 1730s. This part of the Valley was settled by Jost Hite (1685–1761), one of the Valley's first pioneers. This mostly German settlement began to take shape after 1749, when Peter Stauffer (or Stover) laid out a plan for what was called Staufferstadt, or Stover Town. But by 1761, when the settlement was officially chartered as a town, it had been renamed Strasburg, possibly after Strasbourg, in Alsace (now part of France), presumably Stover's birthplace.

Many interesting homes and commercial buildings line the town's streets. For an in-depth look at these structures and their history, pick up the self-guided walking tour pamphlet at the Strasburg Museum. One particular building of interest is today's Hotel Strasburg, which still operates as a hotel and restaurant. It is located at 213 South Holliday Street, just a block off King Street in the downtown area. It was built in 1902 as a private hospital by Dr. Mackall Bruin, a married man who scandalized the town by running off with one of his nurses; he was never heard from again. The building was turned into a hotel in 1915.

From the museum, drive back down King Street into the downtown area. Once upon a time, King Street was lined on both sides with huge old trees; the trees had to be cut down when U.S. 11 was widened in the 1930s. But stately trees still line Strasburg's neighborhood streets. The streets east of King in particular are reminiscent of small-town America from decades past.

During its long history, Strasburg has experienced the terror of war more than once. Several early residents were the unfortunate victims of random Indian attacks (then called "outrages") before and during the French and Indian War. One

Hotel Strasburg

of the oldest structures from that era is Frye Fort, built in 1747 with 32-inch-thick stone walls as a defense against Indian attacks. The fort still stands as a restored private home on Cedar Creek, several miles northwest of Strasburg. Amazingly, the house was occupied by the original owner's descendants or relatives by marriage until the 1970s.

Located off U.S. 11, down a rutted road near the I-81 interchange in Strasburg, is another beautiful old stone house known as Harmony Hall. It was built in 1753 for George Bowman, whose wife, Mary, was a daughter of Jost Hite. The house, which was once known as Fort Bowman, still stands in good condition. It has been purchased by the Belle Grove Foundation, which plans to restore it.

In 1764—a year after the French and Indian War officially ended—George Miller, his wife, and two children were working in a field near their home north of Strasburg when they were killed by a group of eight or nine Indians and one white man, who had organized the raid as revenge against George Miller. After killing the Millers while they were working in the field, the murderers entered the Miller house, placed a burning coal on the family's opened German Bible, and closed the book; on top of the Bible they placed the body of the family's cat. The fire burned through several pages but died out, leaving the volume intact. One daughter, who had been in the house, escaped and ran to Fort Bowman (mentioned earlier) for

Fort Bowman

help. This Bible is on display at the Strasburg Museum.

On that same horrible day in 1764, the murderous group continued their rampage south of town. John Dellinger, his wife, and their infant child were captured at their home near Spengler Hall (which the tour passes later). Mr. Dellinger and the baby were killed, but neighbors were able to rescue Mrs. Dellinger.

Almost a hundred years later, the town found itself mired in the Civil War. Strasburg's location as a crossroads and a railhead made it strategically valuable to both sides, and its proximity to Massanutten Mountain—which begins its 50-mile stretch to the south near here—provided General Jackson with places to confuse and spy on Union troops after the Battle of Kernstown in March 1862.

Throughout the Civil War, the summit of Three Top Mountain—also known as Signal Knob, the prominent northern end of Massanutten Mountain above Strasburg—served as a critical communications and observation post for both the North and the South. Using flags during the day and torches at night, the Confederates sent signals up and down the Blue Ridge from Signal Knob. (Hikers can follow a 7-mile trail to the top of Signal Knob that begins a short distance east of the Elizabeth Furnace Recreation Area; the trailhead location is noted in the Fort Valley section later in this tour).

In the spring of 1862, General Jackson marched 16,000 men through Strasburg several times. Later that fall, he brought 40,000 troops through the town.

Two significant Civil War battles were fought nearby in 1864—the Battle of Cedar Creek (see The Middletown to Winchester Tour, page 43) and the Battle of Fisher's Hill, which is the next stop on this tour.

From downtown Strasburg, continue down King Street (U.S. 11 South) toward Woodstock. Shortly after the road curves to the left out of the main business district, you'll see an old mill—now a restaurant—on the left. This stone structure, once known as Spengler's Mill, was built around 1794 by Anthony Spengler, a local farmer who sent weekly shipments of produce and flour by wagon to Alexandria. It was operated as a mill until 1938. General Sheridan reportedly tried to burn this mill during "The Burning" campaign in 1864, but the fire was put out in time to save it. The large brick Federal-style mansion across the road from the mill is Spengler Hall, also known as Matin Hill, which Spengler built in 1820.

Signal Knob

Spengler's Mill

Drive south on U.S. 11 for 1 mile until you see a brown road sign marking the turn-off for Fisher's Hill Battlefield. Turn right on Route 601 (Battlefield Road) and carefully follow the signs to the battlefield as Route 601 twists and turns for about 2 miles to the site. As the road traverses a low concrete bridge and enters the hamlet of Fisher's Hill, note the restored old mill, which can be seen on the left through the trees on the left. It is now a private residence. Once known as Keller's Mill, it dates to the 1700s. A combination post office and general store—a rare sight anywhere these days—occupies a low white building on the right a little farther up the road.

Fisher's Hill, often called "the Gibraltar of the Confederacy," was the scene of five different Civil War engagements. The best known took place in September 1864. General Jubal Early had retreated to Fisher's Hill after the Confederate defeat at Winchester. General Sheridan's surprise attack with 20,000 men here proved too much for General Early's 12,000 troops. It was after the Battle of Fisher's Hill, and Early's retreat to Waynesboro, that Sheridan ordered the destruction of the Valley's barns, mills, crops, and livestock—a campaign known as "The Burning"—in an effort to cut off food and supplies destined for Confederate troops in other parts of the state.

In the years following the war, families from as far away as Washington, D.C., came to Fisher's Hill each August to honor war veterans with a grand picnic complete with bands, a merry-go-round, speeches, and dancing. Today the battlefield is maintained by the Association for the Preservation of Civil War Sites.

From the battlefield, retrace your route back to U.S. 11. Turn right and proceed 3.4

Keller's Mill

Old store at Fisher's Hill

miles to the village of **Toms Brook.** Not much is known about the early history of the town, or even how it got its name—which it has had since surveyors first noted it in 1744. Local citizens claim it's the only town with that name in the United States. Toms Brook is a quiet place these days.

The Battle of Toms Brook was fought northwest of town on October 9, 1864, during the period when Sheridan was destroying the Valley. Confederate soldiers found themselves helpless to stop the devastation but continued to attack Federal forces whenever they had a chance. Their actions finally irritated Sheridan to the point that he ordered his men to confront the Confederates at Toms Brook. Far outnumbered, the Southerners quickly retreated down the Valley Pike toward Woodstock. The Union soldiers are said to have referred jokingly to this retreat as "the Woodstock Races." Historic markers for this battle are located on the right less than 1 mile out of town.

Continue along the Valley Pike to the next village, **Maurertown**. Pronounced "Morrytown," this town also dates to the mid-1700s. It was probably named for a German immigrant named Charles Maurer, who owned much of the land in the area. That surname was common in the area and was spelled many ways, including Mowery, which sheds light on the pronunciation of the town's name. Much larger in days gone by, Maurertown once boasted a train station, a chair factory, three mills, and an undertaker.

The Shenandoah River meanders along the foothills of Massanutten Mountain just east of Maurertown. The next stop is the area of the river's famous "Seven Bends," which you may be able to see from the Woodstock Tower, depending on the time of year. In this part of the Valley in 1964, an archaeological team sponsored by the Virginia State Library excavated about 15 percent of the remains of an Indian town that they dated to between 900 and 1600 A.D. The town was about 250 feet in diameter and contained circular structures, food storage pits, and graves.

From Maurertown, continue south on U.S. 11 for 3.5 miles. Less than 0.5 mile after you pass the Woodstock city limits sign, you'll see a large brick building on the left, once the local middle school and now the county administration center. Just past the center, turn left on to Route 665 (Mill Road) and go 1.4 miles to a stop sign at Cemetery Road. Turn left; you are now on Route 758 (Woodstock Tower Road). As you approach Mas-

sanutten Mountain straight ahead, the road curves left and crosses the North Fork of the Shenandoah River in about 0.5 mile. After you cross the bridge, be sure to stay on Woodstock Tower Road. It is mostly gravel but well maintained for the rest of the hairpin-curved, 2.5-mile drive up the mountain. You'll be traveling through the George Washington National Forest. (Note that this road is not suitable for motorhomes, RVs, or trailers, and it is often closed during bad weather.)

When you approach the top of the mountain, park in one of the gravel waysides along the road. Look to the right for a sign mounted on a stone pillar that points the way to the 0.25-mile trail to the 40-foot Woodstock Tower, located high above the town on a ridge of Massanutten Mountain. (If you begin to descend the mountain, you've passed the trail entrance.) The short and relatively easy climb to the top offers magnificent views in two directions. Facing west, you'll see the town of Woodstock directly below, with Great North Mountain and layers of Allegheny ridges in the distance. In winter, spring, and late fall, you'll enjoy a great view of the often-photographed "Seven Bends" of the North Fork of the Shenandoah River, some 1,200 feet below. In fact, the meandering Shenandoah twists and turns to form 16 bends between Woodstock and Strasburg, traversing a river distance of 35 miles over just 12 linear miles of land. Turning around to face east, you'll see Fort Valley (the next stop on the tour) and the Blue Ridge Mountains.

The tower was built by the Civilian Conservation Corps as a joint venture with the people of Woodstock in the 1930s.

Leaving the tower, continue driving east down the mountain. After about 0.5 mile the road forks; keep to the right to stay on Woodstock Tower Road. This road descends into Fort Valley past Little Fort Recreation Area. In about 4 miles, you'll come to a stop sign at Route 678 (Fort Valley Road) at **Detrick**. *Turn left.* The Fort Valley Country Store is located to the right near this intersection, in case you need picnic supplies to take to the park a few miles down the road.

Fort Valley is a "valley within a valley," carved out by Passage Creek and enclosed by two parallel ranges of Massanutten Mountain. Until you look at a map of the area, you may not even realize this little valley exists. Its peaceful farms and rolling hills take you back to a time and place far removed from the stresses of modern life. There are no shopping centers, no fast-food restaurants, no billboards, no signs of commercialism anywhere.

Fort Valley measures about 5 miles across at its widest point and extends 23 miles from the town of Waterlick in the north to near New Market Gap in the south. (This tour covers the northern part of Fort Valley; see The Fort Valley to Page Valley Tour, page 164, for more about the southern portion.) The northern part of Fort Valley was part of the area George Washington surveyed for Lord Fairfax in 1748 and 1749. The story goes that Washington remembered this valley during the Revolutionary War, thinking it could provide him with a military advantage if the British drove him west. Some people say that he even had General Daniel Morgan build a road into the valley, which can still be seen today along the Veach Gap Trail.

Many arrowheads and stone tomahawk heads have been found on farms in Fort Valley, confirming that this secluded area was long used as a hunting ground

Barn in Fort Valley

by various Indian tribes. An Indian burial ground has been discovered near one of the farms here. According to the reports of one early settler, the Indians called the valley *Massanutton*, an Indian word for basket, supposedly because its shape was similar to that of baskets they made.

Fort Valley's first non-Indian resident is thought to have been a man named Powell, a reclusive character who claimed he had found gold and silver in the surrounding hills. He is said to have made high-quality counterfeit coins from his finds, but the authorities were never able to find him in the wilds of the mountains. Powell's operation was so secure, in fact, that the locals took to calling the place Powell's Fort. The German settlers who arrived in the 1730s called the area Powell's Fort Valley.

By the 1800s, Fort Valley's mineral deposits were attracting industrial activity. Manganese mines were developed, as were two iron-ore mines, which supplied the Fort Valley iron furnaces owned by a man named Blackford. He named those furnaces after two of his daughters, Elizabeth and Caroline. (Another Blackford-owned furnace, near Luray, was named for a third daughter, Isabella.) The furnaces were burned by Union forces during the Civil War and never rebuilt.

In less than 1 mile down Fort Valley Road from the turn, you'll pass a sign for the small settlement of **Seven Fountains**. A resort of the same name once stood here; also called Burner's White Sulphur Springs, it was one of Virginia's many popular mineral springs resorts. From 1850 until the Civil War, as many as 600 people at a time filled the large hotel and private cottages to escape the city heat and take the waters. Most visitors came from the Washington, D.C., area, riding the train into Strasburg and then taking a horse-drawn carriage into Fort Valley. In 1853, Seven Fountains became the location of the first post office in Fort Valley; before then, residents had to travel over the mountain to Woodstock to get their mail. The resort never reopened after the Civil War.

Continue on Fort Valley Road for about 0.5 mile to the Fort Valley Museum, the small red-brick building on the left. This structure originally housed the Old Brick Church at Dry Run, built in 1841. It was a "free" church, used by several denomina-

tions until its congregations could build their own churches. Today, the museum features textiles, local fossils, tools, and an exhibit of a one-room school. It is staffed by volunteers and is open on weekend afternoons from Memorial Day weekend through late October.

Past the museum, Fort Valley Road begins to curve alongside Passage Creek, passing several marked hiking trails along the way. In some places, trail information is posted at parking places; for additional information, contact the U.S. Forest Service (see the listing in the appendix).

Drive almost 7 miles to Elizabeth Furnace Recreation Area. This recreation area includes a campground, a picnic area, a group campground area, and the ruins of Elizabeth Furnace. The park offers rest rooms, picnic tables, shelters, trails, and fishing along Passage Creek. The entrance to the picnic area is about 0.5 mile past the campground area. One mile past the picnic area entrance is the beginning of the hiking trail to Signal Knob.

From the recreation area, continue for 3 miles to the settlement of **Fortsmouth;** *note that it may not have a town sign.* On the left side of the road, across the street

John Lederer, Early Valley Visitor

One of the earliest European explorers in this area was the German physician and scholar John Lederer. Although other explorers may have seen the Shenandoah Valley earlier, Lederer was the first European to record (in Latin) his journeys here. He made three trips to the Blue Ridge in 1669 and 1670. On the first, it appears he reached the top of the Blue Ridge at or near Swift Run Gap in the area of what is now Shenandoah National Park above Elkton. From that vantage point, he saw many more mountain ranges to the west—a discouraging finding for those wishing to expand settlement westward. On his third trip, in August 1670, he reached the top of the Blue Ridge near Manassas Gap or Chester Gap (his descriptions do not make the spot clear), southeast of Front Royal. (Route 522 passes through Chester Gap today.) Lederer later wrote, "They are certainly in great errour, who imagine that the Continent of North America is but eight or ten days journey over from the Atlantick to the Indian Ocean." A small roadside monument recognizing Lederer can be found along Route 55 in Linden, east of Front Royal, in the area of Manassas Gap.

from the Fortsmouth Fire and Rescue building, is a 1785 home built by Samuel M.C. Richardson, who was a Revolutionary War soldier, a Shenandoah County magistrate, and the planner of the town of Front Royal. The painted brick house, still used as a residence, is partially hidden by a stand of trees.

In 1 mile, Fort Valley Road ends at a stop sign at Route 55 (Strasburg Road); turn right. This is **Waterlick**. *In about 4 miles, you'll reach the* **Front Royal** *city limits. In another mile, the road meets U.S. 340 (North Shenandoah Avenue); turn right and cross the Shenandoah River bridge into town. In less than 1 mile, you'll start to see tourism signs pointing to the historic downtown area and the visitor center. Following these signs, turn left at the first traffic light to stay on Routes 340 South/522 South/55 East. Continue through two traffic lights. Turn left on to Main Street at the third light to reach the historic district and the visitor center.* (If you wish to bypass the town and go directly to the entrance to Skyline Drive and Shenandoah National Park, continue straight through the light.)

As you turn on to Main Street, you'll pass in front of the Warren County Courthouse, a handsome stone structure completed in 1936 by the Works Progress Administration (another of President Franklin Roosevelt's Depression-era work programs). It replaced the town's first courthouse, which was built in 1836, when Warren County was formed.

Drive two blocks to the Front Royal Visitor Center, on the left, and park in the lot. The visitor center occupies the 1880s railroad station near the center of downtown. It shares a parking lot with the Village Commons, which has a distinctive domed gazebo. The friendly, well-staffed visitor center offers plenty of information about local history and Civil War events in the area. You can also pick up a pamphlet describing a self-guided walking tour of the historic district.

Front Royal began as a crossroads where the trails through Manassas Gap and

Skyline Drive and the Shenandoah National Park

The north entrance to Skyline Drive is off U.S. 340, south of Front Royal. Skyline Drive winds for 105 miles atop the Blue Ridge Mountains through Shenandoah National Park and ends at the Blue Ridge Parkway near Waynesboro.

In the 1930s, the area was not as lush as it is today. There were few trees, the result of decades of farming and logging activities in the area. The park area also suffered greatly from the chestnut blight of the early 1900s—it is estimated that every fourth tree in Appalachian forests was a chestnut tree. Today the park is a nature-lover's paradise, with more than 860 species of wildflowers, 50 species of mammals (including the highest density of black bears of any national park), and more than 200 species of birds that live in or pass through the park annually.

Although especially lovely in the fall, Skyline Drive, the only road through the park, tends to get crowded in October, so be forewarned. The park's 1.5 million visitors a year come for its 500 miles of hiking trails—the Appalachian Trail passes through the park's length—scenic views, picnicking, camping, fishing, and other activities.

Front Royal Visitor Center

Chester Gap—the two lowest gaps across the Blue Ridge from the eastern part of the state—met. Front Royal's early name was Helltown, presumably a reflection of the rough-and-tumble lifestyle of the early residents. Some of the village's more conservative citizens later renamed it Lehewtown, after a French Huguenot settler who owned 200 acres and a tavern here in the mid-1700s.

For many years, reports of Indian attacks slowed the pace of settlement in the area. But after the Revolutionary War, land speculators came to the area and obtained a charter for a town they called Front Royal. No one is quite sure how the name originated. The most popular theory is that the drill sergeant of the local militia, frustrated when his less-than-professional volunteers failed to understand marching instructions, finally took to telling them to "front the royal oak," a huge tree in the area of today's Village Commons. He figured it was the only way he could make all the men face the same direction. Amused onlookers repeated the story, and it is thought the name evolved from there.

The town's strategic location made it valuable to both sides during the Civil War. The North and South Forks of the Shenandoah River meet here, and roads, railroads, and bridges offered transport in all directions. The town suffered heavy

Village Commons in Front Royal

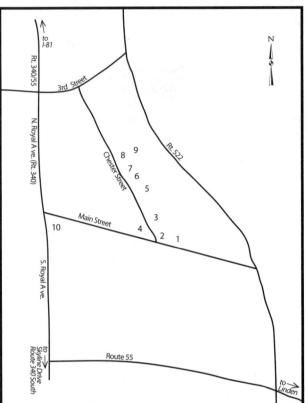

DOWNTOWN FRONT ROYAL

1   Visitor Center
2   Village Commons
3   Garrison House
4   Mullan-Trout House
5   Chester House
6   Balthis House
7   Warren Rifles
     Confederate Museum
8   Ivy Lodge/Warren
     Heritage Society
9   Belle Boyd Cottage
10   Warren County
     Courthouse

losses during the war. After the fighting was over, not a single business was left in Front Royal. Its bridges were burned, its rail lines were gone, and most of its buildings were either damaged or destroyed. By the mid-1930s, the opening of Skyline Drive and Shenandoah National Park and the development of Skyline Caverns (near the park entrance) brought tourism to the area virtually overnight.

Starting from the visitor center, you can take a short walking tour of Front Royal's oldest street, Chester Street (the street across the Village Commons from the visitor center). You'll soon notice that the usual numbering scheme does not hold true. Here you'll find a mix of ascending and descending numbers, as well as odd and even numbers on both sides of the street.

At 12 Chester Street is the Mullan-Trout House. It was built by Thomas Mullan sometime between 1806 and 1815. In 1853, it was bought by a Methodist circuit rider named David Trout.

At 15 Chester Street is Garrison House. Dr. Manley Littleton Garrison built this brick dwelling in 1882 after tearing down a small frame house that once stood here. He was a field and hospital physician during the Civil War and later practiced medicine for 50 years in a small building that stood next to this house.

Chester House at 43 Chester Street, which was once the home of the Samuels family as well as a bed-and-breakfast, is now a law office.

Balthis House, the white frame house at 55 Chester Street, is the oldest house

Mullan-Trout House   *Chester House*

on the street. Built around 1787, it was owned by the William Balthis family from 1838 to 1908. The brick wing in back was added around 1845. The first Mr. Balthis was a blacksmith who had a shop next door, on the lot where the Warren Rifles Confederate Museum stands today.

This museum, which is a memorial to Confederate soldiers from throughout the South, was built and dedicated in 1959; Senator Strom Thurmond of South Carolina cut the ribbon on opening day. It displays many local relics of the Civil War (including Stonewall Jackson's signal gun). The museum was conceived in 1937 by the Warren Rifles chapter of the United Daughters of the Confederacy, which spent more than 20 years raising funds and taking donations of materials and services to build the structure.

Next door at 101 Chester Street is Ivy Lodge, home of the Warren Heritage Society. One local history states that "this venerable house has been the home of more leading citizens, the center of more political, social, religious, patriotic, and cultural events that any other place left standing in Front Royal." For much of its

Balthis House

The Oldest Street in Front Royal

Chester Street is Front Royal's oldest. It was first known as Chester's Road, an early trail across the Blue Ridge that connected Winchester with markets in eastern Virginia and Maryland. The name no doubt came from Thomas Chester, a settler from Pennsylvania who in 1736 became the first licensed ferryboat operator west of the Blue Ridge. Chester also served as sheriff. He once found himself in the unenviable position of having to charge his wife, Sarah, with selling "strong drinks commonly called Rye Brandy or Whiskey and Cyder without License." Fortunately for him, the case was dismissed for reasons never recorded.

existence, it has served as a schoolhouse or as a home for school officials. It was built in the 1850s, but the fact that the window frames and floors are held together by wooden pegs, not nails, seems to date the structure to before 1825. Today, it contains exhibits about daily life in the area and historical archives.

In the yard behind Ivy Lodge is the Belle Boyd Cottage, made famous by its association with a young woman of the Civil War. It is one of the oldest dwellings in town. Belle Boyd was known throughout the United States and England for her exploits—never fully proved, however—as a self-appointed spy for the Confederacy. The cottage welcomes visitors.

It all started when, as a girl of 17, Belle shot and killed a Union soldier in her parents' home in Martinsburg on July 4, 1861. The soldier had told Belle's mother that he planned to raise the Union flag over the house. When Mrs. Boyd, whose husband was serving with the Confederates, declared that she and her children would rather die first, the soldier responded with an insulting comment that prompted Belle to pull out a pistol and shoot him. After a brief investigation, the soldier's commanding officer let Belle off the hook, even placing soldiers around the house to protect the Boyds from further harassment. Belle soon charmed these men, then stole their weapons and passed along information about Union plans to the Confederates.

Presumably to keep her out of trouble, Belle was sent to Front Royal to live with her aunt and uncle, who were the proprietors of the Fishback Hotel at 317 East Main Street. But she was soon back to her old tricks.

In the spring of 1862, at the time General Stonewall Jackson was beginning his famous Valley Campaign, General James Shields made the Fishback Hotel his Union headquarters. Belle, who lived with her relatives in the cottage behind the hotel, found herself in the perfect position to resume her covert activities. (Note that the cottage was moved to its Chester Street location in 1982.)

In her recollection of the times, Belle stated that General Shields "introduced me to the officers of his staff, to one of whom, Captain K., I am indebted for some very remarkable infusions, some withered flowers, and a great deal of very important information, which was carefully transmitted to my countrymen."

One night she hid in a closet above the hotel parlor, where she could overhear, through a hole in the floor, Union war plans being made below. At one o'clock in the morning, after the meeting ended, she quietly saddled her horse and rode 15 miles to tell Colonel Turner Ashby what she had heard. General Stonewall Jackson reportedly used her information to prepare for his surprise attack on Front Royal on May 23, 1862.

On that day, while Union troops in the town were in an uproar upon discovering they were under attack, Belle took revenge on a Union-friendly reporter who was staying at the hotel. Unwisely, the man had left his room key hanging on the outside of his door as he was packing to leave. "The temptation of making a Yankee prisoner was too strong to be resisted," Belle wrote. "Yielding to the impulse, I quietly locked in the 'Special Correspondent' of the *New York Herald*." Later, she watched from the hotel steps as he was taken prisoner; he reportedly yelled to her, "I'll make you rue this!"

Belle claimed that on the same day, in the midst of an ongoing attack, she once again carried military information to the Confederates, bullets piercing her skirts as she ran through the battle lines. According to Belle's journal, her efforts won her a personal note of praise and appreciation from General Jackson.

The Union officers were not amused. She was arrested six times and imprisoned three times in the Old Capitol Prison in Washington, D.C., where it is said she helped Confederate prisoners escape and even talked the warden into shopping for her wedding trousseau.

After the war, she continued to lead an interesting life, marrying a Federal navy ensign who had been assigned to guard her. Later she became a stage actress and married two more times. The docents at the Belle Boyd Cottage can relate many more details about the life of this interesting woman.

These are just a few of the many historic homes in Front Royal; pick up a copy of the walking-tour booklet at the visitor center for more places to walk in town.

Return to your car to complete the tour. Drive north on Chester Street until it ends at Routes 340/522 (Royal Avenue). Turn right and leave town the way you came in. Follow the signs to I-66. To reach I-81, take I-66 West, which merges with I-81 a short distance west of Front Royal.

The Woodstock to Lost City to Columbia Furnace Tour

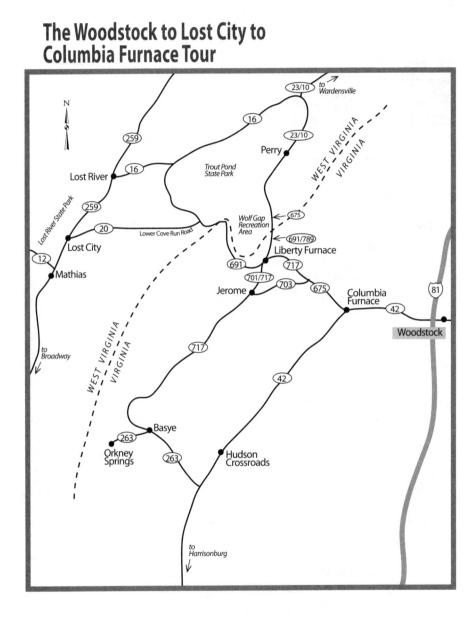

TOUR **6**

The Woodstock to Lost City to Columbia Furnace Tour

This tour starts in Woodstock, one of the Shenandoah Valley's oldest towns, and winds toward Great North Mountain past the communities of Conicville and Hudson Crossroads, which were first settled in the 1700s. It then begins a descent into a picturesque hidden valley and the longtime resort villages of Basye and Orkney Springs. From there, the tour skirts the foothills of Great North Mountain to Liberty Furnace, then begins the climb over this first ridge of the Alleghenies into West Virginia. After passing Wolf Gap Recreation Area, it continues past Trout Pond State Park on to Lost City, West Virginia. A side trip to Lost River State Park is included. The tour returns toward Woodstock by way of a gravel mountain road that offers spectacular views of the valley below and Massanutten Mountain to the east.

The tour includes honest-to-goodness backroads up and over Great North Mountain. These roads mean slow travel times. If you want to visit the two West Virginia State Parks, you might want to save the Woodstock portion of the tour for another day.

Total mileage: 95 miles

The tour begins in **Woodstock***. Take Exit 283 off I-81, then follow Route 42 North to U.S. 11. Turn left on to U.S. 11 (Main Street) at the traffic light.* On your way into the downtown area, you'll pass the campus of Massanutten Military Academy, which held its first classes in 1899. The first stop is the historic Shenandoah County Courthouse, on the left at the fourth traffic light.

Woodstock was part of Frederick County when it was chartered in 1761; the town had been formed in 1752 by German and Scotch-Irish settlers. George Washington, as the Frederick County delegate to the Virginia House of Burgesses, sponsored its charter. In 1772, Frederick County was split and Dunmore County was formed, with Woodstock as the county seat. The new county was named for Virginia's royal governor at the time, Lord Dunmore. But the name was short-lived. During the American Revolution, Lord Dunmore burned Norfolk, among other

Why West Virginia?

About half this tour takes place in West Virginia. Although many sites along the route are not technically part of the Shenandoah Valley, they carry ties to its history. West Virginia was part of Virginia until 1863, when for political reasons—most western Virginia counties had refused to secede from the Union in 1861—it split off. Residents of the trans-Allegheny area (and even the Shenandoah Valley) had long believed that their interests, both political and economic, were not fairly represented in Richmond, where the state assembly had long been controlled by well-to-do plantation owners, lawyers, and businessmen on the eastern side of the Blue Ridge. There were few plantation-like farms west of the Blue Ridge, and relatively few slaveowners. Nevertheless, the two states share a common past, and the portion of West Virginia covered in this tour remains linked to the Shenandoah Valley both socially and economically.

dastardly deeds, prompting county residents to rename their county Shenandoah, then spelled Shanando.

A German settler named Jacob Mueller laid out the town on 1,200 acres he owned here, some of which he had received as a land grant from Lord Fairfax in 1752. He called his town Woodstock, but the locals called it Muellerstadt. Like many other immigrants, he had first settled in Philadelphia but later moved south to Virginia, where land was cheaper and more plentiful.

Woodstock has had several well-known residents. John Sevier, who later became the first governor of Tennessee, moved here from New Market in 1770 but left for eastern Tennessee three years later. Jonathan Clark, elder brother of the Revolutionary War hero George Rogers Clark, was another early resident. Thomas Marshall, father of Supreme Court Chief Justice John Marshall, was the first clerk of the circuit court before the Revolutionary War.

The town's most famous resident was one of its first. John Peter Gabriel Muhlenberg came to Woodstock as a young preacher in 1773. His father, Henry Melchior Muhlenberg, is considered the father of the Lutheran Church in America. The younger Muhlenberg's church in Woodstock was built of logs, like most structures of the day. It stood in the middle of what is now the intersection of Main and Court Streets, almost in front of the courthouse. It is thought that the church was already there when the town was laid out. Some believe that is why Main Street was so much wider in Woodstock than in other Valley towns.

Politically active from the start, Muhlenberg was elected to the Virginia House of Burgesses in 1774, at the age of 28. He soon became involved in local patriots' meetings. By January 1776, the Virginia House of Delegates had made him a colonel in the Eighth Virginia Regiment (also called the German Regiment) of the Continental Army.

Later that month, during a sermon in his little Woodstock church, he made a dramatic appeal to the congregation. Local historian Karen Cooper cites the account given by Muhlenberg's great-nephew, Henry A. Muhlenberg: "[Colonel

Above: *Shenandoah County Courthouse*
Right: *Shenandoah County Courthouse weathervane*

Muhlenberg] ascended the pulpit, his tall form arrayed in full uniform, over which his gown, the symbol of his holy calling, was thrown. After [telling the audience] the story of their sufferings and their wrongs, and telling them of the sacred character of the struggle in which he had unsheathed his sword…he said 'that in the words of the Bible, there is a time for all things, a time to preach and a time to pray, but those times have passed away' and in a voice that re-echoed through the church like a trumpet-blast, 'that there was a time to fight, and that time had now come!' The sermon finished, he pronounced the benediction….Deliberately pulling off the gown, he stood before them a warrior, and descending from the pulpit, ordered the drums at the church door to beat for recruits."

Muhlenberg and his men—mostly German settlers from the Valley—went first to defend Charleston, and then to various places throughout the South. His regiment went on to assist George Washington at Brandywine, Germantown, Valley Forge, and Monmouth. Muhlenberg later fought at Yorktown and rose to the rank of major general, in charge of the Continental forces in Virginia.

The Shenandoah County Courthouse dates to 1795 (replacing an earlier log structure at the site) and is thought to be the oldest courthouse in continuous use west of the Blue Ridge. Made of locally quarried limestone, the building has been altered and enlarged on several occasions; its columned portico was added in 1929.

The weathervane on top of the courthouse cupola may look like an Indian from a distance, but closer inspection reveals that the man in a feathered hat and topcoat holding a spear is a different figure altogether. Its meaning remained a mystery for many years. In 1927, Shenandoah Valley historian John Wayland heard about a monument that had been erected in Lucerne, Switzerland, to the memory of the Swiss Guards who were massacred in Paris in 1792, during the French Revolution. The Swiss Guards were, for the most part, ceremonial mercenary soldiers from Switzerland who served the French monarchy.

On a hunch, Wayland wrote to Lucerne's mayor and requested a list of their names. The surnames on the list were the same as several early Valley residents: Bowman, Kibler, Kaufman, Miller, Hoover, Senseney, Suter, Walker, and others. From this research, Dr. Wayland surmised that the murdered Swiss Guards may have been related to some of the area's settlers, who probably designed the weathervane as a memorial.

From the courthouse, walk one block up Court Street to the Woodstock Museum, located in the Marshall-Samuels House, at 104 South Muhlenberg Street. It is open from May through October on Thursdays, Fridays, and Saturdays from noon to 4 P.M. Staffed by volunteers, this museum includes artifacts, furniture, quilts, maps, tools, Civil War memorabilia, and many interesting items of everyday life in the past, including a 19th-century still. The Marshall-Samuels House, built of brick and limestone sometime before 1772, got its name from Thomas Marshall, mentioned earlier, and Judge Green Berry Samuels. Marshall stayed here when in Woodstock on court business between 1772 and 1781. Samuels, a later owner, was a United States congressman in the 1830s and a Virginia Supreme Court judge.

The museum also maintains the Dick Wickham House, located directly behind the courthouse. The house dates to the 1770s. The current weatherboarding covers the original log construction. Many of the old houses in Woodstock and elsewhere in the Valley were originally log cabins that have since been covered with other materials—a practice that gave the homes a more finished look and helped keep out cold drafts. It can be toured by appointment or when the Woodstock Museum is open.

Return to Main Street to see several homes of historic interest. Woodstock has many interesting old homes and buildings from all eras and of various architectural styles. From the courthouse, head north on Main Street to the end of the next block, at 237 North Main. The John Effinger House, at 201 North Main, was named for a Hessian soldier who fought with the Americans during the Revolutionary War and served for a time as one of George Washington's bodyguards. Effinger bought the lot in 1790 and lived in what is now the rear log section of the house until his death in 1839. Local legend says that the logs in the front part of this house came from the old church where Peter Muhlenberg preached.

Marshall-Samuels House

Dick Wickham House

John Effinger House

Clower House

The Clower House is at 237 North Main. It was named after another Revolutionary War veteran, George Clower. He built the rear log section of the present house and lived here until his death in 1822.

At 402 North Main is a house thought to have been built by Jacob Ott in the late 1700s; the rear brick portion was built by his son in the 1840s.

The Tollgate Keeper's House, at 409 North Main, was also built of logs. Until 1918, a tollgate stood in front of the house during the days when this road was the Valley Turnpike—one of the first macadamized roads in the country, dating to the 1830s.

Return to your car and drive south on Main Street past the military academy. At the traffic light, turn right on to Route 42. The tour continues on Route 42 for about 10 miles. You'll cross I-81 and pass through several hamlets before reaching the intersection with Route 703 just before Conicville. Turn right on Route 703 and drive about 0.5 mile to see the small stone structure known as the Rinker House.

This area was settled by Jacob Rinker, a Swiss immigrant, around 1749. He built this two-room house around that time. It was constructed over a spring, providing a convenient source of water, a common practice in those days. The stone construction suggests that the house may have served as a fort to protect local families from Indian attacks.

This structure was later the home of Rinker's son, also named Jacob, who served as a lieutenant in Muhlenberg's famous Eighth Virginia Regiment during

Rinker House

the Revolutionary War. In addition to his military endeavors, which included service with George Rogers Clark in the Illinois Territory, Jacob Rinker, Jr., was a well-respected county magistrate and surveyor. He was also a member of the Virginia convention that ratified the United States Constitution.

Turn around, return to Route 42, and turn right into **Conicville.** The number of houses lining both sides of the road in Conicville provides a hint of this town's past. The village grew in the years after the Civil War and eventually had three stores and two churches. The schoolhouse on the right at the far end of town, now a private home, was built in 1911 to replace a one-room schoolhouse that had served the community since 1873.

Continue on Route 42 to **Hudson Crossroads**, the next hamlet down the road. A wonderful old stone house built by Henry Baughman in 1800 still stands. Look for it on the left as the road winds toward the two white frame churches that sit to the right of the crossroads. It is often referred to as the Thomas Hudson House, after the man who bought the property in 1815. (The house is easier to see once you get to the crossroads and look back.) Be sure to note the slits in the walls at the basement level. These presumably served two functions—they provided light and air to the lower level and also provided a protected area from which to respond to

Old Conicville schoolhouse

Indian attack. The house's longevity can be partly attributed to the huge timbers used in its construction and the quality of the stonework.

A Lutheran church has stood in Hudson Crossroads since before 1850. Its building was used by a Reformed congregation until its members built their own church across the street in 1852.

Follow Route 42 for another 2.2 miles. Turn right on Route 263 West (Orkney Grade Road). This road, which originates at the southern end of Mount Jackson, had its beginnings as Howard's Lick Turnpike, a privately built and maintained toll road that once took travelers over North Mountain and into Hardy County, West Virginia, to the towns of Lost City and Mathias.

Route 263 soon begins to quickly wind down into an unexpected little valley with dramatic views of North Mountain. As the road levels out, you'll enter the village of **Basye** and the entrance to Bryce Resort. To visit the resort—which is open to the public and offers skiing, golf, boating, swimming, and tennis—turn right on to Resort Drive after crossing the bridge over Stony Creek.

Continue on Route 263, as it veers to the left into Basye, for another 1.5 miles to **Orkney Springs**, *where the road ends.* Orkney Springs has been a travelers' destination since the first pioneers arrived in the late 1700s; Indians apparently visited the springs many years before that. The area was first called Yellow Springs, because chalybeate, which contains iron salts, colors the moss-covered rocks a bright yellow. This is one of the few surviving 1800s-era mineral springs resorts that once were commonplace in the western Virginia

The Virginia Springs Resorts

At least 75 mineral springs resorts have come and gone in Virginia over the past 200 years or so. They peaked in popularity around the mid-1800s as cool summer getaways and "restorers of health" for city dwellers. Most guests came by rail and stayed for a month or longer. Some resorts were run strictly for their so-called health benefits and offered only the basic amenities. But others were fashionable places to stay, where social contacts and business deals were part of the attraction.

Many of the resorts were damaged during the Civil War and never reopened. Later, advances in medicine and the advent of the automobile in the early 1900s hastened the demise of the few that remained. Many hotels burned down around that time, with arson suspected in more than a few cases.

mountains. It is nothing short of amazing that it still stands today.

The area's first settler was John McDonald, who bought more than 300 acres here in 1775. His wife was a daughter of Jost Hite, one of the early Valley settlers. In 1805, the McDonalds' son sold the land to a major in the Revolutionary War, Peter Higgins. Not long after that, the first of two or three small log "hotels" was built at the springs.

In 1850, the owners of the property at the time founded the Orkney Springs Mineral Company. By 1858, the building of the Maryland House, which still stands, was begun. Orkney Springs was on its way to becoming one of Virginia's most popular and enduring mineral springs resorts. The variety of springs at Orkney were reputed to have curative powers for many complaints, including mental and physical exhaustion.

The source of the village's name is uncertain. John McDonald was thought to have come to America from the Orkney Islands, off the coast of Scotland. Another theory is that George Washington, who helped survey this area for Lord Fairfax, named it after the earl of Orkney, the first royal governor of Virginia. For a short time in the 1800s, the village was known as Van Burenville, after Martin Van Buren visited here during his campaign for the presidency in the late 1830s.

The main hotel building today is, and long has been, the Virginia House, built between 1873 and 1876. Even by today's standards, this building is huge, measuring 100 feet wide by 265 long and standing four stories high. In its early days, it boasted 175 guest rooms, a 40-by-155-foot dining room, and a 50-by-100-foot ballroom. The names of the various guest cottages built later on the grounds provide clues to the guests' probable hometowns: Philadelphia, Washington, Baltimore, Richmond, Norfolk, Charleston, and Savannah. The hotel and its cottages could accommodate up to 750 guests.

Most visitors were families who came here for a month's stay in the summer to escape city heat and humidity. The men would commute on weekends from their jobs in the city. Guests from Washington, D.C., would take the train to Mount Jackson and then travel by horse-drawn stagecoaches (which ran twice a day) down an old Indian road—now Route 263—to the springs. The trip from Mount Jackson that takes 25 minutes today required about 4 hours back then. In the 1850s, stages also ran from New Market to Orkney Springs three times a week. Today's visitors can only wonder how horses managed to pull buggies loaded with guests and their

Orkney Springs Hotel, Virginia House

trunks up the steep, winding road out of Basye on the return trip to Mount Jackson.

The springs resort was just as popular with the local residents. In *A History of Shenandoah County, Virginia,* John Wayland wrote, "Before cars, a procession of buggies used to mark the road up Mill Creek [Route 263] and across the hills to Orkney on Sunday and Saturday afternoons. It was the ambition of almost every rural swain to take his best girl to Orkney."

Postcards from the resort's peak period—1870 to 1890—show well-dressed men and women (most of the latter carrying opened parasols) sitting on the hotel's many balconies and porches or strolling the grounds with their children. In those days, the roof of the main hotel building was built in the French mansard style, which gave it an elegant appearance. The largest swimming pool in the South at the time (90 by 50 feet) was built here in 1890. Many other sports and activities were offered, including horse races.

By the 1920s, the resort's success began to fade because of the advent of automobile travel. Travelers were no longer limited to places where railroads could take them. Around that time, the Episcopal Diocese of Virginia built a retreat called Shrine Mont next to the resort. In 1979, the diocese bought the entire 950-acre Orkney Springs complex. It restored the buildings in 1987 and now uses them for church retreats and conferences.

Orkney Springs has been home to the Shenandoah Valley Music Festival since 1963; for a few years before then, it hosted summer workshops of the American Symphony Orchestra League. Every summer, various musical events—from bluegrass to jazz to classical symphonies—take place on weekends in the open-air pavilion on the lawn behind the hotel.

To continue on the tour, head back up Route 263 toward Basye, and turn left on Route 717 (Alum Springs Road) just past a car wash. In 0.7 mile, you will pass the entrance to Creekside Village and Chalet High, a resort rental company that occupies the building that once was known as Bird Haven. The Alum Springs Hotel began operating here in 1852. It became quite popular by the 1870s, evidently as much for its elegant restaurant as for the healing powers of its springs.

In another 0.5 mile, look for the ruins of the Henrietta Furnace on the left; it's also been called Alum Springs Furnace and Myers Furnace. One account says it was built by Samuel Myers, who operated it from 1855 to 1865; another account states it was built in 1820 and was burned in 1864, presumably by Union troops. It was never used again.

From 1780 to 1880, ironmaking was an important industry in this part of the Shenandoah Valley. But area forests were destroyed as a result. Until coke was introduced as a more efficient fuel in the late 1800s, charcoal was needed to create the hot fires in the furnaces. Charcoal was made by burning small pine trees in kilns or "pits." It's been estimated that each furnace required cutting down about 150 acres of woodland a year. This extensive lumbering eventually stripped mountain areas bare in parts.

Other problems contributed to deforestation in the area. For example, most of the yellow pines in the Valley between 1880 and 1890 were killed by an insect

Henrietta Furnace   *Liberty Furnace ruins and mill*

infestation. The chestnut blight affected the northern end of the Valley (and much of the eastern United States) beginning in 1914. (It's been estimated that at one time, chestnut trees made up to 60 percent of some area forests.) Even today, a small insect, the woolly adelgid, has killed off many of the grand old hemlock trees in these forests.

By the 1900s, people began to realize the damage that had been done and began to regenerate the forests. By the 1930s, thousands of seedlings were planted by the United States Forest Service and the Civilian Conservation Corps (C.C.C.), a government jobs program created during the Great Depression to provide work for unemployed men and to help the government conserve and develop national forests and parks.

Conservation efforts continue today. The Valley's forests are probably more heavily forested today than they were during much of the 1800s. Almost all of the mountain forests that form the western boundaries of the Valley are part of the George Washington National Forest, which is run by the United States Forest Service, an agency of the Department of Agriculture.

*Continue past the furnace for another 5.3 miles to where Route 717 meets Route 703 at a stop sign. Turn left toward **Jerome**. Jerome was settled as early as 1785. The road curves around a picturesque white church perched on a hilltop.* Built in 1892, St. Paul's Lutheran Church replaced an 1854 structure. Before then, the congregation met in a nearby schoolhouse.

In less than 0.5 mile, turn right on to Route 701 (Liberty Furnace Road). In 1.8 miles, you'll see a white mansion high on the hill to the left. The ruins of Liberty Furnace and an old gristmill lie below. Turn left on to Cold Spring Road. It will become Route 691, an unpaved road that starts the climb up the mountain.

Walter Newman, whose family had lived in the area since the 1760s, built and began operating this iron furnace in 1822. He turned it over to his son in 1842. In 1886, after changing hands a few times, both Liberty and Columbia Furnaces (mentioned later in this tour) were bought by a Philadelphia company that formed the Liberty Iron Company here. A 12-mile narrow-gauge railroad was built to connect these furnaces to the main railway in Edinburg. But by 1907, the iron-ore industry in the Valley could no longer compete with cheaper sources in the West, and the Liberty Iron Company closed. The railroad tracks are long gone as well,

These Ancient Mountains

Great North Mountain forms part of the first ridge of the Alleghenies, which stretch about 500 miles from northern Pennsylvania to southwestern Virginia. The Alleghenies are the westernmost range of the Appalachians (the other two ranges being the Blue Ridge and the Cumberland).

The mountains that surround the Shenandoah Valley are among the oldest on earth, much older than the Rockies, the Alps, or the Himalayas.

Mountain-building processes had already been going on here for 200 million years when the Appalachians came into being. They were formed when tectonic forces caused the landmass we know today as Africa to push into eastern North America some 250 to 300 million years ago, and the rocky land buckled into a series of high ridges.

View from Great North Mountain

Later, all the earth's continents eventually moved together to form the supercontinent that geologists call Pangaea. The young Appalachians were located in the interior of this massive continent for 50 million years. At one time, these mountains may have been as high as the Himalayas are today, but the forces of erosion have long been at work, wearing down their height and softening their once-sharp peaks.

pulled up and sold as scrap metal during World War II.

Near Liberty Furnace, the (C.C.C.) set up its seventh camp in 1933. This camp was established for African-American men. One of the jobs these men may have performed was the planting of thousands of trees mentioned earlier; it is estimated that C.C.C. workers planted some three billion trees nationwide.

After passing through a mile of dense forest, with Laurel Run rushing alongside the road, Route 691 turns sharply to the left and becomes Judge Rye Road. Do not turn here. Instead, continue straight on what is now Route 789 (Sam Clark Road) for another 0.3 mile until you reach Route 675 (Wolf Gap Road). Turn left. You will soon enter **Wolf Gap Recreation Area**. *The paved road winds up the mountain for almost 2 miles to the* park campground and picnic area on the right; this is where the Tibbet Knob Trail and the Mill Mountain Trail meet. You'll cross the West Virginia line and enter Hardy County at the crest of the mountain.

Although Wolf Gap may have been named after the animal once prevalent in the area (before settlers were paid handsome bounties for wolf heads), it was probably named for Jacob Wolfe, who bought 400 acres of land south of here in 1754. The elevation at the crest is 2,250 feet.

In less than 4 miles, you'll come out of the forest and enter **Perry, West Virginia**. There you'll pass the Perry General Store, which operates a zoo of sorts.

In another 2.9 miles, the ruins of another old iron furnace are on the right. In another 1.3 miles, look for a brown sign pointing left to the road leading to **Trout Pond**; *turn left on to this road (Thorn Bottom Road). In about 6 miles, this tour passes the*

Lost River State Park Side Trip

If time allows, you may want to make a side trip to Lost River State Park. This attractive park offers hiking trails, rental cabins, a swimming pool, tennis and volleyball courts, a softball field, and horseback riding.

Drive south from Lost River on Route 259 for 4.3 miles; the park comes up quickly on the right in Mathias, so watch for the brown state park sign just before the road to the park. Turn right on Howard's Lick Road. The park entrance is 4 miles down this road. The large log cabin (a private home) facing Route 259 at this intersection is the Mathias Homestead, built in the 1790s. A state historical marker, located just before the park turnoff, notes that Confederate general Thomas Jonathan "Stonewall" Jackson's great-grandparents settled in this area around 1750, and that his grandfather was born here. Shortly afterward, the family moved to Clarksburg, where Jackson was born in 1824.

This area was known as Howard's Lick in the early 1800s. The Lee family of Virginia had a summer retreat here. Henry "Lighthorse Harry" Lee was given part of Lord Fairfax's landholdings as a reward for his service in the Revolutionary War. The cabin he built still stands in the park. One of his sons, Charles Carter Lee (Robert E. Lee's brother), built a boardinghouse and cabins here for guests who came to "take the waters" from the sulfur springs. The property was later sold, and the new owners expanded the resort and renamed it Lee White Sulphur Springs. After the hotel burned down in 1910, the resort closed.

The western end of the old Howard's Lick Turnpike, which began in Mount Jackson and led past Basye over the mountains, is a short distance south and across Route 259 from Route 12; it is now known as Upper Cove Run Road. It is not a reliable road.

entrance to **Trout Pond State Park**. The park has camping and picnic areas, short trails, the two-acre Trout Pond and the 17-acre Rock Cliff Lake. The small sandy beach on the lake is especially popular with families in the summer months. No food is available at the park; if you need supplies, be sure to stop on your way.

*From the turnoff to Trout Pond State Park, continue down the mountain for 4.6 miles into the hamlet of **Lost River**, where the road intersects Route 259. To visit the Lost River General Store, turn right; it is a short distance on the right. To continue the tour, turn left on to Route 259. (If you want to take a side trip to **Lost River State Park**, see the sidebar above.)*

The village of Lost River dates back to the 1750s. A battle in the French and Indian War took place here in 1756. This is a good place to stop and stretch and visit the Lost River Artisans Cooperative and the Lost River Museum (in the lower level of the artisans cooperative), located on the left shortly after you turn on to Route 259.

*From Lost River, continue south on Route 259 for 2.2 miles to **Lost City**. Turn left on to Lower Cove Run Road. You'll have to watch carefully for this turn; it is just past the Lost City Baptist Church, which is partially obscured by trees on the left side of the road (look for the small West Virginia Route 59 sign).*

This road, which will put you back in the George Washington National Forest, takes you on a beautiful drive through rocky cliffs and dense forest as it loops along

the crest of Great North Mountain. The road becomes Route 691 in a few miles. The road is unpaved most of the way, but it is well maintained. Although you don't need a four-wheel-drive vehicle, it is not for the faint of heart. It's narrow in parts, and there are no safety rails. But on a clear day, the views are as dramatic as those from Skyline Drive in Shenandoah National Park. Every so often the road widens to provide a place to pull off and take pictures or just admire the view. You may see white-tailed deer. In early June, these woods are full of the pale pink blossoms of mountain laurel.

Continue to the intersection with Sam Clark Road—you were here earlier in the tour. Turn right and drive 1.5 miles, to Route 717 (Liberty Furnace Road), and turn left. From here it is nearly 6 miles to **Columbia Furnace**. Big Stony Creek is on the right much of the way.

Columbia Furnace was once the heart of industrial activity in Shenandoah County. Built around 1804, it continued operations under various owners until 1907, despite being burned three times during the Civil War. At its peak, it employed about 200 people. It supplied pig iron to iron forges, such as Union Forge near Edinburg, where guns, cannons, and ammunition were produced—an important activity during war-time because it allowed the region to be self-sufficient.

The tour ends at Columbia Furnace. *The road veers to the right and passes over a low concrete bridge. After crossing the bridge, turn left on to Route 42 to return to Woodstock.*

View of Route 691 along the crest of Great North Mountain

The Edinburg to Singers Glen to Mount Jackson Tour

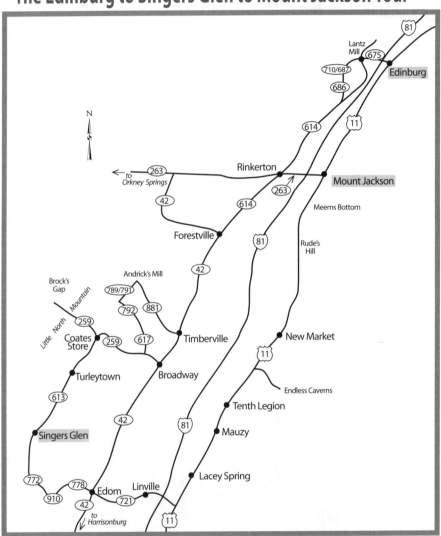

TOUR 7
The Edinburg to Singers Glen to Mount Jackson Tour

This tour begins and ends on the historic Valley Pike, today's U.S. 11. It passes through scenic farmland of the central Shenandoah Valley in the foothills of Massanutten Mountain, Great North Mountain, and Little North Mountain, following routes used in colonial times and even earlier. The tour begins in Edinburg and passes through Lantz Mills, Forestville, Turleytown, Singers Glen, Edom, Lacey Spring, Tenth Legion, and New Market. It ends just a few miles south of where it began, on U.S. 11 at Mount Jackson.

Highlights include several Civil War sites (including the famous New Market battlefield), a farm where Indians staged a brutal attack on settlers in the 1750s, a perfectly preserved 19th-century village that influenced American religious music publishing and education in the 1800s, several restored mills, the place where Abraham Lincoln's father was born, portions of a trail George Washington used to return to Mount Vernon from western Virginia, and one of the last covered bridges in Virginia.

Total mileage: Approximately 65 miles

*The tour begins at the town of **Edinburg**, which is about midway between Winchester and Harrisonburg. Take Exit 279 off I-81 and follow Route 185 East (Stony Creek Boulevard), which ends at U.S. 11 (Main Street) in less than 1 mile. Turn right at the stop sign to see the Edinburg Mill on the right a short distance down U.S. 11.*

Edinburg began as a German settlement in the late 1700s. Today, it is one of the prettiest towns in the valley, with dozens of old homes representing almost every era and architectural style. The Edinburg Mill is probably the most historically significant building in town; it was built in the late 1840s by Major George Grandstaff. In the early 1800s, Grandstaff's ancestors built a dam on Stony Creek at this spot to provide water power for a sawmill, a carding mill, and a boring mill for a rifle factory. The rifle factory, begun by Major George Grandstaff's grandfather, provided guns for the War of 1812.

The Edinburg Mill is one of only a handful of pre–Civil War mills that survived

General Philip Sheridan's campaign of destruction—known as "The Burning"—in the central and northern Shenandoah Valley in 1864; this tour visits three others as well. The Grandstaff Mill, as it was known then, was set on fire at least twice by Sheridan's forces, but the townspeople—mostly women and children, since it was wartime—saved it on both occasions by setting up bucket brigades stretching to nearby Stony Creek.

Legend has it that on one of those occasions, two of the miller's young female relatives begged General Sheridan to spare the mill. Swayed by their pleas, Sheridan instructed his soldiers to help douse the fire. Local historians Mary Ann Williamson and Jean Allen Davis say that Sheridan gave the orders "because of his respect for Major George [Grandstaff], who had been an outstanding strategist in the War of 1812."

The mill, which operated continuously until the 1960s, later housed a series of restaurants and gift shops. Today the mill, completely refurbished after a nine-year town project, houses a visitor center and museum. One of the museum's aims is to focus on the history of the Valley Pike, as well as on the history of rail and water-transport in the Valley.

Major Grandstaff's great-grandfather was one of Edinburg's first settlers. John Amos Bischoff brought his Mennonite family to America from the Palatinate (in today's southern Germany) in the 1740s. They lived in the Hawksbill settlement in Luray, on the other side of Massanutten Mountain from Edinburg. One of John Amos's children, George Philip Bischoff, was kidnapped by Indians in 1758. The Indians named the strapping sixteen-year-old "Grand Staff." When he eventu-

Edinburg's Geology

Edinburg is interesting geologically as well as historically. Like much of the Valley, Edinburg lies above limestone formed millions of years ago when the entire region was covered by a vast sea. The many caves and underground streams in the area took shape when drainage water dissolved the limestone. Some believe that Edinburg lies over a large underground lake, stream, or cavern. Over the years, residents have reported hearing the sound of rushing water beneath their homes after a heavy rain. There have also been reports of local people tapping sticks or poles into the ground and then watching them either disappear or descend to as far as 16 feet below the surface. Sinkholes are fairly common throughout this area.

ally returned home, he decided to make "Grandstaff" his surname. He later fought in the American Revolution.

After the war, George Philip Grandstaff moved to Edinburg and built a two-room log house around 1787. This is probably Edinburg's oldest house. It was enlarged by his grandson, Major George Grandstaff, and remains a private residence at 108 Creekside Lane. Creekside Lane is the short, narrow street that runs behind the VFW Hall (originally the Edinburg Hotel), which you will see on the left as you begin to leave the town. Major George Grandstaff was a lawyer, a justice of the peace, and a state legislator. The story goes that Major Grandstaff's friendship with President James Madison led to naming the local magisterial district "Madison."

Across the street from the mill at 211 South Main Street is the Fairfax Lodge, also known as the Philip Grandstaff House, which dates to 1811. Unfortunately, its modern appearance today belies its long history. A shed behind the house served as Union headquarters during the month-long siege of Edinburg in 1862.

Early settlers in Edinburg were typical of those who came to this part of the Shenandoah Valley in the 1700s and 1800s. Most were Protestants from Pennsylvania. Many were members of the Mennonite faith, which began as a Swiss sect of the Anabaptists, who had been persecuted in Europe because they believed in adult rather than infant baptism. The settlers originally came from three regions of Europe: the Rhineland (or Palatinate) in Germany, Alsace (once part of Germany but today part of France), and Switzerland. From Pennsylvania, most headed south down the old Indian trail that later became the Valley Pike and today's U.S. 11 in their search for cheap, fertile land and freedom from religious oppression. In the Shenandoah Valley, many found what they were looking for and more; the rolling valleys and soft hills and mountains are said to have reminded them of their homelands.

The community here was first called Stony Creek and then Shryock. By the 1840s, Swiss settlers arrived in the area and began to call the town Edenburg, presumably a tribute to the town's picturesque setting—their long-sought Garden of Eden. The spelling somehow changed, and the town was incorporated as Edinburg in 1852. It was fairly prosperous in those days, thanks to the several mills along its creek and its position on the Valley Pike, which was by then a macadamized toll road between Winchester and Staunton.

From the mill parking lot, turn left and go back into town. Leave Edinburg the way you came in, by turning back on to Route 185 and following the signs toward I-81. Instead of getting on I-81, pass under the interstate; the road now becomes Route 675. Continue for about 0.5 mile, then turn left on Route 809 (Union Forge Church Road). The road winds down to Stony Creek, which you may be able to see (depending on the time of year) on your left far below.

This area was the site of the Union Forge Iron Company, which began making iron around 1820, primarily for the Tredegar Gun Foundry in Richmond. The company built the white frame Union Forge Church down the road on the right, as well as a school for its workers' children. Throughout the 1800s, ironmaking was big business in this part of the Valley.

When you reach the stop sign at the intersection at the bottom of the hill, turn left on to Route 691 (Swover Creek Road). Follow the small sign pointing to Lantz Mills. In 0.1 mile, you'll reach the ruins of Lantz Roller Mill, on the left.

The **Lantz Mills** area was settled in 1740 by Jacob Wolfe but was named for another German immigrant, Hans George Lantz. Lantz came to the Shenandoah Valley from Frederick County, Maryland. He acquired land in this area in the 1760s and built a gristmill, a sawmill, and a granary. His sons and grandsons continued the family business until the late 1880s. All the original Lantz properties were burned by Union soldiers.

The Lantz Mill that stands today, a recent addition to the Virginia Landmarks Register, was built shortly after the Civil War to replace the 1813 building that was burned in that war. Unlike the other mills in the area, many of the original workings remain. It was used as a feed mill until the 1970s.

The impressive old Victorian house across from the mill, known today as Campbell Farm, was built shortly after the Civil War for Milton C. Campbell, whose family bought Liberty and Columbia Furnaces in the area. Although they had hopes of starting a prosperous business, the venture failed and the property was sold in 1908.

Archaeologists believe that the area around Lantz Mills was occupied by Indians between 6000 B.C. and 400 A.D., based on a 1996 survey that uncovered more than 600 artifacts here.

Louis Michel, a Swiss visitor to the Edinburg area in 1706, noted in his journal

Lantz Mill

Indians in the Shenandoah Valley

Long before Europeans settled in Virginia and the Shenandoah Valley, native peoples were living along the rivers and creeks here. Scientists have uncovered evidence of settlements in Virginia from 9500 to 8000 B.C. One of the most significant prehistoric sites in eastern North America is known as Thunderbird, south of Front Royal off U.S. 340. Paleo-Indians lived and quarried jasper for tools there for almost 2,000 years.

The people who lived in the northern Shenandoah Valley between 400 B.C. and 200 A.D. built hundreds of low stone burial mounds throughout the area. Later, from about 950 A.D. until the late 1600s or so, another culture lived and built much larger earthen burial mounds in the Valley, some of them almost 20 feet high. Those mounds are largely gone today, destroyed by three centuries of plowing and flooding.

During the early 1700s, the Valley was common hunting grounds for several tribes, including the Shawnees, the Susquehannocks, and the Iroquois. Only a few native settlements remained in the Valley during that time. Possible reasons for their departure include tribal warfare, the introduction of European diseases, and conflicts with settlers.

that "all this country is uninhabited except by some Indians." Around 1754, the Indians living in the Valley left, moving west into the Ohio Valley to join other tribes. That move, historians believe, was instigated by the French, who were at odds with the British over claims to the land west of the Alleghenies. When the French and Indian War began that same year, it became obvious that the French had recruited the Indians' help in their fight against the British.

General Edward Braddock's defeat by the French at Fort Duquesne (today's Pittsburgh) in 1755 was a sign of bad times to come. Soon, forts were being erected every 20 miles or so along the frontier. These forts were built under the direction of a young colonial military officer, George Washington (see The Middletown to Winchester Tour, page 55). But the forts didn't stop the raids. Groups of Indians, often led by a Frenchman or two, began conducting terrorist-style attacks on settlers—such as the raid that ended in the capture of George Philip Grandstaff, recounted earlier in this tour. Women and children were rarely spared.

In the Lantz Mills area, the tale is told about how Jacob Wolfe built a fort—a fortified house, really—to protect his family and neighbors during Indian raids. He was walking on his property one night when his dog began acting strangely. Samuel Kercheval related the story in his *History of the Valley of Virginia*, published in 1833. The dog, he wrote, "repeatedly crossed [Wolfe's] path, endeavoring to obstruct his walk; would raise himself up, and place his feet on his master's chest, and strive to push him back; would run a few steps toward the fort and then return whining." Wolfe took the hint and headed quickly back to his house, narrowly avoiding attack by an Indian lying in wait behind a nearby tree. Many years later, Wolfe couldn't bear to put the beloved dog to a merciful death when it became old and sick.

Continuing past Lantz Mills, turn left on to Route 710 (Hamburg Road), which crosses the creek over a low concrete bridge. Shortly, you'll cross a second concrete bridge.

When you reach the intersection with Lantz Road, go straight. At the intersection with Route 686 (South Ox Road), turn right. Route 686 parallels I-81 for a short distance and provides a great view of Massanutten Mountain on the left and Great North Mountain ahead and to the right.

Drive 0.4 mile on Route 686 to a stop sign; turn right on to South Middle Road (Route 614 South). Like U.S. 11, this road was once an old Indian trail. In the 1800s, drovers used it to take their livestock to market after the Valley Pike was macadamized. The sharp rocks used to "pave" the Pike hurt the animals' feet. Middle Road was still a dirt trail and thus easier on the sheep and cattle.

Drive about 2 miles to a red-roofed white barn on the right with the words "Indian Fort Stock Farm" painted in large letters on the side. Immediately past this barn, a stone chimney stands alone near the road. Fort Painter, a large log house owned by early settler George Painter, stood just beyond it. Painter was a German immigrant whose original surname was Bender. This was the site of one of the worst Indian raids on Valley settlers during the French and Indian War. The cemetery on the hill above the barn contains the remains of some of the victims.

One summer day in 1758, a warning went out that about 50 Indians and four Frenchmen were in the vicinity. Many area residents sought protection at Fort Painter. In the ensuing attack, George Painter was killed, and the rest of the settlers surrendered. At that point, the Indians murdered four infants, burned the house and stables, and took 48 prisoners over the Alleghenies. Only three people evaded capture: two of Painter's sons and a young man who had hidden nearby. That night, two of the boys ran 15 miles to Fort Valley for help. But when the members of the rescue party learned how many Indians had attacked, they gave up hope of pursuit.

About three years later, some of the victims, including Mrs. Painter and three of her children, were able to return home. Three other daughters remained with the Indians, including Mary Painter, who was nine years old at the time of the raid. She was found by an American trader 18 years later. He married her and brought her back to the Valley. But by then she had forgotten her German. For the rest of her life, she primarily spoke the Indian language she had learned as a child.

In the years following the attack, a stone house and barn were built (possibly by one of the family's surviving sons) near the site of the burned log house for defense against any future Indian raids. The lone chimney near the road is all that remains of those structures.

Indian Fort Stock Farm

Many attractively restored homes and barns line the road past Indian Fort Stock Farm. Massanutten Mountain rises into view on the left, offering a good view of New Market Gap. Great North Mountain and the Alleghenies can be seen in the distance ahead. The long metal buildings you'll see at farms along this road and elsewhere in the area are poultry houses, a major part of the agricultural scene in Shenandoah County, and even more so in Rockingham County, which lies a few miles ahead. Llamas are among the farm animals kept in this area. You may see a few grazing in fields along the road.

*Drive about 3 miles past Indian Fort Stock Farm to the ghost town of **Rinkerton**.* On the left is Otterbein United Methodist Church, built in 1913. The current church building replaced Otterbein Chapel United Brethren in Christ, which was constructed in 1845. The church is practically all that is left of a once-bustling community at the intersection of South Middle Road and Orkney Grade Road (Route 263). Jacob Rinker, Sr., a Swiss immigrant from near Zurich, may have been the first member of his family to arrive here. If you look closely on the left at the intersection, you can see the crumbling limestone foundation of Colonel Levi Rinker's large brick mansion. Built before the Civil War, the home burned to the ground in 1920. By then, Rinkerton was already deserted.

Rinkerton may have been the site of the first mill in the Shenandoah Valley, built by John Pennywitt after he came to the area from Alsace around 1747. This mill eventually became known as Rinker's Mill. Many more buildings stood here in the 1800s—a flour mill, a sawmill (both on Mill Creek along Orkney Grade Road), a store, a blacksmith shop, and a shoe shop. The settlement was also a popular speaking stump for local politicians.

At the intersection with Route 263 (Orkney Grade Road), continue straight on Route 614 toward Forestville. The large hill ahead and to the left is called Third Hill. During the Civil War, it was used as a signal station. Its name is a mystery—no First or Second Hill is anywhere around. Oddly, it is not the only Third Hill in the Valley. There is another Third Hill not far away, near Fulks Run in Rockingham County, and a third Third Hill in Berkeley County, West Virginia.

*Turn left at the stop sign at **Forestville** and drive a short distance to the carefully restored Zirkle Mill, located on the right on Holman's Creek behind an old frame farmhouse (parking is available on the left, below the old school).* The present mill was built by German settler Andrew Zirkle and his brother in the 1760s; the exact date is not known. Flour from this mill was provided to the Continental Army during the American Revolution.

The mill was one of the few in the Valley to escape Sheridan's torch in the Civil War. During the time of "The Burning" in the Valley in 1864, miller Samuel Hockman noticed that a nearby mill was in flames. He quickly hoisted the American flag above his mill, found the officer in charge, and convinced him of his Union sympathies. Hockman's actions saved his mill but cost him the respect of his customers. Incidentally, the general in charge of the Union cavalry under Sheridan that day was George Custer.

The mill passed through a series of owners until it closed in the mid-1900s. It stood, neglected until the 1980s, when it was bought and partially restored.

Zirkle Mill

In 2004, the owner at that time sold the mill to the Frontier Culture Museum in Staunton, which wanted to move it to their site (see The Staunton to Steeles Tavern Tour, page 188). A community effort to halt the move, culminating in a plea to Virginia's governor, succeeded. Shortly after, the mill was bought by two Zirkle descendants in the area. They have established a foundation to fund its restoration.

Return to the intersection in **Forestville***.* This community apparently got its name because the surrounding area was covered by dense forest when settlers arrived in the 1700s. By the mid-1800s, the town was prospering, no doubt helped by its location on what was then known as either the Woodstock and Harrisonburg Road or the Alexandria-Tennessee Road (now U.S. 42). By 1919, the town had to build its third school, which sits on the hill across from the Zirkle Mill and is now used as a community center.

Turn left on to Route 42 South/614 South (Senedo Road), heading toward Timberville. In spots, this road offers unbeatable views of Massanutten Mountain (to the left) and Little North Mountain and the distant Allegheny ranges in West Virginia (ahead and to the right). Much of the land in this area is so rocky that it can be used only for grazing. The outcroppings that cover the fields are limestone formations that geologists refer to as karst topography.

Drive about 5.3 miles to the "Welcome to Timberville" sign. Stay alert here, because you will be making a sharp right turn in about 0.6 mile. Turn right on to Route 881 (Orchard Drive) just as the road begins to curve left; if you go into the town, you've gone too far. This tour bypasses **Timberville**, which lies on the North Fork of the Shenandoah River and was a settlement as far back as 1750. Much of this area was burned

The Hatmaker's Gamble

The residents of Forestville have preserved some wonderful stories of area life in the past. Here's one: The town had a hat shop in the mid-1800s. One day a man came to the shop to order two hats—an everyday hat and a Sunday hat—for each of his sons. The hatmaker asked how many sons the man had, and the response was 24. The hatmaker, amazed at the number even in those days of large families, offered to make all the hats for free—and throw in two hats for the father in the deal—if he could see all 24 brothers together. The man returned later with all his sons, and the hatmaker, true to his word, made 50 free hats.

Forestville School

by Sheridan's forces during the Civil War. If you go into town, you will find, on the right, the Plains District Memorial Museum, with displays of life in this area in the old days. The museum is open Thursday through Sunday afternoons.

Drive west on Route 881 toward the base of Little North Mountain. In 1.5 miles, you'll pass the Turkey Knob apple storage facility, which serves the many orchards in the area. About 0.3 mile past the facility, turn left on to Andrick Mill Road (Route 789). Andrick Mill is on the right almost immediately after the turn. Perhaps this mill's out-of-the-way location saved it during the Civil War.

*Follow Andrick Mill Road (which becomes Route 790) to the stop sign at Route 792 (Crossroads Lane). Turn left. In 0.9 mile, Route 792 ends at a stop sign; turn right on Route 617 (Spar Mine Road). In 1.3 miles, you'll reach Route 259 West (Brock's Gap Road) on the outskirts of the town of **Broadway**. Turn right.*

This road leads into West Virginia through the ancient mountain passageway called Brock's Gap, thought to have been used by buffalo and Indians as they traveled into the first range of the Alleghenies. The North Fork of the Shenandoah River, which has its source not far from here in the mountains to the west, follows the right-hand side of the road.

Andrick Mill

Chimney Rock/ Fulks Run Grocery Side Trip

A few miles west down Route 259 past the tour's turnoff at Cootes Store are two interesting stops.

The first—a little over 1 mile down the road, at the intersection with Route 612—is an unusual rock formation known as Chimney Rock. The best way to view this 1,338-foot-high formation is to turn right on to Route 612 and look up to the right.

Chimney Rock

The rock is immense but sometimes partially hidden because of tree cover. It should not be confused with Natural Chimneys near Mount Solon (see The Harrisonburg to Mount Solon to Port Republic Tour, pages 149–50).

Continue 2.6 miles past Chimney Rock on Route 259 West to Fulks Run Grocery, which is the second stop. This old-fashioned grocery sells award-winning sugar-cured Turner Hams. The hams, which are smoked behind the store, have won high praise from former *Gourmet* magazine "backroads" restaurant reviewer Michael Stern, now of www.Roadfood.com.

Route 259 crosses several feeder creeks—first Cedar Creek in 1 mile, then Turley Creek 1.4 miles farther along. About 0.3 mile past the Turley Creek bridge, you'll see a sign pointing left to Singers Glen. Turn left on to Route 613 (Turleytown Road) at the tiny community called **Cootes Store.**

In 1870, merchants began using the Shenandoah River from Brock's Gap to Cootes Store for transporting goods and passengers on flatboats, also called "gundalows." Other parts of the Shenandoah River were put to similar use, but long-held plans to make the river fully navigable (George Washington was an early proponent) were finally abandoned when railroad lines were completed throughout the Valley in the late 1800s.

George Washington noted in his diary that he passed through Brock's Gap on horseback early in the morning of September 30, 1784, as he returned from a trip to the Ohio Valley. He planned to spend the night with his friend Thomas Lewis, who lived near what is now Port Republic (see The Harrisonburg to Mount Solon to Port Republic Tour, page 161). He turned on to Turleytown Road (known in those days as Back Road) and followed a route similar to the one you are currently traveling. Washington noted in his journal that he rode about 40 miles that day and reached Lewis's house at sundown.

Like Middle Road, Turleytown Road was used by farmers in the 18th and 19th centuries to drive their livestock to market and to summer pastureland in Highland County, southwest of here.

Drive almost 2 miles past Cootes Store to the Neff Lumber Mill. The last surviving industry in once-thriving **Turleytown,** the mill is on the site of an earlier combination flour mill and sawmill on Turley Creek. In the early 1900s, the Neff Lumber Mill sawed logs of walnut from nearby West Virginia and sent the wood to furniture makers in Baltimore. During World War II, it provided timber to the army and navy while also making chicken coops for Valley farmers.

The area's first settler was Giles Turley, who was traveling to points south when he stopped and decided to settle here in 1804. The town grew largely because of its location on the drovers' road. Within a few years, Turley built a wayside inn and tavern.

Turley Creek, also called Brock's Creek, is a powerful stream that supported five gristmills, a hominy mill, one or two sawmills, a carding mill (used to prepare wool for spinning), a mill that rolled hemp (once an important Valley crop) for ropemaking, a foundry, a tanyard, and other businesses. Now hard to see from the road, the ruins of the Turley Roller Mill, built in 1880, still stand near the bridge over the creek about 0.2 mile past the lumbermill.

Continue 0.6 mile past the old mill to the unusual-looking stone building, housing a quarry office, on the right. This home was obviously built from rocks from the large quarry below.

*Follow Turleytown Road as it curves to the left through tranquil green hills and lush valleys into the town of **Singers Glen**, which welcomes visitors with a sign calling it the "Birthplace of Sacred Music in the South." At the stop sign, turn right to remain on Route 613, which is now called Singers Glen Road.*

The peaceful little village of Singers Glen seems frozen in time. Many descendants of the original families still live here in the restored homes of their ancestors.

As you enter town on Singers Glen Road, you'll see the post office. This was the town's store from the time it was built in 1890 until 1974; the post office has occupied space in the building since 1914.

Singers Glen, originally called Mountain Valley, was settled in 1809 or 1810, when Joseph Funk built a small log house here. He and many other local settlers were descendants of German Anabaptists who came to Virginia from Pennsylvania in the late 1700s. Funk was born in Berks County, Pennsylvania, in 1777; his grandfather was the first Mennonite bishop in America. His parents settled in nearby Sparkling Springs in 1786.

Joseph Funk raised a large family and became the community's self-appointed teacher. He placed a heavy emphasis on music in his lessons. Around 1816, he published a volume of hymns that became popular among rural congregations throughout the country. By 1847, Funk's music publishing business had grown to

Singers Glen Post Office

Funk-Acker House

the point that he and his sons were able to establish their own printing shop and bindery in town. For the next 30 years, they published music books and periodicals that gained nationwide circulation. In 1861, they began a school for teachers of vocal music, which became the Singer's Glen School for Advanced Scholars in Literary Studies and Music.

The elder Funk died in 1862, but one of his grandsons, Aldine Kieffer, and Kieffer's sister's husband, Ephraim Ruebush, continued the business. In 1878, they moved the publishing operation to Dayton, near Harrisonburg, where it became the Ruebush-Kieffer Company, a well-known music publishing house in the South. Three years earlier, Joseph Funkhouser founded Shenandoah Seminary (later called Shenandoah College) in Dayton, which included music education; later, the Shenandoah Conservatory of Music became a separate school. In 1960, both schools moved to Winchester and later merged. Known as Shenandoah University since 1991, today the school has more than 3,000 students.

Across the street from the Donovan Memorial United Methodist Church is the Swank-Ruddle House, which dates to 1826. This home was built at a different location—back up Turleytown Road near the cemetery on the outskirts of town—as the home of Jacob Freeze. The Funks bought it, took it apart, and moved it to the present location in 1885 for use as a lumber planing mill. It was later used as a carriage factory. In 1903, S. Henton Swank bought it for use as a residence.

A Victorian house in Singers Glen

In the next block, you'll see Singers Glen Baptist Church on the right. Next to the church stand four Funk homes. The first, known as the Funk-Acker House, belonged to Joseph Funk's son, Timothy, who built it in 1850. Its next resident, John Acker (1845–1923), was active in county political affairs and served as a state senator. The two white Victorian gingerbread houses next door were built in the 1890s by Funk grandsons. Next to those is the original Joseph Funk dwelling, constructed around 1810, a small, unassuming house with a tin roof. Its log construction was long ago covered by weatherboarding. A descendant of Joseph Funk owns the house, which is a registered National Historic Landmark.

Leave town by continuing south on Route 613. In about 1 mile, look for a small sign pointing to Sparkling Springs Road, on the right. (If you have 10 minutes to spare, follow this road past a lovely white farmhouse to one of Virginia's many popular old springs resorts. After 1 mile, the road will curve sharply to the left; in 0.1 mile turn right to stay on Sparkling Springs Road. This springs resort, located at the base of Little North Mountain, was a Mennonite facility that began around 1898. Today, the cottages are privately owned, but the place retains the feel of a peaceful summer retreat tucked into the side of a mountain.)

Continue south on Route 613 past the turnoff to Sparkling Springs for 1.5 miles. Watch for St. Johns Lutheran Cemetery on the left just before the road begins to curve to the left. Almost immediately after the cemetery, make a left turn on to Route 772 (Greenmount Road). In 0.6 mile, you'll come to a stop sign at Snapps Creek Road; keep going straight for 1.1 miles to the intersection with Sky Road. (That's Peaked Mountain, at the south end of the Massanutten range, in the distance ahead.)

Turn left, then make an immediate right to stay on Route 772. In another mile, you'll reach the intersection with Route 910 (Grist Mill Road). Turn left, proceed 1.3 miles to Route 779 (Brenneman Church Road) and turn right. This road quickly becomes Route 778; continue straight for 0.4 mile.

On the left side of the road is the old Breneman-Turner Mill. It was built of bricks and limestone by Abraham Breneman around 1800. Like the other mills on this tour, this was among the few to survive General Sheridan's burning during the Civil War. The mill was saved, according to local legend, because Union soldiers

Breneman-Turner Mill

were sympathetic to reports of illness in the mill owner's family. The more likely story is that the family was able to extinguish the flames in time.

The mill is especially interesting because it was operated continuously for nearly 200 years, thanks in part to the single-handed efforts of J. Howard Turner, who bought it in 1933 and ran it by himself until he died in 1988, at the age of 88. At the time, Breneman-Turner Mill was the last stone mill operating in Rockingham County. Turner's family donated the mill to the Valley Brethren Mennonite Heritage Center in 2003, and restoration is underway.

Route 778 intersects U.S. 42 (Harpine Highway) in 0.9 mile. Turn left on to U.S. 42, drive 0.7 mile, and turn right on Route 859 (Jesse Bennett Way). This is the town of **Edom**. Its main street was named for the Edom man who performed the first successful Cesarean operation in North America. In 1794, Dr. Jesse Bennett's pregnant wife became ill, and she and her unborn child were facing almost certain death. Dr. Bennett tried to convince a colleague and teacher of medicine in Staunton to perform surgery on his wife, but the man refused. Dr. Bennett courageously went ahead with the surgery by himself and saved the lives of both his wife and daughter, who lived to be 77.

A short distance after you make the turn, you'll see a large red-brick building on your left. This is the old Edom store and post office, which is thought to have been built in 1835.

Across the street, you can see the ruins of another old mill, this one unusual because it was made of limestone. Overgrown and abandoned for many years, this is the Edom-Burrus Mill, built around 1867 at the site of an earlier mill burned

Old Edom store and post office

Edom-Burrus Mill

during the Civil War. In the early 1900s, the Edom-Burrus Mill produced 50 barrels of "Famous White Rose Flour" a day and was the hub of the town's activities. It burned in 1960.

The man who built the mill, John K. Beery, was obviously speaking from experience when he offered future builders of stone structures this rule of thumb: "First of all, haul twice as much stone as you think you will need, then double that, and you may have half enough."

At the first intersection in town, turn right on to Route 721 (Linville-Edom Road). Continue east toward **Linville**. Notice the lovely arched bridge to the right as you cross Linville Creek—it looks quite old but was built in the early 1900s.

It is 0.1 mile to a charming old brick house on the creek on the right. Known as the J. Owen Beard House, it was constructed in two stages. Joseph Wenger (J. Owen Beard's grandfather) built the original home in 1819. In 1835, a new house was built next to it. The intention was to tear down the earlier structure, but instead the owners decided to join the two. They added a second floor to the original structure so the rooflines would meet, but in doing so, they had to leave a three-foot space between the two buildings. This bricked-up area came in handy years later as a place to hide valuables from looting Yankees during the Civil War. Notice the unusual round brick pillars supporting the porch in back.

Past the Beard House is the Linville-Edom School, which was built in the early 1900s at this compromise location—the exact midpoint between the two towns.

A short distance past the school and on the left is a lovely old red-brick house, Farmingreen, built by Henry Wenger, whose family had emigrated to Lancaster

J. Owen Beard House

Farmingreen

County, Pennsylvania, from Switzerland in the late 1720s. A barn built on the estate around 1790 survived the Civil War but burned to the ground in 1895. The main part of the house was constructed in 1825; the frame and brick additions on the right date to the 20th century.

Daniel Boone's family traveled through the Linville area around 1750 on the way to the Yadkin Valley in North Carolina. Daniel was a teenager at the time. His parents were friendly with the Bryan family, who lived in the area. It was during this visit that he may have met Rebecca Bryan, who became his wife about five years later.

The next intersection is at Kratzer Road in the town of **Linville***. To stay on Route 721, turn left, then make an immediate right. Route 721 now becomes Long's Pump Road.*

The three-story house on the left at the corner is the Sipes-Davis House, sometimes called the Stone House. Now apartments, the structure was built as a barn in 1811 by German immigrant Christian Kratzer. It was turned into a residence following the Civil War. At various times after that, it housed a general store, a cheese factory, and the town's post office.

Continue on Long's Pump Road as it curves past dairy farms and rolling fields. Turn left on to Route 619 (Simmers Valley Road). When you come to an intersection, stay straight even though Route 619 curves left. You are now on Route 806 (Lacey Spring Road), which leads in less than 2 miles to U.S. 11. Turn left on U.S. 11 and head north toward New Market. Soon after you turn, you'll see a state historical marker on the right. It notes the location, some 4 miles west, of the Lincoln Homestead (see the sidebar below) and mentions the existence of an inn owned by members of the Lincoln family at this spot. The inn was destroyed by fire in 1898.

You are driving along one of the oldest and most-traveled roads in America, although it may not look like it today. For about a century, from the 1740s to the

Lincoln Homestead Side Trip

About 2.5 miles north of Edom, on the right side of Route 42, there is a painted two-story brick house known as the Lincoln Homestead. It was built around 1800 by Captain Jacob Lincoln, who was a brother of President Abraham Lincoln's grandfather. The president's grandfather, also named Abraham, served in the Revolutionary War; his parents came here from Pennsylvania in 1768. A state historical marker stands in front of the house (now a private home), which is accessible from a short access road off Route 42. The Lincoln Society of Virginia is trying to buy this property and restore it.

An earlier house located nearby was where President Lincoln's father, Thomas, was born in 1776. That branch of the Lincolns moved to Kentucky when Thomas was only six years old. Many members of the Lincoln family remained in this area of the Valley, however; a graveyard containing the remains of five generations of Lincolns lies on the hill above the house. The Virginia Lincolns were slaveholders and supported the Confederates in the Civil War.

mid-1800s, what is now U.S. 11 was the primary road for settlers traveling from Pennsylvania to points south and west. According to historian Carl Bridenbaugh, "In the last sixteen years of the colonial era southbound traffic along the Great Philadelphia Wagon Road [one of the road's many earlier names] was numbered in the tens of thousands; it was the most heavily traveled road in all America and must have had more vehicles jolting along its rough and tortuous way than all other main roads combined."

The road was macadamized (with stones and gravel, not asphalt) in the late 1830s and became known as the Valley Pike. It was later heavily used by Civil War soldiers of both sides. Many battles took place along it, including one just a short distance ahead. After that time, the road took on yet another name: the Long Gray Trail.

By the mid-1960s, I-81 was built, causing many of the 1940s- and 1950s-vintage motor hotels, tourist courts, and gas stations along U.S. 11 to go out of business. Many of those buildings still stand, in varying states of decay, as lonely reminders of the road's past importance.

Continue 1.8 miles from Lacey Spring to the old stagecoach stop once known as Sparta or Spartopolis and called **Mauzy.** It was named after a local resident and has been known as Mauzy (pronounced Mo-zee, with the accent on the last syllable) since around the mid-1800s. It is located just before U.S. 11 crosses I-81. On the left side of the road is a red-roofed building with porches running along the length of both floors. Now a gift shop, this was once a popular wayside tavern known as the Mauzy House. It was built by William Pickering around 1800. The building is unusual because it seems to have been created by joining two six-room houses.

Continue on U.S. 11, passing over I-81, to the next village, **Tenth Legion.** Local historians claim that its unusual name was inspired by Thomas Jefferson, who is said to have called this part of the Shenandoah Valley his "Tenth Legion of democracy" (a reference to Julius Caesar's loyal Tenth Legion). The people living here had great respect for Jefferson and were strong supporters of his beliefs on religious freedom.

As you enter Tenth Legion, note the stone building on the left next to a larger brick church. The stone structure is Bethlehem Church, named in honor of Moravian brethren from Bethlehem, Pennsylvania. The Moravians left behind a journal that mentioned this area during their "toilsome journey" through Virginia to Winston-Salem, North Carolina, in 1753. The church was built around 1844 and was the second Quaker meeting house on this site. It served as a hospital during the Valley Campaign in 1862. After the Civil War, the Quakers merged with another local church. In 1952, the new church was built next door.

Across the side street to the right of the Bethlehem Church is the old Tenth Legion School, built in 1922. The last classes were held there in 1972. Today, the building has been transformed into a very large private home.

Continue on U.S. 11. Just down the road, look to your left for the large stone marker with a bronze statue of a turkey on top. It marks the Rockingham County line. Rockingham County is called the "Turkey Capital" for good reason—it's one of the top ten turkey-producing counties in the nation.

Bethlehem Church

Old Tenth Legion School

Rockingham County turkey

Drive about 1 mile to see an impressive white mansion on the right, Mooreland Hall, also known as Court Manor. Somewhat hidden from the road by trees, it is an iconic Southern plantation. The house was built by Reuben Moore around 1838 of bricks made on the grounds. In 1925, it was bought by Dr. Willis Sharpes Kilmer, who bred and trained racehorses here, including the winner of the 1928 Kentucky Derby. The home fell into disrepair after Kilmer's death. In the 1960s and '70s, it even housed a hippie commune. A new owner began renovations in 1985, adding two wings and restoring the original structure. The house is surrounded by beautiful lawns and stately old trees today.

The side road to one of the Valley's many unusual limestone-formation caves, Endless Caverns, is on the right 1.4 miles ahead. If you care to make a brief side trip, follow the lovely tree-lined drive for almost 2 miles to the caverns. The caverns were discovered in 1879 by two boys who were hunting rabbits with their dog. The

Mooreland Hall

dog chased a rabbit behind some limestone boulders. When the boys moved the boulders aside, they discovered a large dark opening leading to the caves below.

Another old farmhouse sits on the left side of U.S. 11 about 1.2 miles past the road to the caverns. This is Hardscrabble Farm, built around 1776 by William McDowell, a merchant and tavern keeper. It was named Hardscrabble by its next owner, Major Peter Higgins, who bought it in 1806 and soon discovered that the farm's soil had been exhausted by poor farming practices. For a time during the Civil War, the house served as the headquarters of two Union generals, John P. Gordon and Robert Toombs. After the Battle of New Market, which took place a few miles up the road, the home was one of many in the area that served as make-shift hospitals.

Continue less than 1 mile past Hardscrabble Farm to three state historical markers on the left. One of them notes that at this point, U.S. 11 crosses the old Fairfax Line, which was the southern boundary of Lord Fairfax's immense landholdings in northern Virginia in the 1700s. (See The White Post to Millwood to Berryville Tour, pages 64–65, for more about Lord Fairfax.) When Peter Jefferson and Thomas Lewis surveyed the Fairfax Line in 1746, they referred to the trail as the "Old Indian Road." Another historical marker notes the nearby birthplace of John Sevier. The son of New Market innkeeper Valentine Sevier, John Sevier was a six-time governor of Tennessee. The third marker notes that the Battle of New Market took place to the north.

*As you enter **New Market**, you'll pass The Shenvalee.* The name was created from the words *Shenandoah, Virginia,* and *Lee.* This hotel and public golf course, long popular with Valley residents for its scenic location at the base of Massanutten Mountain, has been around since 1926. During World War II, the U.S. State Department took it over for more than a year to house Italian prisoners of diplomatic rank.

The beginnings of New Market go back to the late 1700s. The town grew because of its location at the junction of the Valley Road (in the days before it was a turnpike) and the road that ran between Massanutten Gap (to the east) and Brock's Gap (to the west). In fact, the settlement's early name was Cross Roads. The town

Two 1950s Eateries on U.S. 11

Two family-run restaurants have managed to survive for more than a half-century on U.S. 11 in and near New Market. Their interiors give visitors a taste of what life in the slow lane might have been like before I-81 came along.

The Southern Kitchen, on the right as the tour enters New Market heading north, has been serving country breakfasts, fried chicken, Virginia ham, and coconut cream pies since 1955. The interior is so dated that it is almost back in style, with mid-20th-century Formica tabletops and uniformed waitresses. There's a small jukebox in every booth. Michael Stern, formerly of *Gourmet* magazine and now of www.Roadfood.com, has high praise in particular for its peanut soup, a Virginia classic.

Heading about 8 miles down U.S. 11 South toward Harrisonburg, you'll come to the unpretentious Blue Stone Inn, in Lacey Spring. Once part of a motel operation dating back to the 1920s—when the Valley Pike was a major north-south artery—the Blue Stone is now a popular dinner-only

Southern Kitchen Restaurant

restaurant, which specializes in steaks and seafood. The same family has owned it since 1949. Like the Southern Kitchen, the décor hasn't changed much in all that time. Its motto, "Where you can always eat under a buck," refers to the taxidermy on the knotty-pine walls above the wooden booths.

was later renamed after New Market, England. The English town had, and still has, a famous horse-racing track; the Shenandoah Valley town had a mile-long racetrack in the old days, west of town.

New Market is full of historic buildings. Several old structures along Congress Street (U.S. 11) are of special interest. Portions of the Calvert House, on the left at 9485 Congress Street, date back to the 1770s. The home once belonged to Major John S. Calvert, who served as secretary of the treasury for the Confederacy. He met an untimely death in Richmond in 1870, when the Capitol dome collapsed on him. He was a descendant of the Calverts who founded Maryland.

Next door to the Calvert House is a building, dating to 1855, that once housed a cabinet- and casket-making shop owned by a German immigrant, Henry Theis. After 1889, the Cushman brothers built carriages and wagons here. Back then, the building had double doors that extended to the ceiling. Next door, at 9475 Congress Street, is Deary's Tavern, which was a stagecoach inn in the late 1700s.

New Market achieved prominence in the 1800s as a printing and publishing center. The building that housed the Henkel Press is at 9445 Congress Street. The press began when Ambrose Henkel, the 16-year-old son of a local preacher, decided

Calvert House

Old carriage factory in New Market

Deary's Tavern

to walk to Hagerstown, Maryland, to learn the printing trade. In 1806, his on-the-job training complete, he bought a printing press in Reading, Pennsylvania, and brought it back to New Market to begin his business. Because the surrounding area was so heavily settled by German immigrants and their descendants, most of the printing he did before 1830 was in German. Henkel's first newspaper, *Der Volksberichter*, was printed here between 1807 and 1809.

Many other newspapers and books followed during the more than 100 years the family owned the press. Among them was an English-language newspaper called the *Shenandoah Valley*. That newspaper survives today; combined with another old newspaper, it is published in Woodstock as the *Shenandoah Valley Herald*. Elon Henkel, grandson of the founder, sold the press in 1925. It ceased operation in 1975.

The Solomon Henkel House, on the left at 9417 Congress Street, was built in 1802. Solomon Henkel was a physician and druggist. His son, Solon Henkel, lived in this house during the Civil War. Note the metal plate tacked to the front door; it is said to cover up damage made when Union soldiers, trying to barge in, struck the door with their bayonets and rifle butts; they were enraged after Mrs. Solon Henkel poured hot water on them from the upstairs window. The shutters on the house are said to be original.

The impressive brick house across the street at 9400 Congress Street (yes, the address is correct) was built by Dr. C. C. Henkel, who was a surgeon for the Army of Northern Virginia during the Civil War.

Three interesting structures are located at the town's main intersection, where Congress Street crosses U.S. 211 West.

At the southeast corner, 9386 Congress Street, stands a brick-and-stone building dating back to the early 1800s. It has seen many uses over the years—most recently as a restaurant, a store, and museum. The portion facing Congress Street was built in 1807 as a mercantile store. In 1864, it was used as General Jubal Early's headquarters. The building later went through several incarnations as a hotel—as the Carrollton Hotel in 1884, as the Hotel Thaxton in 1903 (John Philip Sousa and his family stayed there one night in 1909), as the Battlefield Inn in 1921, and as the Lee-Jackson Hotel from 1928 until the 1950s.

Across the street, on the southwest corner, is a log cabin that now houses a gift shop. John Sevier, who was born in this area in 1745, had a trading post nearby, perhaps as early as 1765. It was located behind the current log cabin (said to have been built using some of the original timbers from Sevier's store) on the southwest corner of the intersection. Sevier, who moved west in the early 1770s and gained fame as an Indian fighter, was the only governor of the short-lived State of Franklin, the first governor of Tennessee, and the first governor west of the Blue Ridge.

One of the oldest buildings in the area, perhaps built before the Revolutionary War, is the structure of gray stone and brick on the northwest corner. Now a bank, it is known as the Abbie Henkel House. In the 1830s, Abe Neff and Samuel Funkhouser ran a general store there.

The town's growth slowed when the Orange, Alexandria, and Manassas Gap Railroad was completed to Harrisonburg after the Civil War. Even though the station was 2 miles out of town, citizens feared that noisy, smoky trains would upset their livestock.

The town is still a busy crossroads, partly because New Market Battlefield State Historical Park receives a steady stream of visitors year-round. This tour does not visit the state historical park, though it does pass by parts of the battlefield. *To visit the state historical park, with its fine museum, turn left on to U.S. 211 West; the park is located down the first side road to the right on the far side of I-81.* The Virginia Military Institute operates the Hall of Valor Civil War Museum on the site. Don't confuse it with the white-columned, private, New Market Battlefield Military Museum, which you will

New Market Battlefield State Historical Park / Hall of Valor Civil War Museum

pass on the way to the historical park; that museum has been closed.

From the main intersection in New Market, which is U. S. 11 (Congress Street) and Old Cross Road, continue north on U.S. 11 for about 1 mile to see the fields where the Battle of New Market took place on a rainy Sunday in May 1864. On the way, you'll pass two more interesting old homes. The first, at 9295 Congress Street, just 0.2 mile past the main intersection on the left, is a restored log home known as the Spitzer-Rupp House. County records show that it was sold to William Menefee in 1804 and was later owned by Henry Spitzer, a gunsmith. His son Charles was also a gunsmith and is said to have made Kentucky long rifles in the house in the mid-1800s. A German immigrant named William F. Rupp, who became well known for frescoes painted in homes and churches in the area, married a daughter of Charles Spitzer in 1862.

Continuing north on U.S. 11, you'll soon see an impressive-looking old brick mansion set back from the road on the left. Originally known as the Rice House and later as Stanley Hall, it was built in 1834 by Dr. John A. Rice, who served in the Mexican War and was an early president of the Valley Turnpike Company. It is said that General Banks used the house as his Union headquarters for a time in 1862. It is now a group residence home.

A short distance past the Rice House, on the left side of U.S. 11, is a historical marker describing the Battle of New Market. General John C. Breckenridge (who had been United States vice president under President James Buchanan from 1857 to 1861) was in command of 4,500 Confederates facing General Franz Sigel's 6,000 Union troops. With nowhere else to turn for help, Breckenridge called on the Virginia Military Institute in Lexington for reinforcements. Of the 300 young men in the cadet corps there at the time, some 250 were sent to New Market.

On their arrival, the cadets assumed reserve positions, but by mid-afternoon they joined the fight. The legend goes that Sigel, in a panic, lapsed into speaking orders in his native German, confusing his troops and contributing to the Union's humiliating defeat at the hands of a much smaller force. When the battle was over, 600 Confederate and 800 Union soldiers were dead, and Sigel's troops were chased down the Valley Pike past Mount Jackson. Ten V.M.I. cadets lost their lives. This battle was the last Confederate victory in the Valley.

Soon afterward, General Grant replaced Sigel with General David Hunter and instructed him to "make all the valleys south of the Baltimore and Ohio road a desert as high up as possible." He further told Hunter to "eat out Virginia clear and clean as far as they go so that crows flying over it for the balance of the season will have to carry their provender with them." Grant was determined to cut off the large supply of food that Valley farmers provided to the Confederate army.

The summer of 1864 saw widespread devastation in the Valley, as Union troops looted, burned, and destroyed every barn, bridge, and railroad in sight, an event that came to be known as "The Burning." General Sheridan, assisted by General Custer and others, later bragged that by October 4, they had burned more than 2,000 barns filled with wheat and hay, more than 70 mills filled with wheat and flour, and some 3,000 sheep. Many homes and fields were also torched. By the fall of 1864, the Valley north of Staunton was a wasteland.

As you continue driving on U.S. 11, you'll be following the path of Sigel's retreat toward

Mount Jackson. In 1.8 miles, on the left, is a historical marker citing the Post-Appomattox Tragedy. A month after the end of the Civil War, four Virginia cavalry soldiers stole six horses from Federal soldiers near Woodstock. Although the soldiers returned the horses to the Union camp near this spot the next day, a month later the Union commander in charge ordered their arrest at their homes in Page County; two of the young men managed to escape, but the other two were brought back to the camp here and executed, without a trial.

*In less than 1 mile, you'll pass another Civil War site on the left, **Rude's Hill**.* General Stonewall Jackson set up camp here for two weeks in early April 1862 after the Battle of Kernstown, before moving his force of 11,000 men to battles to the south and west. Rude's Hill was quiet for two years, until General Jubal Early paused here in October 1864 after his defeat by General Sheridan at the Battle of Opequon, near Winchester. In November, Early was back at Rude's Hill, being attacked by Sheridan again. This time, Sheridan's forces were turned back.

A short distance farther down U.S. 11, after the I-81 turnoff and just past the barn at the intersection on the left, is a nondescript asbestos-sided house. This is the Rude House, used by Jackson as his headquarters while he camped here in 1862; it's said that President Andrew Jackson had been a guest there years earlier.

Just beyond Rude's Hill along U.S. 11 is a flat stretch of farmland called Meems Bottom, named after an early owner of the property. This especially fertile stretch has been enriched over the centuries by the flooding Shenandoah River, which flows around and through it.

During Stonewall Jackson's retreat up (that is, heading south) the Valley in the spring of 1862, Colonel Turner Ashby's beautiful white stallion was struck by a Union bullet during a skirmish at Meems Bottom. Legend says that the horse carried his master off the field of battle and, head held high, walked down the pike with the retreating soldiers before finally falling and dying about a mile past New Market, near Hardscrabble Farm.

Archaeologists believe that the Senedo Indians had a permanent settlement here until they were wiped out by another tribe, possibly the Catawbas. Early Valley historian Samuel Kercheval recorded that in the mid-1700s, a local man was frequently visited by an elderly Indian, who told him that many years earlier a group of invading Indians from farther south had killed his entire nation except for himself and another child. Historians estimate that the massacre occurred between 1650 and 1700. The

Rude House

peaceful Senedos may have been caught up in an ongoing battle between the Catawbas and the Delawares. Early settlers reported seeing tribes passing up and down the Valley on the old Indian trail that extended from New York to South Carolina, part of which is today's U.S. 11.

On the left side of the road is a state historical marker for the covered bridge at Meems Bottom. *Turn left a short distance past the marker, on to Wissler Road.* Lined with Norway maples planted in 1910, this road leads in less than 0.5 mile to the longest covered bridge remaining in Virginia. The small parking area to the left just before the bridge is a good place to stop and take pictures.

During the 1800s, there were hundreds of covered bridges in Virginia, but only eight are left today. Of those, only five are accessible to the public. This one, featuring a single-span Burr arch truss, is 204 feet long. It was built in the early 1890s. Burned by arsonists in 1976, it was rebuilt three years later. At least two other bridges once crossed the Shenandoah at this point. One was burned during the Civil War, and another was destroyed by a flood in 1870.

Return to U.S. 11. In the distance across the road is Mount Airy Farm, which began as a grand old stone mansion built in the late 1700s by Baron Steenbergen. John G. Meems bought the estate in 1841. The mansion was undamaged during the Civil War but most of the farm buildings and fields were destroyed by Union troops; at one time, according to eyewitness reports, as many as 40 fires could be seen burning on the estate.

The Beautiful Shenandoah

It seems probable that the name *Shenandoah*—for which there have been some 30 spellings and variations—came to us from the Senedo tribe. Although no one knows the literal meaning for sure, the word is most often translated as meaning "Daughter of the Stars." Here are a few of the variations that were used in the past:

Cenuntua
Chanador
Chanithor
Gerando
Senantoa
Senedo
Shanando
Shanandoa
Shanandore
Sherundore
Thandore
Tschanator
Zynodoa

Covered bridge at Meems Bottom

By 1909, the house was falling apart, and Daniel Kelleher, whose wife was a Meems granddaughter, bought and rebuilt it. In 1942, the estate was bought by railroad heir Harold S. Vanderbilt, a great-grandson of the railroad magnate Cornelius Vanderbilt. An avid yachtsman, Vanderbilt defended America's Cup three times in the 1930s. He is also cited as the inventor of contract bridge in 1926. Vanderbilt was 56 years old when he became interested in experimental farming and bought Mount Airy. (He and his wife referred to the mansion as their "summer cottage.") He knew nothing about farming but was determined to excel at it. Just two years into this endeavor, he won the DeKalb Virginia State corn-raising championship for growing the largest number of bushels of shelled corn per acre. The following year, he took the national DeKalb prize, which had never been won by a farm outside the Corn Belt. Vanderbilt sold Mount Airy to Joseph A. Kincaid in 1963.

*Turn left on U.S. 11 and drive 0.7 mile toward the bridge over the Shenandoah River into **Mount Jackson***. Before you cross the bridge, look for the crumbling house on the left behind the trees and bushes. This structure is what remains of an old tollhouse, one of many that used to line the Valley Pike every 5 miles between 1840 and 1918, when the toll-taking ended and the state took over maintenance of the road.

Continue across the Shenandoah River bridge into Mount Jackson. In about 0.8 mile, you will see a large white house on the left, sitting on a bluff above Mill Creek; this is the Shenstone Mansion. The land it sits on was part of an original land grant made in 1749 by Lord Fairfax to a man named Riley Moore. This house was built in 1825. A descendant of Moore bought the house after the Civil War, and his daughter lived there until her death in 1969.

Soon after you pass Shenstone, you will pass a log home, also on the left, at 6059 Main Street, known as the Stoneburner House. It was built before 1800 and has been extensively restored over the years.

Mount Jackson was settled in the 1730s. The town was originally called Mount Pleasant but was renamed in 1826 to honor Andrew Jackson, hero of the War of 1812. In the center of town is the red-brick Union Church, built around 1825 and surrounded by an old cemetery, which includes a grave of a Revolutionary War soldier.

Shenstone Mansion

The term *union* meant it was a "free" church, to be shared by various denominations and used for community functions. It was used as a hospital in the Civil War.

The town has a museum at 5901 Main Street that is open on Thursday and Friday afternoons and on Saturdays.

Continue north along U.S. 11. It is 0.8 mile from Union Church to a Confederate cemetery and a monument to Confederate soldiers, located on the left.

Directly across the street from the cemetery, the Confederacy built a large hospital complex consisting of three two-story buildings that could accommodate 500 soldiers. The hospital was run by a local physician, Dr. Andrew Russell Meem, whose staff tended sick and wounded soldiers who arrived by train from places like Gettysburg and Manassas. Colonel Levi Rinker, mentioned earlier in this tour, donated the land for the hospital and cemetery. After the war, the hospital was torn down and the lumber used to build a military installation at Rude's Hill. That installation was used by Union forces during Reconstruction.

The cemetery contains the bodies of about 400 Civil War soldiers from 11 southern states, all of which have been identified.

The tour ends here. To return to I-81, follow the signs just beyond the cemetery.

Union Church

The Harrisonburg to Mount Solon to Port Republic to Peales Crossroads Tour

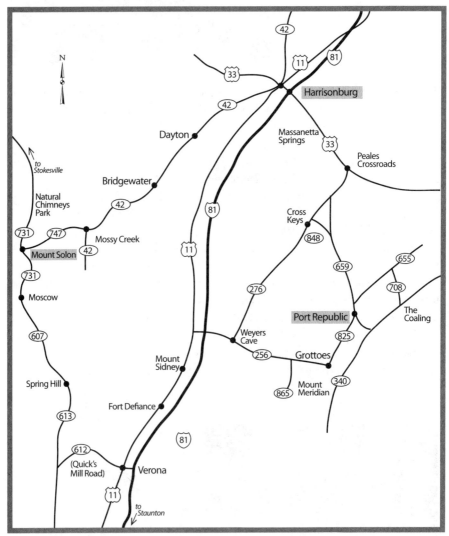

TOUR 8

The Harrisonburg to Mount Solon to Port Republic to Peales Crossroads Tour

This tour begins in Harrisonburg and follows historic country roads through areas of early Valley settlements and Civil War sites. It stops at the Heritage Center in Dayton, then takes scenic Route 42 through the college town of Bridgewater and then on to Mount Solon and Natural Chimneys Park. From there, it winds through hilly farmland until it meets historic U.S. 11 in Verona. The tour then proceeds north to Fort Defiance and the historic Augusta Stone Church and into the town of Mount Sidney. Past Mount Sidney, the tour crosses I-81 and proceeds into the 1890s boom town of Grottoes, long famous for its Grand Caverns. The next stop is the peaceful hamlet of Port Republic, a once-important river port and the scene of Civil War action during Stonewall Jackson's 1862 Valley Campaign. The tour ends near where it began in Harrisonburg.

Note that I-81 intersects the tour at Mount Sidney, making it easy to split this tour into two shorter segments.

Total mileage: Approximately 84 miles.

The tour begins at Courthouse Square in downtown **Harrisonburg.** *From I-81, take Exit 247B, which will put you on U.S. 33 West. In 1.9 miles, you will reach Courthouse Square; you can't miss the domed courthouse building as you approach the downtown area. Park in the area and walk to the first few attractions in this tour.*

Known as Rocktown in its early days because of the prevalence of limestone in the area, Harrisonburg was officially established as a town in 1780. It was named after its founder, Thomas Harrison, who was born to English immigrants on New York's Long Island in 1704. When Harrison was in his early thirties, he, his father, and four brothers traveled to Virginia, drawn by the prospect of plentiful and fertile farmland. The tract that Harrison selected for himself makes up the heart of downtown Harrisonburg today. It was centered on a large spring that flows today under the copper-covered gazebo (an exact replica of the original domed springhouse built here in 1832) at Courthouse Square.

Harrisonburg is the county seat of Rockingham County, which was created in

1778 by splitting off a portion of Augusta County. It was named for the English marquis of Rockingham, Charles Watson Wentworth. Five courthouses have stood at this square since the first log one was built in 1781. The present building was completed in 1897.

The town began here, at the site of the old crossroads of the Spotswood Trail (now U.S. 33) and the Indian Road (later known as the Valley Pike and U.S. 11). As travel on these roads grew, so did the town. Stagecoaches began stopping here on their way between Winchester and Staunton in the 1820s, and traffic increased after the Valley Pike was macadamized a decade later. Another important early road running through Harrisonburg evolved into today's Route 42. It was built in the 1800s as a turnpike to the resort areas in and around Warm Springs, southwest of Harrisonburg.

Several Civil War battles were fought in the area in 1862, the year of General Stonewall Jackson's Valley Campaign. The Battle of Harrisonburg took place at Chestnut Ridge southeast of town on June 6, 1862. General Turner Ashby was killed during that battle; a park containing a monument to him stands off Port Republic Road, about 0.5 mile north of that road's intersection with I-81 (enter from Neff Avenue). The nearby Battles of Port Republic and Cross Keys are described later in this tour. In the spring of

James Madison University

Harrisonburg is the home of James Madison University, which had its beginnings in 1908 as the state-established Normal and Industrial School for Women. The main part of this ever-growing campus (in 2009 it had more than 17,000 students) faces U.S. 11 about a mile south of the downtown area, past a neighborhood of lovely old Victorian-era homes.

The university maintains the Edith J. Carrier Arboretum, 125 acres of natural beauty on the eastern side of the campus. It features forested walking trails, gardens, and many rare and endangered plants native to the mid-Appalachia area. The arboretum is located on University Boulevard a half-block east of the Port Republic Road interchange (Exit 245) with I-81. From Port Republic Road, on Forest Hill Road, turn left on Oak Hill Drive, and then turn right on to University Boulevard. The arboretum is about 0.5 mile on the right.

Rockingham County Court-house

1862, about 2,000 Union prisoners taken during the First Battle of Winchester were held near the courthouse before they were marched to Richmond.

In 1864, General Sheridan's men occupied the town during the devastating thirteen days of "The Burning," when Union soldiers killed or confiscated farm animals and destroyed Valley crops, barns, mills, and other commercial structures.

The intersection of U.S. 33 (Market Street) and U.S. 11 (Main Street) at Courthouse Square remains the main crossroads in Harrisonburg today. From the square, walk two blocks south on Main Street to Bruce Street.

The Hardesty-Higgins House, the handsome red-brick Georgian building on the corner of Main and Bruce Streets (across from the Rockingham Regional Library and the Asbury United Methodist Church) is the city's visitor center. Henry Higgins began building this house in 1848. It was completed five years later by Harrisonburg's first mayor, Isaac Hardesty. Hardesty was a Union sympathizer who allowed General Nathaniel Banks to use this house for three days in May 1862.

The visitor center is worth a stop. In addition to providing tourism information, it contains the Valley Turnpike Museum, the Harrisonburg-Rockingham County Civil War Interpretive Center, a gift shop, and Mrs. Hardesty's Tea Room, where light meals are served.

Just a short walk across the street from the visitor center is the Thomas Harrison House. Around 1750, Harrison built a stone house, which is the oldest in the city. It still stands as the rear portion of the building at 30 West Bruce Street. The

Thomas Harrison House

brick portion was built in the mid-1800s. It's not open to the public.

Return to Main Street and turn right. Just a short walk south of the Harrison House is the Virginia Quilt Museum, at 301 South Main Street. This historic home, an 1856 residence known as the Warren-Sipe House, contains a permanent collection of more than 60 quilts and features changing exhibits of local and international quilts. Begun in 1995 with donations from quilt guilds all over Virginia, it is dedicated to preserving the heritage of quilt making. The museum is open daily except Sunday and Monday.

To resume the driving tour, follow U.S. 33 West for 1.7 miles. Turn left at the traffic light on to Garber's Church Road and drive 1 mile. Turn right just before Harrisonburg High School into the driveway for the CrossRoads Heritage Center.

CrossRoads, the Valley Brethren-Mennonite Heritage Center, tells the story of two Protestant denominations that came to the Shenandoah Valley in the late 1700s; their origins date back to Germany in the 1700s. The Brethren and the Mennonites believe in living a simple life based on peaceful action and service to others. Like the Quakers and the Amish (a denomination that split from the Mennonites in the late 1600s), Mennonites do not believe in military service, which caused them problems during both the Revolutionary War and the Civil War. Because some Old Order Mennonites believe that living a plain and simple life means doing without modern technology, it's not uncommon to see a family riding in a horse and buggy in this area.

The CrossRoads "farmstead" is a 14-acre site that depicts daily life in this religious community during the 1800s and 1900s. Volunteers give tours of the Burkholder-Meyers House, an 1800s homestead on the grounds. The center is open Wednesday through Saturday.

Return to U.S. 33 and turn left. In about 1 mile, after you pass the town limits sign for Dale Enterprise, turn left on to Route 701 at the small sign pointing to Dayton.

The large hill on the right is Mole Hill, a remnant of one of two known ancient volcanoes in Virginia (Trimble Knob in Monterey, described in The Monterey to Hot Springs to Goshen Pass Tour, page 207, is the other). Molten lava from the eruption at Mole Hill more than 45 million years ago has been found 10 miles away at Natural Chimneys. Today's hill, which rises about 500 feet off the Valley floor, has eroded greatly since its creation. Local lore says that area residents celebrated the end of the War of 1812 at the top of Mole Hill. There, it is said, they had

Silver Lake, with Mole Hill in the background

a picnic that featured a barbecued ox, whose last act was to walk up this steep hill.

This part of Rockingham County, with its rolling fields and picturesque farms, reflects the county's longstanding importance as a leading agricultural center. It is one of the top poultry producers in the nation.

Continue on Route 701 to **Dayton**. *Before entering the town, you'll see Silver Lake on the right.* This lake was formed when a dam was built on Cooks Creek to provide water power for two mills that operated here as early as the 1820s. Bowman's Mill, which stands here today, is also called Silver Lake Mill. Named for the man who bought one of the original 1820s mills in 1839, the mill burned down in 1855. It was rebuilt the following year, only to be burned down again nine years later by Union troops led by General George Custer during "The Burning" of the Shenandoah Valley in 1864.

The story goes that Bowman, like the previous owners, was a member of the Church of the Brethren, which opposed slavery and supported the Union cause. For that reason, General Sheridan ordered Bowman's flour mill spared. But General Custer went ahead and destroyed not only Bowman's mill but one of his homes as well. Rockingham County suffered terrible losses during "The Burning"; it is said that more than 60 mills and 450 barns were destroyed here. Afterward, several hundred Brethren and Mennonites packed up what little they had left and moved to West Virginia, protected by Sheridan's troops.

Rebuilt by 1866, Bowman's Mill went through several more owners. Flour was ground here until 1986, and animal feed was ground and mixed here until 1996. Renovated in 2001, the structure now houses a porcelain decorating business. Although it is no longer a working mill, you can still watch the waterwheel turn and see the old grain elevator lift products to the gift shop. It's open Thursdays through Saturdays.

From Bowman's Mill, continue into Dayton and turn left just after the Dayton town limits sign on to Route 732. Soon after, turn right on to Route 42 Business (Main Street), where you'll see Fort Harrison (also known as the Daniel Harrison House). Daniel Harrison was a brother of the founder of Harrisonburg and was Dayton's first settler. He arrived in the area in 1745 and built the front portion of this stone house in 1749.

Stone houses like this one were often called forts, because their thick walls served to protect area families against Indian attacks, which were frequent in the

Daniel Harrison House

Valley during the mid-1700s. Early settlers in Dayton were especially vulnerable because they were near the old trail leading to Warm Springs, a favorite Indian destination. At this house, the settlers built an underground passage that led to a spring by Cooks Creek, providing them with access to water in case they were confined to the house for a long period. The Daniel Harrison House is open on weekend afternoons from May through October.

As early settlement here grew, the community came to be known as Rifetown or Rifesville after Daniel Rife, who owned much of the land the town occupies. It was formally established as Dayton in 1833. By then, the town had become important because of the many mills in the area and the iron works at Mossy Creek, visited later on this tour. No one is sure why the name Dayton was chosen.

From Fort Harrison, continue on Main Street to the next intersection, Mill Street, and turn right. Go one block and turn right on College Street.

Many of the old homes and businesses that line College Street have a connection to the town's past as a center for music education and publishing. In 1878, the music and book publishing firm of Ruebush-Kieffer moved here from Singers Glen (see The Edinburg to Singers Glen to Mount Jackson Tour, page 124). Dayton was also home to the institution that later became the Shenandoah College and Conservatory of Music; founded in 1875, it is now Shenandoah University in Winchester. Ephraim Ruebush, a president of the college, lived in the Victorian house at 315 College Street. He and Aldine Kieffer were grandsons of Joseph Funk of nearby Singers Glen, whose interest in music and education led him to establish both the publishing company and a school for music educators.

After driving three blocks on College Street, turn left on Route 732 (Bowman Avenue), then turn left on High Street. On your left is the Heritage Center, operated by the Harrisonburg-Rockingham County Historical Society. The main level contains a gift and bookshop that specializes in local folk arts and crafts of high quality, as well as books and publications used for genealogical research. The museum contains permanent and changing exhibits about local history and folk art, including a large map and a film that tell the story of Stonewall Jackson's Valley Campaign of 1862. Upstairs, the society manages a genealogical research library. The center is open daily except Sundays.

From the parking lot at the Heritage Center, turn left on High Street and go two blocks to Mill Street; turn left and go two blocks to Main Street. Turn right, drive to the stop sign at Mason Street, turn left, then turn right on to Route 42 South (John Wayland

Highway). In about 0.2 mile, you will see the Dayton Farmers Market, on the right. The building houses a collection of shops and a cafeteria-style restaurant and bakery run by area Mennonites. The Dayton Farmers Market is open Thursdays, Fridays, and Saturdays.

Continue on Route 42 South to **Bridgewater***, where Route 42 becomes Main Street.* One of this area's early settlers, in the 1740s, was a man named Alexander Herring. He married one of Daniel Harrison's sisters, Abigail. Their daughter, Bathsheba, married a man from the Linville Creek area named Abraham Lincoln. One of their children, Thomas Lincoln, was the father of the future president. (See the sidebar about the Lincoln Homestead on page 128.) The Lincoln family moved to Kentucky when Thomas was a small boy. Until a few years ago, the house Herring built stood on Cooks Creek between Dayton and Bridgewater. It has since been moved log by log to a spot about 11 miles west.

The area was settled by Scotch-Irish immigrants as early as 1740. By the early 1800s, many Pennsylvanians of German descent were moving to the area as well. Bridgewater was first called Dinkletown, after the two Dinkle brothers who built mills and a tavern here around 1800. The many local mills sent their flour and other products to market on flat-bottomed boats on the North River, which flows through the southern end of town. Of the eight bridges that have spanned the river here since 1820, the most famous was a 240-foot covered bridge said to be the longest single-span wooden bridge in the world at the time.

Today the town is home to Bridgewater College, a private school operated by the Church of the Brethren. It was established in 1880 at Spring Creek as the Virginia Normal School and later moved here. On the campus is the Reuel B. Pritchett Museum, which contains some 10,000 items that were part of a private collection owned by Pritchett, a minister and farmer from Tennessee. The museum owns more than 175 rare books and Bibles, including a copy of the Venice Bible published in 1482. Other items on display include fossils, Civil War artifacts, antique guns and swords, jugs, glassware, and carpentry tools. The museum, which is on the lower level of Cole Hall on East College Street, is open Monday through Friday afternoons (visitors are asked to call ahead; see the appendix listing) or by appointment.

Many interesting old homes line Main Street. A former mayor of Bridgewater owned the Barbee House at 403 North Main, built in 1818. This brick house was

Barbee House

J. G. Brown House

later turned into a tavern; after the Civil War, it became a girls' school. It is claimed that both Henry Clay and Andrew Jackson once slept here.

J.G. Brown, a captain in the Civil War, built the imposing white house with columns at 111 South Main in 1849.

At least six of the town's doctors have lived in the T.H. Brown Home at 115 South Main, which was built about 1838.

Dinkle Tavern, a red-brick structure built by one of the Dinkle brothers who helped develop the town in the early 1800s, still stands at 215 South Main Street, just before the North River Bridge. The tavern became a popular stopping place for travelers from Washington, D.C., to Warm Springs before the Civil War. At that time, Route 42 was known as the Harrisonburg–Warm Springs Turnpike.

Just past Dinkle Tavern, on the right before the North River Bridge, is a river-

Dinkle Tavern

side park and walking trail. A Civil War Trails interpretive sign tells the story of the town's importance during the Civil War.

Follow Route 42 across the North River bridge and drive 3.2 miles. At **Mossy Creek,** *Route 42 veers sharply to the left. Don't turn here; instead, stay straight on Route 747 (Mossy Creek Road).* The stone-and-brick house on the left at this junction is now mostly hidden by trees. It was once known as the Miller House and is one of the oldest homes in Augusta County. The stone portion was built in 1784 by Henry Miller, who founded the large ironworks nearby. Miller was a cousin of Daniel Boone and is thought to have learned iron making from Boone's father, Squire Boone.

Continue straight on 747. Just past the intersection of Routes 42 and 747 is a field on the left that was once the site of a lake created by a dam built on Mossy Creek to provide power for the ironworks and mill. The lake, which had a pavilion and dance hall, was a popular weekend gathering spot from the mid-1800s until the early 1900s. The Chesapeake and Western Railroad brought day-trippers from Harrisonburg on Sundays. After the ironworks and mill shut down in the early 1900s, the lake was drained and returned to farmland.

On the right 0.6 mile past the intersection, you'll see a driveway on the right leading to a handsome red-brick house with white pillars. Now a private home, this is the George Craun House, which was built near the site of the Mossy Creek Academy. The academy was established by Jedediah Hotchkiss around 1853. Hotchkiss was an engineer and teacher who later played an important role in the Civil War as General Stonewall Jackson's topographical engineer and mapmaker. While it existed, the school is said to have produced many promising young people. It shut down when the Civil War began and was used for a while as a Confederate hospital. A fire destroyed the building soon after the war.

Continue 0.7 mile to the Mossy Creek Presbyterian Church, beautifully situated on the hill to the left. The church was founded in 1768 by Scotch-Irish settlers. It was one of several early Presbyterian churches in this part of the Valley.

As you continue toward **Mount Solon,** you'll pass the area where Stonewall Jackson's army camped after the Battle of McDowell in Highland County in May 1862 (see The Monterey to Hot Springs to Goshen Pass Tour, page 204).

Drive 1.9 miles to the stop sign in Mount Solon. Turn right on Route 731 (Natural Chimneys Road). Before you turn, note the white frame building directly across the street. During the Civil War, Generals Jackson and Ewell met here to lay out a plan to pursue General Banks's Union troops.

About 0.7 mile outside Mount Solon, you'll see a green-and-yellow sign marking the entrance to **Natural Chimneys Park.** The park has picnic tables and shelters, a campground, and a swimming pool. It is operated by the Augusta County Parks and Recreation Department, which charges a small admission fee. There are seven limestone "chimneys," the highest of which measures 120 feet. They are about 500 million years old, formed from the sediment of an ancient sea that covered the Shenandoah Valley. Once part of a huge cavern, the chimneys are what was left after the roof caved in. The stone markers scattered around the area tell the geological story of their formation.

William Cullen Bryant described the Natural Chimneys in his popular book, *Picturesque America,* published in 1872. He said they resembled ancient castle ruins. As such, they provide the perfect backdrop for the park's most famous activity—the Natural Chimneys Jousting Tournament, which the park claims is the oldest continuously held sporting event in America. Participants reenact the sport of knights, but instead of knocking each other off horses, they try to guide their lances through small suspended metal rings while galloping.

The games began here in 1821 as a way for two local men to settle a claim on the young woman both wanted to marry. Today, riders come from surrounding states to compete in a sport that originated—in a slightly more deadly form—in France in the 11th century. The tournament is held on the third Saturday in August. Call the park for more information; the number is listed in the appendix.

From the park entrance, head back to Mount Solon. When you reach the stop sign at the intersection, stay straight on Route 731.

Stokesville Side Trip

If you turn right as you leave the entrance to Natural Chimneys Park and drive 4.5 miles west, you'll end up in **Stokesville.** This sparsely settled community once was the terminus of the old Chesapeake and Western Railroad—called the "Crooked and Weedy" by locals at the time. The line began in Dayton in 1895 and primarily transported lumber from Mount Solon to Elkton. When

Restored train station in Stokesville

the lumber supply was exhausted in the 1930s, the line ceased operations. *To reach the train station from Natural Chimneys Park, turn right when leaving the park and continue to the yield sign at North River Road and turn left. At the stop sign at Route 718, turn left and cross the old iron railroad bridge; the Stokesville station is on your right.*

Tucked into the base of the Alleghenies, the restored train station (now a private home) still stands, with a cheery red caboose parked to the left. The village of Stokesville was named after a local millionaire, W.E.D. Stokes, who helped finance the rail line from Mount Solon. Heading 1 mile in the other direction, Route 718 continues to the entrance to Todd Lake, North River Campground, and several mountain hiking trails in the Dry River Ranger District of the George Washington National Forest.

Mount Solon has been around since the 1700s and is thought to have been named for the ancient Greek lawgiver. As you pass through this small village, you'll see several old buildings. On the outskirts as you leave, you'll see a beautifully restored old home on the right side of the road. Spring Meadows, which is now a special-events facility, was built by J. Marshall McCue in 1838. Here, on the evening of May 17, 1862, it is said that Mr. McCue, a member of the Virginia House of Delegates, entertained Stonewall Jackson and members of his staff at dinner, while Jackson's men camped in the area.

Continue on Route 731. In 2.2 miles, you'll come to a stop sign at Route 42 at **Moscow**; *continue straight on what is now Route 607 (Mount Solon Road). Stay on this road toward* **Spring Hill**. On the 5 miles to Spring Hill, the road leads through rolling farmland with dramatic views of the Blue Ridge Mountains to the east and south. *Drive another 4 miles past Spring Hill. Almost immediately after you pass Pleasant View Lutheran Church on the left, turn left on to Route 612 (Quick's Mill Road). About 2 miles down the road, a panoramic view of Massanutten Mountain and the Blue Ridge range comes into view as you descend for another 3 miles toward U.S. 11 and the town of* **Verona**. *Turn left on U.S. 11.*

The city of Ann Arbor, Michigan, was named for Ann Allen, a pioneer woman who once lived in the Verona area. She left here in 1824 to join her husband, John, who had moved west—as many Valley residents did during that period. He and another man, Elisha Rumsey, settled at a place in the Michigan Territory that they named "Ann's Arbor," after both their wives. A few years later, John Allen left Ann Arbor, without Ann, to take part in the California gold rush and was never heard

Old Mount Solon bank building

Spring Meadows

Mount Airy Farm, once home to Grandma Moses

Grandma Moses in Augusta County

Not many people know that Anna Mary Robertson Moses, better known as the folk artist Grandma Moses, lived in the Shenandoah Valley for 18 years. She came here as a farmer's wife (and entrepreneur) when she was twenty-eight years old.

She and her husband were on their way to North Carolina for their honeymoon in 1887 when they mistakenly got off the train in Staunton and decided to stay. They first rented a dairy farm near Verona. Not long after, they rented another dairy farm nearby, where Anna Moses learned to make especially tasty butter that she sold in large quantities (160 pounds a week!) to what is now the Greenbrier Resort in White Sulphur Springs, West Virginia.

A few years later they moved to another farm northwest of Verona. By 1901, she and her husband were able to buy the first Verona farmhouse they had rented, which they called Mount Airy Farm.

The family returned to their native New York state in 1905 to take care of Mr. Moses' parents. When she was in her late seventies, Mrs. Moses took up painting. About 40 of her works, including one of Mount Airy, are thought to be Shenandoah Valley scenes. Born in the year the Civil War began, she died in 1961 at the age of 101.

Grandma Moses' house at Mount Airy Farm still stands, but it is in rickety condition. It barely escaped demolition by the county in 2007 because it stood in the middle of the county's new industrial park. Preservation efforts are under way.

from again. She returned to Verona and died here; her grave is at the Augusta Stone Church, the next stop on this tour. The Allen family's home is still standing along U.S. 11 as you leave Verona; it's the red-brick structure on the hill just after you cross the low concrete bridge over the Middle River.

Continue north on U.S. 11 for 3 miles to **Fort Defiance**. On the left is Augusta Military Academy, which has closed and is now owned by a church. Charles S. Roller, a Confederate veteran and state delegate, founded the school in 1879 to teach the classics. Perhaps because so many of his students were Confederate veterans, he also ran the school partly as a military academy. It later became a traditional military academy and was a well-respected school for more than a century. In 1920, it formed the first Junior Reserve Officers' Training Corps in the country. It was operated by Roller's descendants until it closed in 1984 because of financial difficulties. The alumni association operates a museum in the alumni house on the grounds; it is open daily except Sundays and holidays.

Next door to the military academy is the Augusta Stone Church. The original part of this church, which is the oldest Virginia church west of the Blue Ridge and

Augusta Military Academy

Augusta Stone Church

the oldest Presbyterian church in continuous use in Virginia, was completed in 1749. Set in a grove of towering old oak trees, the church grounds and cemetery are well worth a stop. The main church building was enlarged in the early 1920s, but the original walls and roof remain.

The area's first settlers were Scotch-Irish who were on a continual search for freedom from religious persecution. Their ancestors moved (or were forced to move) from Scotland to Ireland in the early 1600s. By the mid-1700s, many then moved from Ireland to America. Settling first in Pennsylvania, they found they didn't fit in well with the established German and Quaker settlements. Many came to the central and southern part of the Shenandoah Valley, places that were largely unsettled at the time.

In 1738 a group of Scotch-Irish settlers formed a "Christian society" here. They worshiped in a log cabin located on the site of what is now the church cemetery. Their first minister, John Craig, arrived from Ireland via Delaware in 1740. He made an observation about the Shenandoah Valley, describing it as "a wilderness in the proper sense, and a few Christian settlers in it with numbers of heathens travelling among us. . . [The local people] generally march about in small companies from fifteen to twenty, sometimes more or less. They must be supplied at any house they call at, with victuals, or they become their own stewards and cooks, and spare

The "Ungainly" Parson Speece

The fourth minister of the Augusta Stone Church began his tenure in 1813. He was an educated and colorful character named Conrad Speece, whom a local historian described as follows: "Parson Speece chewed tobacco excessively, even sleeping with a quid in his mouth. He was tall, heavy, and ungainly; and his clothes, always too large for him, hung loosely on his large frame. His voice was loud, deep, and resonant. He was very sociable and an able conversationalist, sprinkling his remarks with droll and curious phrases. He was a bachelor, whether from choice or because Shenandoah women could not discern his sterling worth beneath his rough and ungainly exterior, the records do not state."

nothing they choose to eat and drink." Reverend Craig obviously had his work cut out for him.

For many years, Craig also served as minister (every other Sunday) at another Presbyterian church in the area, Tinkling Springs. His Sunday morning sermons lasted from ten o'clock to noon, and his afternoon service lasted from one o'clock to sundown. *The Annals of Augusta County* notes that the latter service was "sometimes so late that the clerk found it difficult to read the last Psalm."

In 1747, he and his congregation—men and women alike—began building the Augusta Stone Church, completing it in 1749. By the 1750s, during the French and Indian War, many settlers feared for their lives and had moved out of the Valley. The Reverend Craig felt strongly that residents should stay, and he became a strong supporter of fort-building in the Valley. In 1755, he urged the settlers to build a stockade around the church. Fortunately, the church—which would also have served as their fort—was never attacked. The courage of these residents was probably the source of the name of Fort Defiance, given to the community much later, in the late 1800s.

The Session House Museum, in the small old stone building next to the church, contains a museum that tells the church's history. It is open on Sunday mornings by request or by appointment at other times; see the appendix for contact information.

Continue on U.S. 11 to the next town, **Mount Sidney.** In the late 1700s, this was the only stage stop between Keezletown, at the base of the Massanutten (to the east), and Staunton (to the south).

A farm near Mount Sidney was the birthplace of Dwight D. Eisenhower's mother, Ida Elizabeth Stover, in 1862. Her first three years were spent in the shadow of the Civil War. When Ida's mother died when she was eight, her father sent her and her siblings to live with relatives. She spent the next 11 years with her grandfather, William Link; he was a grandson of Mathias Link, who had come to the area in the 1750s. Ida moved to Kansas in 1883, where she met and married David Eisenhower. In 1952, President Eisenhower visited Mount Sidney to see where his mother had spent her childhood.

This section of U.S. 11 was not part of the original Indian Trail, which ran closer to Massanutten Mountain. Historians say that the trail left what is now U.S. 11 near Mauzy, north of Harrisonburg, and rejoined it above Mount Sidney. Most of the old route followed the path of today's Route 276 (Keezletown Road), which is still called the Indian Trail in some places.

As you leave Mount Sidney, turn right on to Route 750, which passes over I-81 and intersects Route 256 (Weyers Cave Road) at a traffic light in 2.8 miles. At this point, you have completed the western half of this tour.

To continue the tour, turn right and continue straight for about 5 miles to **Grottoes.** The mountains you see to the left are the southern end of the Massanutten range; to the right and ahead are the Blue Ridge Mountains, topped by Skyline Drive. The tallest peaks here range in elevation from 3,300 to almost 3,600 feet.

In nearly 4 miles, you may want to take a quick side trip to see a most unusual octagonal barn. Look for the sign pointing right to **Mount Meridian** *and turn right. Just* *after the turn, you'll be able to see the barn in the distance ahead on the right.* A Virginia state historic landmark, this barn was built in 1867 by Samuel Harnsberger, whose ancestors were Swiss-Germans who came to the Valley in the early 1700s. He was inspired by the octagonal house in Grottoes built by his brother (see below). During its construction, the barn's design reportedly stumped local carpenters. An outside expert had to be called in to help them fit everything together. It was restored in 1978.

Mount Meridian provided a peaceful place for Stonewall Jackson's army to rest for five days in mid-June 1862, with "the men reposing under the shade, or bathing in the sparkling waters of the [river], and the horses feeding in the abundant pastures," as a Major Dabney recorded.

Turn around and turn right to return to Route 256 to continue toward Grottoes. Grottoes is just across the South River, which joins the North River at Port Republic in about 3 miles to form the North Fork of the Shenandoah River. Just before the South River bridge, you'll pass a state historical marker on the left, near the driveway of a private home. It says that in 1811 artist George Caleb Bingham was born nearby. Bingham was well known for his paintings of the American West.

Grottoes was named for the large cave now known as Grand Caverns. *To reach Grand Caverns, follow the signs as you enter the town and turn right at Route 825 (Dogwood Avenue).* Located in the foothills of the Blue Ridge, the caverns were discovered in 1806 by a young man named Bernard Weyer (the source of the name of the nearby town, Weyers Cave). They contained deposits of potassium nitrate, used for making gunpowder, a product that was in great demand in the early 1800s and again during the Civil War. The caverns were originally called Madison's Cave, for John Madison, the first clerk of Augusta County, who lived in nearby Port Republic.

Thomas Jefferson visited the caverns and described them in his only book, *Notes on the State of Virginia,* published in 1787. Jefferson wrote: "It is in a hill of about 200 feet perpendicular height. . . . It extends into the earth about 300 feet, branching into subordinate caverns." The largest of these caverns is Cathedral Hall, which is 280 feet long and more than 70 feet high, making it one of the largest cavern rooms on the East Coast.

In 1836, the owners opened the Grand Ballroom chamber as a dance hall. Tourists could view all the caverns on one day a year, when each room was lighted

An unusual octagonal barn near Grottoes
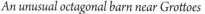

with candles. During the Civil War, General Stonewall Jackson's troops, who were camped nearby, visited the caverns, and like tourists through the ages they wrote their names on the walls. Jackson, though, declined to enter the caves, the story goes, explaining that "I fear I shall be underground soon enough, and I have no desire to speed the process!" By 1889, permanent lighting was installed.

Grand Caverns is open daily. The adjoining park has a swimming pool, hiking and biking trails, playgrounds, and picnic shelters.

To continue into Grottoes from the caverns, turn left back on to Dogwood Avenue. Go to the stop sign on Route 256 and continue straight to stay on Dogwood Avenue. The town's gridlike layout, with numbered streets intersecting with avenues named for trees, reflects the ambitious plans of the town's founders during its heyday in the late 1800s. Besides the tourism potential of the caverns, the area was rich in mineral deposits and iron ore. Also, the railroad made it a convenient shipping point for the many agricultural products that this part of the Valley produced then. Grottoes—then known as Liola—grew after a group of investors (including Jedediah Hotchkiss, mentioned earlier in this tour) organized the Grottoes Company of the Shenandoah in 1888, with the hopes of establishing a thriving new city. They improved the caverns, built a large hotel (which burned to the ground after only four years of operation), and planned factories. By 1891, the town had a newspaper, two brick factories, a tile factory, a woolen mill, a brass factory, and a sash-and-blind factory. An electric power plant was under construction. Their dream for Shendun (their new name for the town) included a 30-mile long street-car system that would use mules for power. The first leg of the line began running in 1892. A year later the company went into receivership.

As elsewhere in the nation, the boom went bust for various reasons: the panic of 1893, the overall weakness of the Grottoes Company, the abandonment of plans for an east-west railway, and the discovery of cheaper-to-mine iron ore in Minnesota. By 1912, the town's population dropped to almost half its 1891 high of 709. That year, the locals renamed their town Grottoes. They no doubt felt like crawling into the cave.

Route 663, which runs out of Grottoes up into the Blue Ridge, was the original part of the old Brown's Gap Turnpike, the most direct route between Harrisonburg and Charlottesville in the early 1800s and an important route from the Valley over the mountains to eastern Virginia during the Civil War. The turnpike was closed when Shenandoah National Park was created.

To see an unusual house, take a short detour off of Dogwood Avenue. Turn left at 14th Street and drive to its end, at Holly Avenue, and turn right; the house is almost immediately on the left. Stephen Harnsberger, a member of the Harnsberger family mentioned earlier, built this octagonal house in 1856. He based it on a plan he found in an 1853 book on octagonal houses, which had become something of a fad in the mid-1800s. Such homes were thought to have been healthier living spaces because they allowed more light into the interiors, remained cooler in the summer, and were easier to heat in the winter. Two well-known octagonal homes were built in America well before the mid-1800s: Thomas Jefferson's Poplar Forest, in

Lynchburg, Virginia, and William Thornton's Tayloe House, better known as the Octagon House, in Washington, D.C. Several thousand octagon houses were built all over America in the mid- to late-1800s, many of which still stand today. The Harnsberger House has been restored and remains a private home.

Return to Dogwood Avenue and turn left. In about 3 miles, you'll come to a stop sign; turn left on to Route 253 West (Port Republic Road). Immediately after you cross the South River Bridge after the turn, at the intersection with Water Street, on your right you'll see the Port Republic Museum, located in the Frank Kemper Home, sometimes called the Turner Ashby House. Little is left of this once-important river town of **Port Republic**, partly because of General Sheridan's campaign of destruction in the Valley during 1864 and partly because of two destructive floods in the 1870s. The museum describes the last four days of Jackson's Valley Campaign and tells the story of the river port and industrial community that thrived here from the mid-1700s through the 1800s. The museum is open on Sunday afternoons from April through October or by appointment; see the appendix for details.

The body of the beloved General Turner Ashby was brought to this house after his death during a skirmish with Union troops at Chestnut Ridge, southeast of Harrisonburg. After his horse was shot out from under him, he continued to lead his men on foot and was soon killed by enemy fire. Stonewall Jackson and others came to this house to pay their last respects.

Port Republic is one of Rockingham County's oldest inhabited places. Shawnee Indians are said to have lived in the area in the early 1700s. In 1733, a German

Port Republic Museum

immigrant named Jacob Stover received an 800-acre tract of land from the king of England that included the area that would later become Port Republic. As was the practice in those days, land grants were issued on the condition that the grantee settle a certain number of families on the land within a given period. Although the story was never confirmed, local wags of the day claimed that Stover, after failing to meet this requirement and not wanting to lose the land, gave fictitious human names to his horses, cows, hogs, dogs, and even a few chickens. He supposedly drew up a report that designated these animals as heads of households and sent it to the king. The grant was approved, after which Stover divided the land into small parcels and sold them.

Today, Port Republic retains the feel of the old settlement. Its layout remains much as it was in 1802, and the streets are lined with houses spanning three centuries. A pamphlet describing a walking tour of the town is available at the museum. Interpretive signs along Water Street also tell the background of the sites. A short distance down the other side of Water Street, across Route 253 from the museum, is Bradburn Memorial Park, where you can have a picnic lunch along the South River. It was here that Union forces forded the river to enter the town in 1862.

Drive west on Water Street past the park and then a short distance left on Route 605 (Main Street) to the site of the old Madison Hall. One of the town's more famous homes, it was built in the mid-1700s. That house was replaced in 1916 by a Victorian-style house on the same site. Madison Hall originally belonged to John Madison (whose cousin was the father of President James Madison). John's son, James, was the first Episcopal bishop in Virginia and was president of William and Mary College for many years.

During the Civil War, Stonewall Jackson used Madison Hall as a temporary headquarters during the Battles of Cross Keys and Port Republic. Traveling along what is now U.S. 11, Jackson arrived in the Port Republic area in June 1862 after winning important battles in Front Royal and Winchester. At the time, he was being pursued by two Union armies, one led by General John C. Fremont and the other by General James Shields.

While staying at Madison Hall, Jackson barely escaped enemy capture. He had planned to attend church on Sunday morning, June 8, 1862, but around 8 A.M. the sound of guns and cannons announced the unexpected presence of Union cavalry,

Patterson House, Port Republic

A Shenandoah River Port

After the South Fork of the Shenandoah was made navigable, the town of Port Republic began to grow in the 1820s and 1830s. To ship their goods to market, merchants used flat-bottom boats that curved up at each end. They were called floatboats or gundalows—most certainly derived from the Italian word *gondola*—and were constructed of heavy timbers. They carried lumber, iron ore, flour, and other items downriver—meaning northward on the Shenandoah—to Harpers Ferry, from where they could be transported down the Potomac River and the C&O Canal to Georgetown and Alexandria. Because the boats could not make the return trip against the current, they were broken apart and sold as lumber. It is said that much of the town of Harpers Ferry was built from the wood scavenged from these boats.

It took some clever engineering and a lot of dangerous work to get the boats north. Prominent Valley historian John Wayland recorded in *The History of Rockingham County* how the boats were moved down the Shenandoah, which is shallow and rocky in places: "The floatboats used were made of heavy undressed lumber, and were guided by rudders at each end. At the dams in the river, next to the shore, chutes were placed, constructed of strong timber, for the passage of the boats. When the rise in the river was sufficient, the boats would go over the dam."

The boats measured about nine feet wide by 80 to 90 feet long. They could carry a load of up to 12 tons of iron, 12,000 feet of lumber, or 110 barrels of flour—if the water was high enough. The boatmen were paid from $14 to $18 to make the trip; after reaching Harpers Ferry, they had to walk home. One report noted that a typical trip took five to seven days—three or four days on the boat, then two or three days to walk back. The fact that it took less time to walk the route reveals something about the difficulties involved in navigation.

Wayland's book contains an eyewitness report of a local man, who as a boy in the late 1800s watched the boats on the Shenandoah near Luray:

> We got in sight just in time to see the first boat go thro, strike a great rock, split in twain, and the whole cargo of pigiron went to the bottom. Each boat was manned by six men, and when the boat broke those on it were carried to such deep water that they had to swim. There were 18 boats in this fleet, and soon the men began to wade in and gather the iron together in a pile. The broken boat was taken to the bank and repaired, reloaded, and started on its way again. . . .
>
> Nearly all the boats were provided with tin horns about 8 feet long, and when they would start from the stations on the River, all would blow. War songs were the favorite tunes, and the music they made would make your hair stand on end. These horns could be heard for 5 miles.

Gundalows were a common sight on many parts of the Shenandoah and North Rivers throughout much of the 1800s (see The Natural Bridge to Lexington Tour, pages 223–27). Early town names revealed the importance of river trade: Bridgewater, on the North River and visited earlier on this tour, was once Bridgeport; Timberville, on the North Fork of the Shenandoah, was first known as Williamsport.

The days of floatboats on the Shenandoah River came to an end by 1890; they were put out of business by the growing network of railroads in the Valley.

which had crossed the South River. Jackson found himself separated from his army by the raging North River, swollen by recent spring rains. He and several of his staff officers made a mad dash on horseback across the river's covered bridge, attracting enemy fire as they ran. When they came out the other side, they found themselves face to face with Federal troops. Some members of his staff were captured, but Jackson was somehow able to rejoin his troops. Later that day, the Confederates regained the town.

On that same harrowing day, Richard Ewell, one of Jackson's generals, and his 5,000 men defeated General Fremont's army of 10,000 at Cross Keys, 4 miles northwest of here.

That night and early into the next day, June 9, Jackson moved most of his army to a location called "The Coaling," east of town above the Shenandoah River. This area was used to burn wood for making charcoal, the fuel used to fire the local iron furnaces. General Shields had placed a division of men there to hold this strategic spot high above the surrounding fields while waiting for Fremont to move his troops there from Cross Keys.

Jackson knew he had to capture the hill before Fremont's troops arrived. During heavy fighting that morning, the Union lost and re-won the hill twice before the Confederates managed to take it back for good. By the time Fremont's army arrived at the Coaling, Jackson was in an advantageous position to deal with them. The fighting began shortly after daybreak, and by 10:30 A.M. the bloody battle was over. Federal casualties totaled 1,100 and Confederate casualties 1,000.

In the end, the victorious Confederates chased the Federals to Elkton. The Battle of Port Republic was the last engagement in Jackson's brilliant 1862 Valley Campaign, during which he successfully diverted Union forces from other parts of the state to prevent them from taking the Confederate capital of Richmond.

The tour continues with a visit to the Port Republic Battlefield at "The Coaling." *From the Port Republic Museum on Water Street, go back down Route 253 and across the South River bridge (the way you came into town) for about 1 mile to its intersection with Route 340 (East Side Highway). Turn left and go 1.1 miles on U.S. 340 North, where you'll pass a battlefield marker on the left side of the road. Continue 1 mile past to the brown historical-site road sign near Route 340's intersection with Route 708; to visit the Coaling, turn right after the sign on to Route 708 (Ore Bank Road). (If you don't wish to visit the Coaling, turn left on to Ore Bank Road to continue the tour.) To* the left of a parking area is a self-guided walking trail through the battlefield. The trail goes up a fairly steep hillside that is maintained by the Blue and Gray Education Society and the Association for the Preservation of Civil War Sites.

From the Coaling, go straight across Route 340, staying on Route 708, which becomes Lynnwood Road. In about 0.5 mile, you will pass an old home named Lynnwood, located just after the railroad crossing and set back from the road on your right; the drive going in to the property is marked Dilworth Drive. This painted brick mansion was built by the son of the original landowner, Thomas Lewis, in 1812. Lewis's earlier white frame home on the property was George Washington's destination on the night of September 30, 1784, after he spent the day riding 40 miles across the Val-

Lynnwood

ley from Brock's Gap (see The Edinburg to Singers Glen to Mount Jackson Tour, page 122).

Lewis bought the surrounding 530 acres (much of it part of the original Stover grant mentioned earlier) from a Pennsylvanian named Christopher Franciscus in 1751. He named the house after his mother, Margaret Lynn Lewis. Thomas Lewis was one of four distinguished sons of John Lewis, the early Scotch-Irish Valley settler and founder of Staunton. Thomas Lewis worked with Peter Jefferson (Thomas Jefferson's father) to survey the Lord Fairfax grant in the 1750s. In 1788, he became the first surveyor of Rockingham County.

Continue for about 0.5 mile on Route 708 across the Shenandoah River bridge to another historic mansion, Bogota. Almost impossible to see from the road because of surrounding trees, this beautiful Greek Revival-style brick home was built in the mid-1840s by Jacob Strayer. In 1862, the Strayer family watched the Battle of Port Republic from the home's balcony. Clara Strayer, the 19-year-old daughter of the owner, recorded her impressions of the battle, which soon descended on the house itself:

> A rifle shell passed about 15 feet from the southwest corner of this house, another fell through the roof of a cabin on the upper edge of the orchard, within two feet of old Uncle Daniel who had been on the retired list. He yelled lustily, being more scared than hurt as the shell did not explode. . . .
>
> They next came to the house in search of Rebels. . .[they] poured in every door, and such clanking of sabers, ransacking of presses, trying to break open doors, I never saw. They came into our chamber, when I remarked, "This is a lady's chamber and as such will be respected by *gentlemen.*" The leader, a big bluffy Dutchman [the local term for German immigrants], replied, "Yah, yah! If dere be any Dutch gentlemen! Come boys, let's go to town!"

The property was originally purchased in 1751 by Gabriel Jones, a descendant of settlers from Wales. Jones was born in Williamsburg and educated in London. It appears that the property was called Bogota from the time of this original owner; the name is derived from the South American Indian word *bacata*, meaning planted fields. Jones built a house just a few hundred feet south of where Bogota stands now. When Rockingham County was created in 1777, Jones was named deputy attorney for the county; he had earlier served as the head of the Augusta County court. George Washington dined with Jones here when he passed through the area in 1784.

Continue on Route 708 past Bogota until it meets Route 655 (Lawyers Road, named after Gabriel Jones by the locals because it was the route he took on his frequent trips to court in Harrisonburg).

Turn left and continue for about 2 miles to Route 659 (Port Republic Road) and

The Geology of the Massanutten

Past Cross Keys, the tour passes the southern end of the Massanutten Mountain, which divides the Shenandoah Valley for 50 miles from Strasburg south to this point. The Massanutten is geologically quite different from both the Blue Ridge to the east and the Alleghenies to the west. Unlike those mountains, the Massanutten is largely composed of hard, slow-to-erode sandstone, the remnant of a huge sand shoal that lay beneath the ancient Lapetus Sea, which covered the Valley some 430 million years ago.

turn right. Heading north, you'll be passing much of the area where the Battle of Cross Keys took place. Drive for 3 miles (just a short distance past the Mill Creek Church of the Brethren on the left) and turn left at the bottom of a hill on to Route 848 (Artillery Road). This road will take you through the old hamlet of **Cross Keys**. *After 1.7 miles, the road intersects with Route 276. Turn right on to Route 276 North and head toward the village of Cross Keys.*

An old tavern, sadly torn down in 2002, gave Cross Keys its name. A member of the Kemper family, which had owned the house, said the name was taken from an old bookstore in London; the sign above the door probably bore a picture of two keys crossed. The building served as a post office in 1804 and later a store, run by the Rodham Kemper family from 1823 to 1845. It was, like so many homes and buildings in the area, used as a hospital during the Civil War.

The southern end of the Massanutten, known as Peaked Mountain, will soon come into view on the right.

Local legend holds that gold was buried in the side of Peaked Mountain by a wealthy local settler, who returned to Germany. In the early 1800s, treasure hunters tore up the side of the mountain searching for it.

One day, the story goes, a local Irish tailor decided to take advantage of the treasure hunters. The tailor claimed that he had recently traveled to Ohio, where he visited a factory that made spyglasses that could look into the earth. Noticing their lack of success in locating the buried treasure, he offered to return to Ohio and purchase one of these helpful instruments for them—with their money, of course. They pooled their resources and sent the tailor to Ohio. A few months later he returned. He said that he had bought the special spyglass but had lost it, along with most of his possessions, while crossing a swift-running creek. When he offered to go back for another one, the trusting locals once again came up with the required amount. The tailor left the area and was never heard from again.

When you reach the traffic light at the intersection with Port Republic Road, continue straight. About 0.3 mile after the light you will pass Meadow View Farm on the left. This red-brick house with white trim was built by Edward Kemper in 1870. He was not the first to enjoy this picturesque spot. For hundreds of years, Indians traveling through the Valley camped here, as evidenced by the many arrowheads that have been uncovered in the surrounding fields. A house stood on the property as early as 1745. One of the land's early owners, John Stephenson, built a horse-racing track across the road around 1780.

*Continue for about 1.5 miles past Meadow View Farm to **Peales Crossroads**, where Route 276 meets U.S. 33.* The old red-brick house on the right was built by Jonathan Peale in 1844; the Peales acquired the land in 1811, having come here from England by way of Pennsylvania. This home may have been used as headquarters by Stonewall Jackson before the Battle of Cross Keys. Mrs. Peale used to tell stories about entertaining Jackson and his staff during the war; she claimed that she once fed and housed 60 men here. The house was the center of the community's social activities for many years, but by the 1930s it had been converted into a guesthouse. Today, it is a private home.

Turn left on to U.S. 33 West. Although not part of the tour, an old mineral springs resort called **Massanetta Springs** is 1.5 miles down the road (you will see a sign on the left marking the turnoff.) These hot springs were originally owned by the Taylor brothers, Jonathon and William, who bought the land in 1814. The property has been owned by many others since. In 1888, it was purchased by Dr. Burke Chrisman, who owned a mineral water company. He named the springs Massanetta, combining his wife's name, Henrietta, with Massanutten. He bottled the water from the springs and sold it throughout the eastern United States as a cure for various ailments. The water's popularity brought people to the springs, so Chrisman built a small hotel to accommodate them. A later owner built a large brick hotel and turned the grounds into a summer resort. Since 1922, the property has been owned by the Presbyterian Synod of Virginia; it is used as a national Bible conference center.

Continue for about 3 miles on U.S. 33 to I-81 in Harrisonburg, where the tour ends.

The Fort Valley to Page Valley Tour

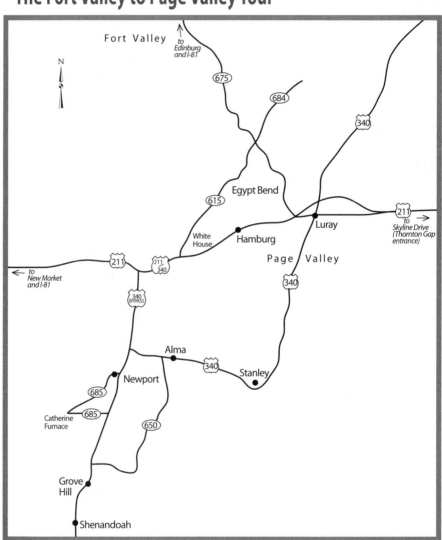

TOUR 9
The Fort Valley to Page Valley Tour

This tour begins by climbing the western range of Massanutten Mountain near Edinburg and then descending into Fort Valley at Kings Crossing. In a few miles, the road traverses the eastern range of the Massanutten and then drops down into Page Valley and the town of Luray.

Page Valley was one of the earliest settled areas in the Shenandoah Valley. Late Woodland Indians lived here around 950 A.D. (as the Paleo-Indians probably did thousands of years earlier). Swiss and German immigrants arrived in the early 1700s. If you've ever stood along the Skyline Drive overlooks near Loft Mountain or Big Meadows and faced west, then you've seen Page Valley. Two of the first Europeans to reach the top of the Blue Ridge and look west did so from near those same spots.

The tour also visits a Civil War site, the ruins of an old iron furnace, and the 1800s industrial town of Shenandoah before ending with a scenic drive along the Shenandoah River's South Fork.

Total mileage: Approximately 60 miles

To begin the tour, take Exit 279 off I-81 and turn on to Route 185 East toward **Edinburg** at the bottom of the ramp. Drive 1 mile to the stop sign at Main Street. Turn left on to U.S. 11 North and go through the town (described in The Edinburg to Singers Glen to Mount Jackson Tour, page 113). Just after you pass the car dealership on the edge of town, turn right on to Route 675 East (Edinburg Gap Road), following the signs toward Kings Crossing, Fort Valley, and Camp Roosevelt.

The road crosses the North Fork of the Shenandoah River and then winds through Edinburg Gap (and George Washington National Forest) over the western ridge of Massanutten Mountain. It soon descends into the southern part of Fort Valley, a scenic and secluded "valley within a valley." (The northern part of this valley is covered in The Strasburg to Fort Valley to Front Royal Tour.) This tour passes through Fort Valley's southern section on the way to yet another valley within the larger Shenandoah Valley—Page Valley, bordered by the Massanutten range on the west and the Blue Ridge on the east.

In almost 6 miles, Route 675 intersects Route 678 (Fort Valley Road) at **Kings**

Crossing. Turn right toward Luray and follow the signs to Camp Roosevelt. The road forks almost immediately after the turn; keep to the left to stay on Route 675, now called Camp Roosevelt Road. In about 3.2 miles, the road meets Moreland Gap Road. Turn left to stay on Route 675. The entrance to Camp Roosevelt is up the road a short distance on the left.

This was the first of 1,500 Civilian Conservation Corps (C.C.C.) camps established in the United States in the 1930s. During the Depression, the federal government created the C.C.C. with two aims in mind: to provide paying jobs for unemployed young men and to restore and conserve dwindling national forest resources. During that decade, the C.C.C. built roads, blazed trails, planted trees, controlled erosion, and developed recreational areas and parks, including Shenandoah National Park. Today at Camp Roosevelt, you can see the foundations of that first C.C.C. camp, which employed 200 men. A campground, a picnic area (with restrooms), and hiking trails are available to visitors.

From Camp Roosevelt, continue on Route 675 as it begins to climb the eastern range of Massanutten Mountain. In about 1.5 miles, you'll reach an overlook on the left with panoramic views of Page Valley below. As the road levels off, you'll reach a stop sign at the intersection where Route 615 (Egypt Bend Road) goes to the right and Route 675 goes to the left. Turn left, then right, continuing on Route 675 across the Bixler's Ferry bridge toward Luray.

The land along the Shenandoah River in Page Valley was one of the earliest settled areas in the Shenandoah Valley. Around 1726 or 1727, Jacob Stover, a Swiss immigrant, was granted several thousand acres here and began to sell tracts to Swiss and German settlers who came from the Lancaster, Pennsylvania, area. Most were Mennonites or Lutherans. Originally known as the Massanutten Patent, this land

Early Settlers Under Attack

For many years, early settlers in the Page Valley faced the prospect of surprise Indian attacks. A tragic tale is told of a man named John Roads (probably originally Roodt, also later spelled Rhodes). Roads was a Swiss Mennonite minister whose family lived peacefully in a log cabin beside a river bend near Luray for more than 30 years. One day in August 1764, a year after the official end of the French and Indian War, eight Indians and "a worthless villain of a white man" (in the words of 19th-century Valley historian Samuel Kercheval) came looking for the family's hidden money.

The attackers shot and killed the reverend and his wife. They also brutally murdered several of the couple's children. One of the family's older daughters grabbed her toddler sister and escaped by running to a neighbor's house. One son was kidnapped by the Indians but managed to return to the Valley about three years later. The attackers couldn't find the money, which was stashed in a cellar wall, so they set the home on fire before they left.

One of the family's grandsons later built a log-and-stone house on the site using some of the charred timbers from the original structure. That home, called Fort Rhodes, survived well into the 20th century, only to burn down several years ago.

grant stretched 10 miles up and down the Shenandoah River from near what is now Luray.

South of the Bixler's Ferry bridge is an area along the river called Egypt Bend. One of the early settlers, Abraham Strickler, called this land Egypt, apparently comparing the settlers' flight to Virginia from religious persecution in Europe and Pennsylvania to the Israelites' flight to Egypt. The surnames of other early settlers—which can still be seen on area mailboxes and businesses—include Miller (Anglicized from Mueller), Long, Kauffman, Burner, Brubaker, and Ruffner. Fort Egypt, built here by Abraham Strickler's son, Jacob, has been carefully restored and still stands near the river off Egypt Bend Road. Unfortunately, that house cannot be easily seen from the road and so is not part of this tour.

After crossing the Bixler's Ferry bridge over the Shenandoah River, you'll enter the outskirts of **Luray**. To the right just across the bridge, a driveway leads to the Old Stone House, also called the Heiston-Strickler House. The house, a private residence, is not visible from the road; it's down Stagecoach Lane, at the end of a gravel drive leading past a poultry farm. Built around 1790 by Jacob Heiston or his son Abraham, it was later owned by Daniel Strickler, a descendant of one of the early settlers. It remained in the Strickler family for many years. Compared to the typical log houses of the time, this stone structure was a substantial and impressive home.

Drive 3 miles, passing over the U.S. 211 bridge, to Lee Street and turn right. Go two blocks to the stop sign; prepare to turn left. Directly across Main Street before you turn is the Mimslyn Inn, a 1931 brick building on 14 acres. The inn has been extensively

Old Stone House

Mimslyn Inn

Aventine Hall

renovated and is once again a gracious small hotel and restaurant.

The Mimslyn is not the first structure to stand on this hill. Aventine Hall was built here in 1852 by Peter Bock Borst, the commonwealth attorney for Page County at the time. During the Civil War, soldiers were housed in Aventine Hall. In the 1920s, it became the main building of Luray College. After the Mimslyn Inn was built in the 1930s, Aventine Hall was taken apart and reassembled a few blocks away, where it stands today.

To see this unusual old home, turn left on to Main Street and go one block. Turn right on to South Court Street. The house is at 143 South Court, on the left past the Page County Courthouse and partially hidden behind an iron gate and a tall white fence. Called one of the purest examples of Greek Revival architecture in Virginia, Aventine Hall was named for one of Rome's seven hills. It was built without nails; every piece of wood in the house was mortised and pinned with pegs. Marble mantels from Italy top the seven fireplaces in the house. It remains a private home and is listed on both the National Register of Historic Places and the Virginia Landmarks Register.

The Page County Courthouse, across the street, was constructed in 1833 by some of the same men who built the University of Virginia for Thomas Jefferson.

Beginning in the late 1700s, area citizens lobbied the Virginia legislature to form a new county. For years, they had to cross Massanutten Mountain (as this tour did, but on roads that were nothing more than rough trails) to get to Woodstock, the county seat of the then-much-larger Shenandoah County. It took a while, but 20 years af-

Page County Courthouse

ter town founders optimistically laid out the town of Luray to serve as the county seat, the assembly agreed, naming the new county for former Virginia governor John Page.

The county administrative building, located directly across the street from the courthouse, was built as Luray High School in 1880 and was one of the early public high schools in Virginia.

No one is sure how the town came to be called Luray. One theory is that the name was derived from an Indian word—Anglicized as Lorrain—for Hawksbill Creek, which runs through the town. Another suggests that the grandfather of one of the town founders, William Staige Marye, came to America from the Lorraine region of France. The most amusing theory is that the town was named after early lot owner Lou Ramey, a well-known blacksmith. But records show that the town had already been named several months before Ramey bought property here. The best thing about this theory is that it explains the local pronunciation of the town's name— "Loo-ray."

Return to Main Street and turn right to pass through the downtown area. Several buildings date to the 1800s. Luray citizens have been working hard to improve the attractiveness of their downtown area in recent years; the addition of the Luray-Hawksbill Greenway walking and wildlife trail entices visitors to get out of their cars and take a stroll along the creek than runs through town. Green herons, black-crowned night-herons, belted kingfishers, downy woodpeckers, pileated woodpeckers, eastern bluebirds, and American goldfinch can be seen along the trail. In the summer, killdeer and tree swallows are often spotted.

Continue east on Main Street. Cross the railroad tracks, go past the large cemetery on the right, and prepare to turn right at the next traffic light. The Barbee Confederate Monument, dedicated in 1898, is ahead and to the right. Well-known sculptor Herbert Barbee was born in Luray, the son of William Randolph Barbee, a famous sculptor of the 1800s. Herbert, following in his father's footsteps, studied art in Florence, Italy. He later established studios in New York, Baltimore, St. Louis, Cincinnati, and Washington, D.C. The soldier depicted in the monument is standing next to a wall made of stone, a symbolic reference to General Stonewall Jackson.

At the light, turn right on to Reservoir Avenue, then make an immediate right turn on to First Street. Continue on First until it intersects Luray Avenue across from Luray High School. Turn right on Luray Avenue. At the stop sign at Amiss Avenue, turn right again. In two blocks, turn left at the stop sign at Cave Street. Turn left again at the next street, Zerkel Street.

The log building to the left of the Page Public Library is a restored one-room schoolhouse. Known as the Massanutten School, it was moved to this location in 1972 and restored by the Page County Heritage Association. It contains 16 original desks, an old cast-iron stove, an 1880 schoolhouse bell, and other historical objects and photos. You can see the town's recently restored railroad station behind the schoolhouse; it houses the town's visitor center. For many years, this train station was a hub of activity as horse-drawn coaches met arriving tourists and took them across town to Luray Caverns.

Luray Singing Tower

Luray schoolhouse

Inn Lawn Park, across the street from the library, was originally the grounds of the massive (153 feet by 160 feet) Luray Inn, constructed in 1883 by the Luray Cave and Hotel Company. It was a grand place, built in the English Tudor style, designed to lodge the hundreds of tourists who came by train to see Luray Caverns. Like so many other Valley hotels of the time, it burned to the ground, in 1891.

Luray's growth as a town took off with the coming of the railroad and the discovery and development of Luray Caverns in the early 1880s. But when an economic depression hit the nation a few years later, the Shenandoah Valley Railroad (which had begun service in 1867 and eventually connected Hagerstown, Maryland, with Roanoke, Virginia) went bankrupt. It was auctioned off in 1890. Its 238 miles of track, 48 locomotives, 29 passenger cars, and 961 freight cars were purchased by the Norfolk and Western Railroad.

Return to Cave Street and turn left; you'll pass Luray's second statue to Confederate soldiers. Turn right at the yield sign, then turn left at the traffic light on to Main Street. As you pass out of the downtown area, Main Street becomes U.S. 211 (Business) West. On the edge of town, you'll see a large stone tower on the right. This is the Luray Singing Tower, which houses a carillon containing 47 bells that are played using a keyboard.

Carillons are popular instruments in Europe, where they originated more than 400 years ago; the bells for the Luray carillon were cast in England. The largest bell weighs more than 7,000 pounds and the smallest just 12.5 pounds. The tower was built as a memorial to Belle Brown Northcott by her husband, T.C. Northcott, and their daughter in 1937. Recitals are given here from spring through fall.

Colonel Northcott was born in Virginia but later moved to Illinois, where he served in the Union army. He bought Luray Caverns in 1900 and moved there. He built a home he called Limeair on the grounds of the caverns. Northcott came up with the idea of cooling the house in summer by blowing in the 54-degree-Fahrenheit air from the caverns. Some say Limeair was the first "air-conditioned" home in America. The house burned down in 1940, and Northcott died at age 97 a year later.

Luray train station

Continue on U.S. 211 (Business) past the tower to the intersection with U.S. 211. To visit the caverns, go straight across U.S. 211; to continue the tour, turn left on to U.S. 211 West.

The caverns were discovered in 1878 by Andrew Campbell, a local tradesman, and Benton Stebbins, a 50-year-old man from Maryland who had recently arrived in Luray seeking a new home for his photography business.

As Russell Gurnee relates in his 1978 book, *Discovery of Luray Caverns, Virginia*, Stebbins had learned about an underground cavern in Cave Hill, on the edge of town. Knowing that the railroad was going to come through Luray, he wondered about the possibility of developing it into a tourist attraction. He became acquainted with Campbell, who felt that the known cave was too small for development. They began to look for a bigger and better cave and after a few weeks of intense searching found the huge underground complex they named Luray Caverns.

They kept their discovery quiet until they could buy the land above the caverns—coincidentally, land that was about to be auctioned by the county to pay the debts of the current owner. Successful in their bid, Stebbins, Campbell, and their partners immediately began illuminating and building trails, floors, and stairs in the caverns, all the while admitting visitors to help finance development. Tourists began arriving in large numbers within the year, thanks to the publicity that began appearing in newspapers and magazines in New York and elsewhere.

Representatives of the Smithsonian Institution visited the caverns in 1880 and included in their report this statement: "It is safe to say there is probably no cave in the world today more completely and profusely decorated with stalactitic and stalagmitic ornamentation than that of Luray." That endorsement soon put Luray on the map.

While the development of Luray Caverns continued, the previous owner of the property, William Biedler, became painfully aware of what he had lost. He brought a lawsuit against Stebbins and Campbell, stating that the sale was fraudulent, since they had prior knowledge of the existence of the caverns.

In 1879, the case came before the county court, which ruled in favor of Stebbins and Campbell. Biedler then appealed to the state supreme court in Richmond, which overturned the lower court's decision two years later, giving the land back to Biedler. Biedler paid his debtors and wasted no time in selling the property to a company that built the Luray Inn.

Stebbins and Campbell were left with nothing for their three years of investment and hard work. Campbell remained at the caverns as a tour guide, but Stebbins moved his family to the nearby town of Stanley, then called Marksville. There, he spent the remaining years of his life futilely attempting to develop an ocher mine (ocher was in demand as an ingredient in paint) and later a copper mine. Both endeavors failed. Stebbins died in Stanley in 1906.

Luray and several other caverns in the Shenandoah Valley proved to be popular tourist attractions throughout the 1900s, thanks first to the railroads and later to automobile travel. In 1921, the number of visitors to Luray Caverns topped 100,000 for the first time. Today, more than 500,000 people a year come to Luray to see the caverns.

From Luray Caverns, continue west on U.S. 211. In 1.6 miles, turn right on to Route 766, just 0.5 mile past the turnoff for the Luray Caverns Airport. You will enter **Hamburg**. Most of this village's early residents were Mennonites from Switzerland and Germany.

On the right a short distance down the road is an old log structure, Mauck Meeting House, originally called Union Church. Built around 1770 by Mennonites from Germany and Switzerland, it has been restored by the Page County Heritage Association and is a National Historic Landmark. The structure was used by Baptists after 1790. A tin roof has replaced the original chestnut shingles. Next to the meeting house is the old Hamburg Grocery; peek in the windows to see what a grocery store looked like in the 1940s.

Across the street from the meeting house is Calendine, a house built around 1840 for Townsend Young, who operated a stagecoach stop and general store here. Calendine was later purchased by William Barbee, the sculptor mentioned earlier, who used the general store as his studio. The structure now houses the Page County

Hamburg Grocery

Mauck Meeting House

Heritage Association Museum (see the appendix entry for more information).

Return to U.S. 211 and turn right. In 1.3 miles, you will see a Virginia Civil War Trails roadside monument in a small parking area on the right. The historical marker commemorates the Shenandoah River bridge and the old structure known as the White House, located to the right of the bridge just beyond the farmhouse. Turn right just before the bridge to get a closer look at the White House.

The bridge across the Shenandoah here has long been called the White House Bridge. General Stonewall Jackson and his army crossed it on May 21, 1862, on their way to Strasburg to try to outflank General Banks's troops. Two days later, Jackson defeated Banks in Front Royal and then turned south to escape the Federal forces pursuing him—General Shields, who was coming from Page Valley, and General Fremont, who was coming from the Valley Pike, to the west.

To prevent the two Union forces from meeting, Jackson ordered Turner Ashby to burn the bridges over the Shenandoah (which at the time was rising because of heavy rainfall) at the White House and at Columbia Mills near Alma, just east of here. The Confederates carried out the burnings early on the morning of June 2. With the bridges gone, Shields's troops were delayed in crossing Massanutten Mountain and uniting with Fremont. As a result, Jackson was able to defeat Shields and

Recycled church steeple, Calendine

Calendine

White House

Fremont in separate battles in early June at Cross Keys and Port Republic (see The Harrisonburg to Port Republic Tour to Peale Crossroads, pages 158 and 160).

Historians believe the White House was built in 1760 as a residence and Mennonite meeting house by Martin Kauffman II, the son of one of the area's first settlers. Both Kauffman and his father were Mennonite ministers. The need for a combination structure apparently arose because of a statute passed by the Virginia Assembly in 1662 that prohibited Quakers (and presumably Mennonites) from assembling. Area Mennonites skirted the issue by worshiping in private homes. Many of the Mennonites in this area became Baptists by the end of the 1700s, largely due to the efforts of the Reverend John Koontz of Front Royal. Martin Kauffman II was one of Koontz's early converts; he became a Baptist minister. One of Kauffman's 10 children, Martin III, later accompanied several members of White House Church to Ohio, where they established a Baptist church in the early 1800s.

Continue driving west. In less than 0.5 mile, look on the right side of the road for a 1929 monument to the early Massanutten settlers. Follow U.S. 211 West for another 2.3 miles, then turn left, toward Stanley and Shenandoah, on to U.S. 340 South. The area along U.S. 340 was another part of the original Massanutten settlement. In later years, this road was known as the New Market and Gordonsville Turnpike, which cut through Fishers Gap to connect eastern and western Virginia in this part of the state.

Continue 4 miles to the village of **Newport***. Turn right on to Route 685 just before Kite's Store.* This road leads through an area of old barns, smokehouses, and springhouses to the once-bustling Catherine Furnace. Kite's Store, a general store, service station, and camp store has stood at this location since 1929 and is a local landmark.

In 2.2 miles, Route 685 curves sharply to the left. To reach Catherine Furnace, veer right to go down the unpaved road marked "Katherine Furnace Road" (a misspelling). In less than 0.5 mile, you'll see the ruins of the furnace to the right, across a low concrete bridge over Cub Run, a scenic trout stream.

The origin of the many iron furnaces near the Shenandoah River can be traced to the ideas of George Washington, who had the river surveyed in the 1780s to determine its suitability for commercial navigation. His plan was to build a gun factory at Harpers Ferry, to which pig iron could be shipped by Shenandoah River flatboats (also called floatboats or gundalows). By 1808, the river was cleared, dredged, and opened to commercial boating. By 1833, when the C&O Canal was completed from Georgetown to Harpers Ferry, the people of the Valley had a cheaper and faster way of getting local products to and from markets in the East. During the mid-1800s, pig iron from Catherine Furnace, Shenandoah Iron Works, and other iron furnaces and forges throughout the Valley was one of many products shipped by river to Harpers Ferry.

Catherine Furnace was built in the 1820s and reached its peak production in the 1850s. It shut down in 1888. The stone furnace that remains on the site was just one part of a large complex of structures and machinery needed to operate the furnace. A bridge connected the top of the furnace to the top of the hillside above it. Workers would dump iron ore (mined less than a mile away), limestone (in plen-

tiful supply throughout the Valley), and charcoal (made by burning timber, also plentiful) into the top of the fiery furnace. The resulting product was large blocks of pig iron, which were then taken to a forge for shaping into nails, horseshoes, tools, kettles, and other products.

In 1836, two sons of an ironmaster from Pennsylvania, Daniel and Henry Forrer, began building a complex of structures called the Shenandoah Iron Works, a few miles up the road from Catherine Furnace. The settlement that grew up around the ironworks later became the town of Shenandoah, the next stop on this tour.

Catherine Furnace, along with two other furnaces built by the Forrers, provided the pig iron for their forge, which produced iron used to make ammunition for the war with Mexico in the 1840s. Two decades later, the ironworks provided iron for Confederate weapons and ammunition during the Civil War.

Return to Route 685 (Newport Road) and turn right. In a little over 1 mile, the road meets U.S. 340 South; turn right again. As you approach the town of **Shenandoah***, which is 4.5 miles away, you will pass through the community of Grove Hill. Shortly after you pass St. Peter's Lutheran Church in Shenandoah, turn right on to Virginia Avenue, following the sign to the business district. At the bottom of the hill, turn left on to First Street.*

The business district sign is a bit of an overstatement today. Although several

Catherine Furnace

nice residential areas surround the town, the "downtown" section of Shenandoah is in transition, with revitalization efforts underway. At its peak in the late 1800s, this community was a major rail and industrial center—and the largest town in Page County. But the town lost its economic base in the 1950s, when rail traffic shrank. To add insult to injury, the business district was devastated by two fires in 2006 and 2007.

In 1866, the Forrers sold their businesses to William Milnes and his partners, who were coal operators from Pennsylvania. In 1870, the growing town and the ironworks had to be rebuilt after a flood wiped out 60 commercial buildings and numerous homes.

Around that same time, Milnes began working with other Valley investors to bring a railroad through the area. When the line, which would eventually reach Roanoke, was finally begun in Hagerstown in 1880, Milnes borrowed money to expand his ironworks and build what he called the Shenandoah Iron, Lumber, Mining, and Manufacturing Company.

The Shenandoah Valley Railroad arrived in town in 1881. The next year, the enormous Gem Furnace was built. The site had 24 boilers and a brick stack rising 100 feet. This furnace—fueled by the more efficient coke—produced over 100 tons of iron a day and employed up to 400 people.

In 1882, the town's name was changed to Milnes; some citizens proudly called it "the Pittsburgh of the Valley." But the town's prosperity was short-lived. The depression of 1884 caused William Milnes's business to go into receivership. By 1885, the Shenandoah Valley Railroad also failed.

The town of Milnes was renamed Shenandoah City in 1890. It began to recover during the boom years of the late 1800s, like so many other towns in the Valley. By that time, the offices of the Shenandoah Land and Improvement Company were bustling, buying up land and selling lots. People were optimistic—one

The town of Shenandoah

Norfolk Southern train station in Shenandoah

citizen predicted that the town would one day have 10,000 residents. But around 1905, the ironworks operation shut down, put out of business by the discovery of far richer iron deposits in Michigan.

The railroad helped keep the town on the map for the next four decades. The yard at Shenandoah was located at the midpoint of the line between Hagerstown and Roanoke. Its engine repair shops and other operations employed more than 400 men during the first half of the 1900s, peaking during World War II. Today, Shenandoah boasts the only working train station (non-passenger) between Hagerstown and Roanoke.

When you reach the end of First Street, turn left on to Maryland Avenue. The unusual-looking house on the left at Second Street is Stevens Cottage, which is listed on the Virginia Landmarks Register and the National Register of Historic Places. It was built in 1890 as offices for the Shenandoah Land and Improvement Company. The architect was William M. Poindexter, who also designed the state library in Richmond. When Shenandoah's boom went bust, the building was sold to two sisters, Mary and Edna Stevens. Mary Stevens was a much-loved schoolteacher here for 50 years; she died at the age of 93 in 1968. The caboose on the property is a

Stevens Cottage

restored Norfolk and Western model from 1917.

*Continue up Maryland Avenue to the traffic light at U.S. 340, turn left, and retrace your route to **Grove Hill**.* Near here is an Indian mound measuring 75 feet long and 20 feet wide, one of many mounds found in Page County. The local farmer who discovered it unearthed 17 bodies that had been placed head to head like spokes in a wheel; tools and other artifacts were also found. The flood of 1870 uncovered between 200 and 300 fire beds near the river, further evidence of an Indian town here.

An 1894 expedition by the Smithsonian Institution found 24 mounds and several town sites in Page County—far more than in any other county it had investigated in the Potomac and James River Valleys.

After you pass through Grove Hill, look for a small sign for Route 650 just before the Shenandoah River bridge. Turn right on to Route 650 (Grove Hill River Road).

This road follows the bends of the South Fork of the Shenandoah River, which is quite wide here, with rapids in places when the water is high. Vacation cottages line the hills above this peaceful tree-lined road. Portions of Shenandoah National Park extend almost to the river in places. Two markers put up by the Virginia Civil War Trails group have been placed along this road. They describe General Jackson's order to burn Red Bridge in late April 1862 to prevent Federal troops from entering the area. A skirmish known as the Battle of Somerville Heights took place here in May 1862.

If you were to climb the mountains on the right side of the road, you would eventually arrive in the vicinity of Big Meadows in Shenandoah National Park. Just south of Big Meadows is Milam Gap. Some historians believe that it was the point where Governor Spotswood's first official expedition across the Blue Ridge descended into the Shenandoah Valley in 1716. Others think that he descended several miles south, at Swift Run Gap, where U.S. 33 crosses the Blue Ridge at Skyline

South Fork of the Shenandoah River

Blue Ridge from the east at Swift Run Gap.)

Alexander Spotswood, the royal governor of the Virginia colony and a proponent of increased westward settlement, organized the trip to claim this unknown area for England. At that time, only a few Europeans had seen the wilderness on the other side of the mountains. The first to do so and record what he saw was John Lederer, a German physician and scholar sent to explore the area in 1669 by Governor William Berkeley. Lederer made three trips to the Blue Ridge and probably (based on his general descriptions) reached Big Meadows and Milam Gap. His last expedition took him to Chester Gap or Manassas Gap, near Front Royal.

Spotswood and 63 men, along with 74 horses, began their trip from Germanna, west of what is now Fredericksburg. When they discovered the Shenandoah River—which they described as wide, deep, and northward flowing—they named it Euphrates. That evening, they set up camp on the riverbank and proceeded to celebrate their successful journey over the mountains. One of the men recorded the raucous evening in his journal:

> The governor buried a bottle with a paper enclosed on which he wrote that he took possession of the place in the name of and for King George the First of England. . . . We had a good dinner, and after it we got the men together and loaded all their arms, and we drank the King's health in champagne, and fired a volley, the Princess's health in Burgundy, and fired a volley, and the rest of the Royal family in claret, and a volley. We drank the Governor's health and fired another volley. We had several sorts of liquors, viz: Virginia red wine and white wine, Irish usquebaugh, brandy shrub, two sorts of rum, champagne, canary, cherry punch, water, cider, etc.

The men of this expedition later became known as the Knights of the Golden Horseshoe. Because of the rocky terrain they had to cross, they needed horseshoes to protect their horses' feet—a practice often not necessary in the soft soil of eastern Virginia. After the expedition, Governor Spotswood gave each man a small

Who Was the First Valley Settler?

No one can be sure which family or families first settled the Shenandoah Valley because no written records have survived—or perhaps were ever made—of their arrival. Historians often point to a German immigrant named Adam Miller (originally Mueller) from the Rhineland town of Schriesheim (near Heidelberg) as the first settler for whom proof can be established. His request for citizenship, dated March 1741, stated that he had lived in the Valley for 15 years, which puts the year of his arrival at 1726 or 1727. Miller lived near what is now Bear Lithia, south of the town of Shenandoah and just north of Elkton. Immigrants apparently arrived in the Luray area about the same time.

The land here was extremely attractive to settlers because it was ready-made for planting—the Indians had long before done the hard work of clearing the fertile Massanutten fields of trees, brush, and rocks.

The People of the Park

Beginning in the mid-1700s, people gradually began settling in the hollows, mountainsides, and ridges of what is now Shenandoah National Park. Some took refuge there to avoid military service for religious reasons during the American Revolution and the Civil War. Others were tenant families who tended cattle for Valley farmers who owned meadowland on top of the mountains.

In the years after the Civil War, life became difficult for these mountain families, and many began to leave. The area had been overlogged and overhunted, and large game was scarce. Families who operated water-powered mills at the base of the mountains were put out of business by steam-powered mills in the 1880s. After that, some residents began to sell tanbark to supply the tanneries in the Valley; others collected and sold bushels of chestnuts. But in the early 1900s, the chestnut blight began killing those grand old trees, and tanneries stopped using tanbark.

When Shenandoah National Park was established in 1935, about 465 families still resided within the park boundaries, and fewer than half owned the property they lived on. In an attempt to resettle these people, the federal government built seven communities outside the park, in which the families could buy farms below cost and with no money down. About 170 families eventually moved to those communities, one of which was Ida, a few miles east of Alma; in 1934, the government built 18 farms there. None of the original Ida families remains, although many of the homes are still there.

Only 43 people were allowed to live out their lives in the park; the last person to do so died in 1979.

horseshoe made of gold and encrusted with jewels. The gifts were inscribed in Latin. "This will enable you to cross the mountains," was written on one side, and "Knights of the Golden Horseshoe" on the other.

Because the mountains were so difficult to cross, settlement from the east was slow for many years. But the route from the north was relatively flat and easy. That is why the Valley came to be inhabited by Swiss, German, and Scotch-Irish immigrants from Pennsylvania. They followed the old Indian route that later developed into the Great Valley Road, one of the many names used for what is now U.S. 11.

Route 650 passes through the hamlet of **Honeyville** *before it ends at U.S. 340 Business just south of* **Alma**. *Turn left at the stop sign on to U.S. 340.*

General Stonewall Jackson's army camped near Alma in June 1862 on the way to fight battles at Cross Keys and Port Republic to the south.

The area above the bridge near Alma was once known as Columbia Mills. In the mid-1800s it was a busy place. Traffic on the river here was bustling by 1868, when the local newspaper reported the following: "During the last week in February, 41 gondola boats passed Columbia Mills in different groups with the following freight: 8 boats with flour, 85 barrels each, 11 with lumber, 80,000 feet, . . . 22 with bloom and pig metal, ten tons each."

Columbia Mills was the site of a family tragedy during the disastrous Shenandoah River flood of 1870. Noah Kite (who operated the mills), his wife, and four of their children were swept away and drowned by some of the worst floodwaters the area has ever experienced.

The tour ends here. Continue on U.S. 340 Business until you see the signs for U.S. 211 (Trucks). Turn right here on to Route 615, which will take you to a stop sign at U.S. 340. Turn right. Drive to the intersection with U.S. 211. To return to I-81, turn left; this will take you across New Market Gap and into the town of New Market in about 6 miles. In New Market, follow the signs to I-81.

To return to Luray and points east, turn right on to U.S. 211.

Walks in the Woods

At the top of Massanutten Mountain, about 12 miles west of Luray on U.S. 211, four interpretive walking trails offer backroads travelers a chance to get out of the car and stretch. The Discovery Way Trail, which begins at the now-closed Lee District (George Washington National Forest) Visitor Center, is quite short—only 0.2 mile—and is wheelchair accessible. The 0.5-mile wildflower trail, which also begins at the center, follows Stonewall Jackson's route over New Market Gap and ends at a picnic area. It is not a level trail.

About 100 yards down U.S. 211 from the closed visitor center (on the right as you drive toward New Market) is Crisman Hollow Road (Forest Road 274, which may not be marked as such but is the only road in the area leading off U.S. 211). This road, which soon becomes unpaved, passes the trailhead for the Storybook Trail in about 1.5 miles. This trail features interpretive signs describing the geology of Massanutten Mountain and is suitable for wheelchairs. A 0.4-mile walk along level paths and boardwalks leads to a cantilevered metal platform offering superb views of Page Valley and the Blue Ridge mountains.

Eight miles farther down Forest Road 274 is the trailhead for the Lions Tale Trail. This 0.5-mile universally accessible loop trail was specially designed for the visually impaired by the Lions Clubs of Virginia. Forest Road 274 ends near Caroline Furnace at Route 675, which is the road you took through Fort Valley near the beginning of this tour. If you turn left on to Route 675, you will eventually reach U.S. 11, south of Mount Jackson.

The Staunton to Steeles Tavern Tour

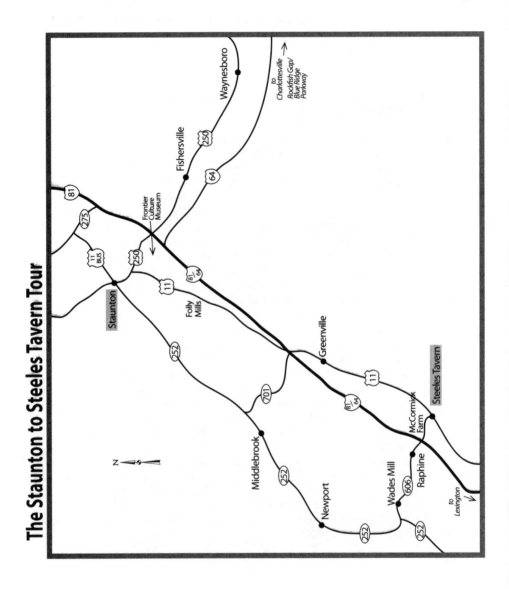

TOUR **10**

The Staunton to Steeles Tavern Tour

This tour begins in Staunton, settled by Scotch-Irish immigrants in the 1730s. Staunton has several attractions of historic interest, including the house where President Woodrow Wilson was born, several old schools and churches, many beautiful old homes, a restored historic wharf and railroad depot, and the Frontier Culture Museum. The tour continues south on historic U.S. 11, the Valley Pike, past a Jefferson-inspired old home, toward Greenville. From there, it heads west and then south down one of the prettiest county roads in the Valley through the 1800s villages of Middlebrook and Newport. It skirts a working gristmill near Raphine before ending near Steeles Tavern at the Cyrus McCormick Farm.

Total mileage: Approximately 70 miles

*The tour begins in **Staunton**. Take Exit 225 off I-81, marked "Woodrow Wilson Parkway/Staunton/Route 262," and veer to the right at the end of the ramp. Follow the signs for the historic downtown district. In 1.3 miles, turn left at the traffic light on to Routes U.S. 11 South/250 East.* Shortly after you turn, notice the large estate on the right side of the road. Hidden by trees, the lovely old home with four tall white columns, which is called Merrifield, is more than 200 years old.

Follow the well-placed tourism signs for about 3.5 miles to Staunton's downtown. At the traffic light at Frederick Street, stay straight. Continue straight through the traffic light at Beverley Street and turn right on to West Johnson Street. In one block, on the left, you'll see a large public parking lot that charges tourist-friendly rates; park here.

Staunton (pronounced "Stanton") is one of the Valley's earliest towns. It was incorporated in 1761 on land that was part of a 1736 grant to William Beverley of Essex County, England, who called the tract Beverley Manor. He built a mill and a house where an 1810 mansion called Kalorama stands today.

Another of the town's fathers was Irish immigrant John Lewis, who moved from Pennsylvania with his family and settled in the area in 1732. Lewis built a house called Bellefonte about 2 miles east of the present downtown area. He had four well-known sons. One of them, Thomas, later became the official surveyor for Augusta County and Rockingham County; in 1747, Thomas Lewis surveyed and platted Staunton. (For more about the patriotic Lewis family, see The Monterey to Hot Springs to Goshen Pass Tour, pages 207–9.)

Augusta County was formed from Orange County in 1738 and named for Princess Augusta, the wife of Frederick, Prince of Wales. Settlers started arriving here in the 1720s; some were of German and English heritage, but most were immigrants or children of immigrants from the Ulster province of Northern Ireland. At the time, Augusta County stretched westward to include parts of what are now Illinois, Indiana, Ohio, Kentucky, western Pennsylvania, and West Virginia. In 1745, the first courthouse was built in the newly designated county seat, Staunton. The town is thought to have been named for Lady Rebecca Staunton, the wife of Royal Governor William Gooch.

By the 1790s, Staunton had grown to a town of 800 people and 200 dwellings. The first volunteer fire department in Virginia was created here in 1790. By the early 1800s, the development of roads in the area helped establish Staunton as a transportation hub. The first graded road in the county was the Staunton and James River Turnpike, which led to Scottsville on the James River south of Charlottesville; completed in 1824, it gave farmers an improved route to markets in the eastern part of the state. The Valley Pike—the macadamized version of the Great Philadelphia Wagon Road and the precursor of today's U.S. 11—connected Staunton to Winchester, 95 miles north, by 1840. Also around that time, construction began on the Staunton-Parkersburg Turnpike—what is now U.S. 250. Finally, the Middlebrook and Brownsburg Turnpike, parts of which followed what is now Route 252, began carrying traffic in 1851. It is traveled later in this tour.

Staunton also became an educational center. Its three schools for women—the Presbyterian-founded Augusta Female Seminary (now called Mary Baldwin College), the Episcopalian Virginia Female Institute (later called Stuart Hall School), and the Methodist Wesleyan Female Institute, which no longer exists—were founded in the 1840s with the goal of truly educating young women, not just serving as finishing schools. Young men came to Staunton to attend Staunton Military

Augusta County Courthouse

STAUNTON
HISTORIC
DISTRICT

1   Woodrow Wilson Presidential
    Library
2   Kalorama
3   American Hotel
4   C&O Train Station
5   Wharf Warehouses
6   Stuart House
7   Trinity Episcopal Church
8   Stonewall Jackson School
9   Stuart Hall School
10 Towne Centre (old YMCA)
11 Mary Baldwin College
12 Augusta County Courthouse

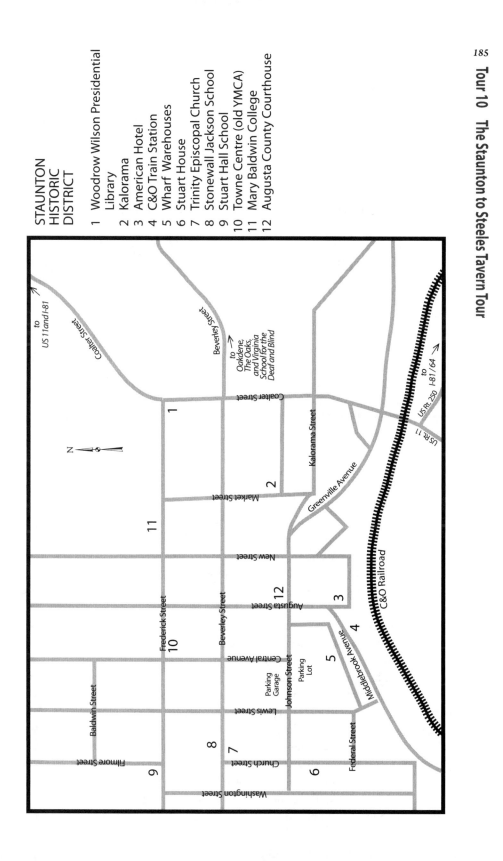

Academy. It was founded here in 1860 but closed in 1976; United States senator and presidential candidate Barry Goldwater was a graduate. Its buildings are now part of Mary Baldwin College.

By the Civil War, Staunton had grown to a town of 4,000 people, 400 houses, and 80 businesses. But when Union major general David Hunter took the town the day after the Union victory at the Battle of Piedmont in 1864, it was the beginning of the end for the Southern cause. While headquartered at the Virginia Hotel (which was located on the site of today's New Street parking garage, next to the Stonewall Jackson Hotel), General Hunter proceeded to destroy everything in Staunton that could help the Confederates, sparing only the area's charitable and educational institutions, private homes, and retail establishments. The railroad station, shops, factories, mills, and foundries were turned to rubble.

The town recovered fairly quickly after the war, however. By the 1870s, a boom began that lasted until the bust of the 1890s. Staunton had streetcars (drawn by mules), an opera house, a YMCA, a public library, a municipal park, and a professional fire department.

Mad Anne Bailey

"Mad Anne" Bailey—whose nickname supposedly reflected her quick temper—came to the Shenandoah Valley from Liverpool, England, as an indentured servant in the mid-1700s. Her happy marriage in Staunton to James Trotter at age 23 came to a sad end nine years later when he was killed by Indians at the Battle of Point Pleasant. Leaving her only child in the care of others, Mad Anne became a scout against the Indians, promising to avenge her husband's death. She scandalized Valley settlers of the time by wearing men's clothes and living the life of a frontiersman. She made good on her promise—legend has it that she "put more than one Indian out of the way."

At the age of 49, she was still at it, saving the day for the besieged Fort Lee in what is now West Virginia. She rode her horse through Indian territory to Fort Union (now Lewisburg) to fetch needed gunpowder, then returned with it to Fort Lee.

For a time, she lived alone in a cabin near Falling Spring, where a plaque honors her memory today (see The Monterey to Hot Springs to Goshen Pass Tour, page 216).

Staunton continued to serve as the commercial center of the Shenandoah Valley well into the mid-20th century. But by the 1950s, the town's dozens of historic buildings began a long decline. In the 1970s, concerned citizens formed the Historic Staunton Foundation, and their extraordinary efforts have turned the town around. In 2002, Staunton won the Great Main Street Award, presented by the National Trust for Historic Preservation.

Today, Staunton's compactness and fascinating mix of architectural styles make it a great town for walking. The National Register of Historic Places has recognized five historic districts in downtown Staunton: The Wharf, Newtown, Stuart Addition, Beverley, and Gospel Hill. A short walking tour is provided in the following paragraphs. For more in-depth information on these areas, pick up the free brochure, "A Self-Guided Tour of Historic Staunton's Historic Districts," at the visitor center at 35 South New Street. The Historic Staunton Foundation offers free one-hour guided walking tours on Saturday mornings at 10 A.M. from June through October. The tours (no reservations required) begin at the Woodrow Wilson Presidential Library at 24 North Coulter Street.

This abbreviated walking tour begins at the historic wharf buildings, which face the public parking lot on Johnson Street. Built after the Civil War and into the early 20th century, most of these former warehouses have been restored to their original appearance and are filled with shops and cafes.

Behind the wharf area is Staunton's restored railroad station. Here, Amtrak provides passenger service (its *Cardinal Line*, which runs from New York City south and then west to Chicago) and freight trains still move through the area. *To get to the station, walk behind the wharf buildings down Augusta Street (located to your left as you face the wharf buildings from the parking lot).*

This is the third railway station at this site. The first small depot, built for the Virginia Central Railroad in 1854, was burned by General Hunter's troops during the Civil War. The present structure was built in 1902 to serve the Chesapeake and Ohio (C&O) Railroad. The restored American Hotel, across the street from the station, has stood since the 1850s. It hosted General Ulysses S. Grant in 1874. The

Woodrow Wilson Presidential Library and Museum

Woodrow Wilson, the nation's 28th president, was born in 1856 in the Greek Revival house at 24 North Coulter Street. His father was the pastor of First Presbyterian Church at the time. The Wilson family had recently moved into this house, which had just been built as the manse for the church. Wilson spent the first two years of his life here, until the family moved to Augusta, Georgia.

Wilson became president in 1912. Following World War I, he helped establish the League of Nations, the forerunner of the United Nations. The Woodrow Wilson Presidential Library and Museum, open daily, offers tours of the house where Wilson was born. The museum, located at 18-24 North Coulter Street, contains Wilson family photographs and possessions, including the president's snazzy Pierce-Arrow limousine.

hotel had shut its doors by the late 1800s; in the early 1900s the building was being used as a warehouse and office space. In the early 21st century, a Staunton architectural firm specializing in historic preservation studied old photos and drawings and came up with a plan to save and restore the building for retail and office use.

Return to the parking area on Johnson Street and turn left, continuing two blocks down Johnson Street to Church Street. Turn left. One of the oldest brick-and-stone homes in Staunton—and one of the first truly large homes in the Shenandoah Valley—is located at 120 Church Street. Built in 1791 by Judge Archibald Stuart, it has remained in the same family for more than 200 years. Known as the Stuart House, it is one of the earliest neo-classical homes in America. The beautiful Chinese Chippendale gates are original to the house. Stuart, son of an Irish immigrant, attended the College of William and Mary, served in the Revolutionary War, and was elected to the Virginia House of Delegates after that war. Judge Stuart was a

Staunton's restored railroad station

friend of Thomas Jefferson, and some think his classically inspired house was in-fluenced by Jefferson's architectural designs. Stuart served as judge of the General Court of Virginia for more than 30 years. The gambrel-roofed structure to the right of the house was built in 1785; it was where Stuart and his family lived while the mansion was under construction.

Turn around and walk one block back up Church Street to Beverley Street to see the historic Trinity Episcopal Church on the right. This 1855 building is the third church on the site. The first was built here in 1763; brick from the first church was used in the keystone of the present building. The church is worth a visit for both its historic value and its twelve stunning Lewis Tiffany stained-glass windows. The Madonna-and-child window was signed by Tiffany himself. The cemetery at Trinity Episcopal has many old tombstones, the oldest of which marks the grave of Roger North, who died in 1776.

The original church building on this site served as the meeting place for the Virginia General Assembly for two weeks in June 1781, after the members fled here

The Frontier Culture Museum

The Frontier Culture Museum is a fascinating outdoor living-history museum consisting of several representative farms that provide a realistic look at the people who settled colonial America. They represent 18th-century Germany, 19th-century Ulster Ireland, 17th-century England, and 18th- and 19th-century America.

The American and European farmhouses are the real thing. They were taken apart in their original locations, shipped to the museum, and rebuilt. The most recent exhibit is a reproduction of an 18th-century West African farmhouse. Costumed interpreters offer demonstra-tions and answer questions about the daily life of the place and period represented by each farm.

The museum is open daily except Thanksgiving, Christmas, and New Year's. The visitor center has exhibits and a 15-minute film. To see the farms, you will follow a self-guided walking tour that takes about two hours. *To get there from downtown Staunton, follow the signs for I-81, I-64, and U.S. 250 East. Continue straight on U.S. 250 East for 1.7 miles. The entrance to the Frontier Culture Museum is on the right.*

Stuart House

Trinity Episcopal Church

The Stonewall Brigade Band

Still going strong today, the Stonewall Brigade Band had its beginnings as the Mountain Sax Horn Band in 1855. It changed its name after five of the band's members served in the Stonewall Brigade during the Civil War.

After the Confederate surrender, General Ulysses S. Grant allowed the band members to keep their instruments rather than turn them over as spoils of war. Indebted to Grant after this kind act, the band later participated in his presidential inaugural parade as well as at the dedication of his tomb in New York City.

Today, Staunton claims that the band is the oldest continuously performing band in the nation. It gives free concerts on Monday evenings from June through August at Gypsy Hill Park, the lovely city park just west of the downtown area.

to escape attack during the Revolutionary War. During the Civil War, the church once again served as a safe haven, this time for the Virginia Theological Seminary, whose students and teachers fled here from Alexandria.

Across Beverley Street from Trinity Episcopal Church is the unusual-looking Stonewall Jackson School. This building housed the city's first public school beginning around 1887; it was remodeled in the Tudor-revival style in the early 1900s. During President-elect Woodrow Wilson's visit to Staunton in 1912, Wilson watched a parade in his honor from a reviewing stand in front of the school. A recent renovation has turned the building into retail and office spaces.

Turn left from Church Street on to Beverley Street. Walk one block on Beverley, then turn right on Washington Street. Walk one block to Frederick Street. Straight ahead is Stuart Hall School's "Old Main." This 1846 building originally housed the Virginia Female Institute. In 1907, the school was renamed to honor its headmistress from 1880 to 1899, Flora Stuart, the widow of Civil War general J.E.B. Stuart. After the war, General Robert E. Lee served on the institute's board of trustees, and his daughters went to school here.

Turn right on Frederick Street and walk three blocks to Augusta Street. The attractive brick building on the corner, now called Towne Centre, was built in 1914 as the town's YMCA and the public library, thanks to a generous donation from the estate of Cyrus McCormick, the local man who became world famous when he invented the mechanical reaper. The building has been renovated and contains of-

Stonewall Jackson School

Old Main, Stuart Hall

Old Staunton YMCA

Mary Baldwin College

fices and condominium lofts. (McCormick's farm is visited later in this tour.)

Continue one block down Frederick Street to see the lovely main building of Mary Baldwin College, at the corner of Frederick and New Streets. This institution had its beginnings as the Augusta Female Seminary, a Presbyterian school, in 1842. An early graduate of the school was Staunton native Mary Julia Baldwin. Miss Baldwin, who came from a well-to-do local family, used her own money to start a free school for the town's poor children. She later became principal at the seminary. In the 1870s, the seminary became independent of the Presbyterian Church. Two years before Baldwin's death in 1897, it was renamed for her.

Turn right on to New Street, cross Beverley Street, and stop in the Staunton Visitor Center at 35 South New Street for more local information. Just across the street from the visitor center is the R.R. Smith Center for History and Art, which houses the offices of three local non-profit groups. Originally the building was the Eakleton Hotel, the finest in the city when it was built in 1895. But when rail travel declined in the mid-1900s, Staunton suffered. The hotel—by then called the Woodrow Wilson Hotel—closed, and the building was turned into a furniture store. When that store shut down in 1989, flocks of pigeons moved in and a long period of decay set in. In 2006, Historic Staunton Foundation used the original architect's plan to restore and renovate the building's interior and its lovely French Second-Empire–style façade.

Return to Beverley Street. Turn right and walk one block to Market Street and turn right. On your right in the middle of the block is the Blackfriars Playhouse, home to the American Shakespeare Center. This theater is the world's only re-creation of London's original Blackfriars Playhouse, the world's first English-speaking indoor theater. Shakespeare has been performed in the Shenandoah Valley for more than twenty years, ever since the founders of the American Shakespeare Center formed a traveling troupe in 1988 called the Shenandoah Shakespeare Express. Today, performances take place year-round in this architecturally accurate reproduction. The audience sits on all four sides of the stage and is often drawn into the action; this is the way Shakespeare liked his plays to be performed. The playhouse offers a backstage tour; check with the Staunton Visitor Center for details. Plans are in the works to build a replica of Shakespeare's Globe Theater nearby.

Just beyond the playhouse is the renovated Stonewall Jackson Hotel. Its old neon sign is a Staunton landmark. Built in 1924, this grand hotel ceased operations in the 1960s. It's said that Amelia Earhart once stayed here. A thorough renovation was completed in 2005.

Across the street from the hotel, at 19 South Market Street, is Kalorama. Mentioned at the beginning of this tour, it is an impressive 1830s building that's been used over the years as a school, a hotel, and the public library.

Blackfriars Playhouse

Stonewall Jackson Hotel

The former Eakleton Hotel

The Oaks   *Oakdene*

Beverley Street's Historic Homes

If you have time, you may want to venture across Coalter Street a few blocks east of Beverley Street's shops and businesses to see some of Staunton's lovely historic homes.

The home at 324 East Beverley, the Thomas J. Michie House, once belonged to the engineer who built bridges for General Stonewall Jackson during the Civil War, Claiborne Rice Mason. The house was probably completed sometime before 1848. Mason was a self-taught engineer who worked on the C&O Railroad before the war. He was legendary for getting jobs done quickly. The story goes that General Jackson once told him that draftsmen were planning to work through the night to draw up plans for a bridge. The next morning, Jackson asked Mason if he had received the plans. Mason supposedly answered, "The bridge is finished. I don't know if the pictures are or not."

The Oaks, at 437 East Beverley, was once owned by Jedediah Hotchkiss, who served as General Jackson's mapmaker. Hotchkiss was a longtime educator who founded Mossy Creek Academy northwest of Staunton in the 1850s (see The Harrisonburg to Mount Solon to Port Republic to Peales Crossroads Tour, page 149). He added the unusual front portion to his house in 1888.

Oakdene, at 605 East Beverley, is an elaborate Victorian home built in 1893 by Virginia's lieutenant governor at the turn of the century, Edward Echols.

Across and just down the street from Oakdene is the Virginia School for the Deaf and Blind, which was established by the state legislature in 1838. The porticoed main building was completed in 1846. This school served as a military hospital during the Civil War; during that period, the students were moved to what is now Stuart Hall School.

Beverley Street

Wright's Dairy-Rite

Backroads travelers of a certain age may want to take a trip back in time by stopping at Wright's Dairy-Rite, just south of Staunton's downtown area on U.S. 11 (Greenville Avenue). Owned by the same family since it opened in 1952 (predating McDonald's hamburger restaurants by three years), Wright's continues to offer drive-in curb service, with treats like made-to-order hamburgers and old-fashioned banana splits. Inside seating is also available, where you place your order using telephones mounted at each table.

As you leave downtown Staunton on the tour, look for Wright's Dairy-Rite on the right, not long after you pass under the railroad bridge on U.S. 11 (Greenville Avenue).

Turn around and walk back to Beverley Street and turn left. This is Staunton's Main Street. After years of renovation and improvement, Beverley Street has been brought back to life with an impressive array of shops and restaurants. The varied architectural styles of many of its buildings deserve a closer look.

Walk along Beverley Street for two blocks and turn left on to Central Avenue. Walk one block to Johnson Street to the parking lot in the wharf area to conclude the walking tour.

To leave downtown Staunton, exit the parking lot and turn right on to Johnson Street. Proceed to the intersection of Commerce Road and Coalter Street. Turn right and stay in the right lane. You are now on U.S. 11 (Greenville Avenue). After passing under the railroad bridge, continue straight on U.S. 11 for about 4.5 miles to Folly Farm.

The old brick buildings you will see on the left just after passing under the railroad bridge once belonged to Western State Hospital, which is now housed in newer facilities nearby. In 1825, this became the second state mental hospital established by Virginia; the first was started in Williamsburg in 1773. The Staunton hospital was one of only five in the United States at the time. The architect was Staunton resident Thomas Blackburn, who had helped build the "academical village"—the University of Virginia—for Thomas Jefferson and who may have studied architecture under Jefferson's guidance.

After Western State Hospital was moved to smaller facilities in the 1970s, the buildings housed the Staunton Correctional Center. A few years after that facility closed in 2003, an ambitious project began to convert the complex's dozen buildings into a residential and commercial complex called "The Villages at Staunton."

When you see the sign for the tiny village called Folly Mills, start to look for a roadside picnic table on the right just down the road. Pull over here to see Folly Farm.

Folly is one of the area's most interesting and little-mentioned old homes. The house sits behind a stand of trees a good distance from the road, but you are able to see the home's historic serpentine brick wall.

Folly was built between 1818 and 1820 by Joseph Smith, who was a planter, a member of the Virginia legislature, and the operator of nearby Folly Mills. The home remained in the same family for several generations. It features a brick serpentine garden wall that "is the only early 19th-century example of this unusual form in the state. Its prototypes, Jefferson's walls at the University of Virginia, have been [re]built at least twice," reads the description of Folly in the Virginia Landmarks Register. The house is also listed in the National Register of Historic Places. The house, built in the Classical Revival style, is similar to those Jefferson designed; it appears that Smith borrowed some of Jefferson's ideas.

Continue south on U.S. 11 for more than 4 miles. Turn right on to Route 701 (Howardsville Road), following the sign for Middlebrook.

This hilly road curves gently through a scenic area seldom traveled by tourists. In 2.2 miles, it passes Bethel Church, on the right. The original Bethel Church, one of the early Presbyterian churches in the area, was built as a result of the efforts of Colonel Robert Doak around 1772. Many of the men who belonged to the Bethel congregation fought in the Revolutionary War. The Bethel Church men were commanded by Captain James Tate—one of the church's elders—in the Battles of Cowpens and Guilford Courthouse in 1781. Twenty-three soldiers from that war are buried in the cemetery here. The present church building was completed in 1888.

The Statler Brothers

The hugely successful country-music singing group known as the Statler Brothers had its start in 1955, when three of the group's four members began singing gospel music in churches in Staunton.

In 1964, the young men began singing backup for Johnny Cash, a gig that lasted for nearly eight years.

After hosting their own cable television show and winning dozens of music industry awards, including induction into both the Country Music Hall of Fame and the Gospel Music Hall of Fame, the group retired in 2002. Three members of the group (only two of whom were brothers) still live in Staunton.

Historic brick wall at Folly Farm

Bethel Church

Bethel Green

Down the road from the church on the left is Bethel Green, a beautiful old red-brick farmhouse listed on the Virginia Landmarks Register. Bethel Green was built on land owned by the first settler in this area, Christian Bumgardner, who arrived in 1772. His grandson, James Bumgardner, a farmer and distillery owner, had this house built in 1857. It is quite striking architecturally, with its unusual Jacobean-style enclosed chimneys and Gothic-style porches.

In about 1.4 miles, you'll reach a stop sign at the intersection with Route 252. Turn left and head 1.4 miles south to **Middlebrook**. Route 252 is one of the prettiest drives in the entire Shenandoah Valley. It passes horse and dairy farms without a hint of civilization to mar the natural beauty of the landscape. This area was settled by Scotch-Irish immigrants in the 1790s.

The village of Middlebrook seems preserved in time. It looks as it must have a century ago, when what is now Route 252 ceased to be a major road from Staunton to Lexington. The entire town has been designated a historic district in the Virginia Landmarks Register, which describes it as "one of the oldest rural villages in the region. . . . The rows of closely spaced dwellings and stores lining the main road maintain the character and scale of the village as it appeared during the height of its prosperity in the 1880s."

About 6.3 miles past Middlebrook, the road passes through another 19th-century village, **Newport**, *and then begins to wind through the hills, following the path of Moffatt's Creek. In 3.9 miles, look to the right for New Providence Presbyterian Church.* This church was established in 1746. Its cemetery contains many interesting old

Waynesboro Side Trip

Waynesboro is about 12 miles east of Staunton on U.S. 250. The town is set against a backdrop of the Blue Ridge Mountains; in fact, the Appalachian Trail runs just above Waynesboro. The settlement was first called Teasville, after an early family, but it took the name of Waynesboro in 1797 in honor of Mad Anthony Wayne, a well-loved Revolutionary War general.

In addition to the Waynesboro Heritage Museum, housed in an old bank building on the corner of Main and Wayne Streets, those interested in area history should visit the Plumb House Museum at 1012 West Main Street, just past Waynesboro High School. This clapboard-over-log home was built around 1804. In 1820, it was purchased by Francis Plumb, a printer from England. It is the oldest wooden building in the city.

Amazingly, it remained in the Plumb family until 1994. It is currently open to visitors Thursdays through Saturdays.

During the Civil War, the Plumb House was in the middle of the Battle of Waynesboro. General Sheridan's Union forces defeated Jubal Early's troops—the last Confederate force left in the Valley—at the town in March 1865, just a month before the war ended. Early was outnumbered, since many of his men had been sent to Petersburg to help General Lee.

If you were to continue east on U.S. 250, you would reach I-64 east of town at Rockfish Gap, the main route over the Blue Ridge to Charlottesville, Richmond, and the Tidewater area. Rockfish Gap also marks the end of Skyline Drive and the beginning of the Blue Ridge Parkway.

headstones. The sign in front of the church notes that this was the birthplace of the Presbyterian synod of Virginia in 1788 and the location of one of the nation's first Sunday schools.

About 0.7 mile after the church, turn left (there's no stop sign) on to Route 606 (Raphine Road). In about 0.5 mile, this road passes historic Wade's Mill (on your left), a restored gristmill that sells its products and kitchen items to the public. The road then winds through the woods; in about 3 miles, it passes one of the Valley's many wineries, Rockbridge Vineyard.

*Continue past the winery to the town of **Raphine**.*

This village was named for the farm of James E.A. Gibbs, who was born near

A historic home in Middlebrook

New Providence Presbyterian Church

Wade's Mill

here. In 1856, Gibbs invented the chain-stitch sewing machine. Unlike the lock-stitch machine invented by Elias Howe, Gibbs's machine used only a single thread, which he believed created a stronger stitch. He went into partnership with a Philadelphia businessman named James Wilcox, who improved the machine and named it the Wilcox-Gibbs. Wilcox began to manufacture and sell the machine in 1859.

When the Civil War began two years later, Gibbs became an active supporter of the Confederate cause and paid little attention to his business venture up north. After the war, he found himself short of funds, so he returned to Philadelphia to see how Wilcox was doing. The story goes that Wilcox gave him $10,000—Gibbs's share of the earnings to that time, a huge sum in those days. One Rockbridge County historian reported that more than a million Wilcox-Gibbs sewing machines had been sold by the early 1900s.

After receiving his money, Gibbs returned to the Shenandoah Valley and improved his home, which he called Raphine, from the Greek word *raphis,* meaning "needle." A self-educated man, he used the money to build an impressive library and travel all over the world.

Leaving Raphine, mentally prepare yourself for a blast of reality as you approach the truck stops surrounding the I-81 exit just ahead. Continue straight under I-81, staying on Route 606 East toward Steeles Tavern. In less than 0.5 mile, look for a sign on the left for the McCormick Farm; it says "Virginia Tech Shenandoah Valley Agricultural Research and Extension Center, McCormick Farm." Turn left at this sign on to McCormick Farm Road. Drive past the old house and the farm buildings to the parking lot behind the restored farm buildings.

Cyrus Hall McCormick was born in 1809. He grew up in the brick house on this property, called Walnut Grove. The house is now used as offices by Virginia Tech. Cyrus's father, Robert, tried for years to invent an automatic reaping machine but never succeeded. Cyrus picked up the challenge as a young man. Working in a shop on the farm, he developed a prototype that he first publicly demonstrated— rather unsuccessfully—on a farm near Steeles Tavern, just up the road, in 1831.

In those days, farmers everywhere were still harvesting wheat and other grains using scythes and sickles, centuries-old tools. It was time-consuming, backbreaking work. The reaper that McCormick developed could cut and stack crops five

McCormick Farm

times faster, a huge improvement that made large-scale farming possible. Most historians agree that the full potential of the American Midwest—which was being settled at the time—could not have been realized without McCormick's "Virginia Reaper."

His first attempts to sell the reaper were discouraging. The biggest demand was from farms farther west—meaning across the Alleghenies—which made shipping the large machines a huge problem. In 1848, he decided to relocate his business to Chicago, then just a small town. McCormick proved to be a creative businessman. He was one of the first to extend credit to farmers and to use advertising to spread the word about his product. His company eventually grew to become International Harvester.

News of his labor-saving device spread throughout the world. McCormick's reaper won top honors at the Crystal Palace Exhibition in London in 1851; he was later awarded France's Legion of Honor and received similar recognition from the emperor of Austria. He was even elected to the French Academy. Historians cite the reaper as being important in providing Union troops with a supply of wheat from the Midwest during the Civil War. But in a broader sense, the reaper represented the first real breakthrough in agriculture since its beginnings 10,000 years ago. Ultimately, it freed millions of people from working on farms and allowed business and industry to develop at a more rapid pace.

McCormick Farm is a National Historic Landmark. Three buildings are open for view—the original blacksmith's shop, which houses a museum containing scale models of McCormick's reapers and audio recordings describing his life and inventions; a gristmill; and the manor house, all dating back to McCormick's days here. The farm is open daily; picnic tables and restrooms are available.

*The tour ends here. Return to Route 606 and turn right to reach Exit 205 off I-81; **or** you can turn left onto Route 606 and drive 1 mile to U.S. 11 and the village of Steeles Tavern. From here, turn left to return to Staunton, about 20 miles south.*

The Monterey to Hot Springs to Goshen Pass Tour

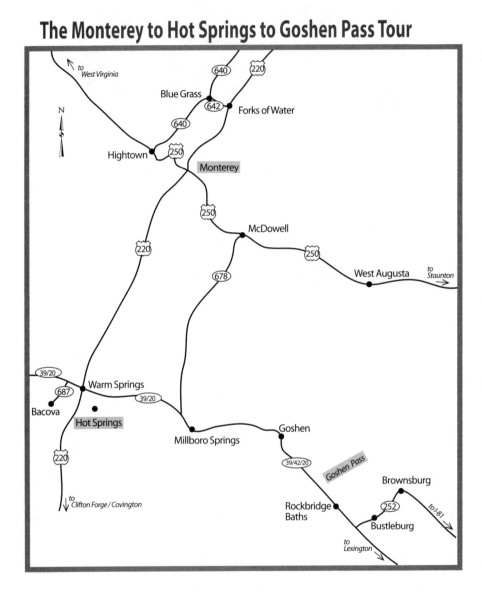

TOUR 11
The Monterey to Hot Springs to Goshen Pass Tour

This tour ventures into some of the most rugged and sparsely populated areas of the Shenandoah Valley. It is concentrated in two western counties—Highland and Bath. Bath County, home of famous mineral springs resorts, including the Homestead, has not a single traffic light—not even a blinking one, as its chamber of commerce proudly asserts. And Highland County is the least populous county east of the Mississippi, having many more sheep than people. The tour ends north of Lexington after passing through the dramatic mountain gorge called Goshen Pass.

Although lengthy in mileage, the tour can be completed in a day. For travelers who want to spend additional time enjoying this mountainous and remote part of the Valley, several side trips to nature preserves and recreation areas are included. For longer stays, this tour combines nicely with both The Staunton to Steeles Tavern Tour and The Natural Bridge to Lexington Tour.

Total mileage: Approximately 140 miles

The tour begins at Exit 225 off I-81 at **Staunton***, marked "Route 262 South/ Woodrow Wilson Parkway/Monterey." At the end of the exit ramp, go straight on Route 262 South. After 4.8 miles, turn right on to U.S. 250 (Churchville Avenue) toward Monterey. You'll be following U.S. 250 all the way to Monterey.*

Continue on U.S. 250 West. It is about 4.5 miles to the town of Churchville, then less than 2 miles to Lone Fountain. About 3.4 miles after passing Lone Fountain, the road enters George Washington National Forest and starts to climb over Jennings Gap. In another mile, look for the historic Buckhorn Inn on the right. This building was once the well-known Buckhorn Tavern, known even earlier as the Dudley House. It dates to around 1811 and was a popular stop for visitors heading to the mineral springs resorts in Bath County.

Two of the tavern's guests in 1854 were Thomas J. Jackson, a professor at the Virginia Military Institute in Lexington, and his first wife, Elinor. Eight years later, Jackson passed by the Buckhorn Tavern again, but this time he was known as

General Stonewall Jackson. He was leading his Confederate troops toward Mount Solon after their victory at the Battle of McDowell (described later in this tour). During the Civil War, the Buckhorn became a makeshift hospital; it later reopened as a tavern. Today, 200 years after it began, the Buckhorn Inn still offers lodging to travelers.

U.S. 250, which was originally the Staunton-Parkersburg Turnpike, was built in the 1840s to connect the Shenandoah Valley with the Ohio River. Claudius Crozet, a civil engineer from France (he had served in Napoleon's army), revised earlier plans for the 220-mile toll road, not an easy task in such mountainous terrain. Crozet had come to the United States in 1816 to teach at West Point. By 1823, he had been appointed Virginia's chief civil engineer. He later helped found Virginia Military Institute, where he also taught. Crozet was the mastermind behind the first railroad through the Blue Ridge, at Rockfish Gap, an engineering feat that involved carving several tunnels through the mountains.

It is about 3.5 miles from the Buckhorn Inn to the hamlet of West Augusta. About 4 miles past West Augusta, you'll see Mountain House Recreation Area on the right. This is an entrance point to one of the most popular hiking and nature areas in this part of the Valley—Ramsey's Draft Wilderness Area. This preserve encompasses 6,500 acres, most of which is old-growth forest, a rarity in the eastern United States. Trails pass through dense, dark woods here, giving hikers an idea of what the eastern forests must have looked like before the European settlers arrived. Not long ago, Ramsey's Draft was also known for its stands of virgin hemlocks, some of which were 500 years old. What's left of these ancient beauties can be seen about 4 miles into a 6-mile trail that runs to the peak of Hardscrabble Knob, which measures 4,282 feet in elevation. As is happening all over the Appalachians, the woolly adelgid insect has been destroying these lovely trees. The dead trees you see near the road in this area were mostly hemlocks. It's been estimated that 90 percent of Virginia's hemlocks have been lost.

Two miles after passing the recreation area, the road begins to climb Shenandoah Mountain (3,760 feet). The scenic overlook at the top of the mountain is worth a stop to take panoramic pictures of the Alleghenies in the distance and visit the Confederate breastworks and the ruins of Fort Edward Johnson. General Edward "Allegheny Ed" Johnson and his men built these fortifications in 1862 to

Feisty Frontier Women

Shenandoah Valley history is full of stories—perhaps embroidered over the years, perhaps not—of tough times and tough women. One of these stories describes a surprise Indian attack on a farmer as he worked outside his log cabin near Fort Lewis in the 1750s. As he ran for the safety of his home, a flying tomahawk struck his head. His wife pulled him into the house and put him to bed.

When the attacking Indians tried to enter the cabin, the woman bolted the door and threatened them with a gun. Like the wolf in the story of the three little pigs, the Indians decided to come down the chimney. The woman quickly pulled the straw mattress from beneath her husband and threw it on the smoldering fire. The resulting clouds of smoke confused the Indians in their descent, whereupon the brave woman—the story goes—tomahawked them as they fell to the floor.

discourage Union troops from invading the Shenandoah Valley from the west. A short loop trail—at points steep and rocky—takes visitors to the ruins; interpretive signs along the path tell the story of the Civil War in this area.

From here the road descends into Highland County. It crosses the Cowpasture River and then climbs once more, this time up to Bullpasture Mountain (3,240 feet). These names were already in use when the first deeds were applied for in the 1720s, and no one is sure of their origin. One story says that when drovers brought their cattle to the mountains for summer grazing, the calves needed to stop and rest at what was called the Calfpasture. The cows could make it to the Cowpasture before stopping, and the bulls could go nonstop to the Bullpasture River. But it seems unlikely that any living thing could make it over two mountains to the Bullpasture River without resting. A more plausible theory suggests that the bulls, cows, and calves referred to in the names were actually the woodland buffalo living in the area.

From Bullpasture Mountain the road quickly drops into a valley, passing stunning vistas on one side and snug cabins in the forest on the other. Called "Virginia's Switzerland" by the local chamber of commerce, Highland County was formed in 1847 after the Staunton-Parkersburg Turnpike opened up the area. But even today, the highway has not spoiled what is still mostly farmland and wilderness.

The area's remoteness attracts lovers of outdoor activities. Three of the state's best trout-fishing rivers are in Highland County: the Cowpasture, the Bullpasture, and the Jackson. Three major Virginia rivers have their headwaters here: the James, the Jackson, and the south branch of the Potomac. Numerous hiking trails cross scenic mountain streams in the George Washington National Forest, which stretches across much of the county. Free pamphlets published by Virginia's Department of Conservation and Recreation describe wildflower and birding trails in the Western Highlands region. These pamphlets are available at local shops.

The view to the west from Shenandoah Mountain

It is hard to believe that a county of less than 2,500 people is just a morning's drive from the major population centers of the mid-Atlantic region. More people lived in Highland County in the 1800s (about 4,000) than do today. Highland County also has the highest mean elevation of any county east of the Mississippi River. There is no industry to speak of. The main enterprise here is cattle and sheep production, with a little maple syrup on the side.

The population grows dramatically for two weekends in mid-March, when Highland County's Maple Festival, held since 1958, draws visitors to watch maple syrup being made at the area's several sugar camps. Visitors feast on maple doughnuts (be prepared to wait in line for these) and pancake breakfasts. The same trees that are tapped for syrup in the spring provide a blaze of yellow, red, and orange in mid-October, when the county holds its Hands and Harvest Festival.

Continue on U.S. 250 West to **McDowell** *on the Bullpasture River, after descending Bullpasture Mountain.* This valley was settled around 1727, but the first land deeds were not recorded until the mid-1740s. In 1757, when the French and Indian War threatened area residents, the settlers built the 80-foot-square Fort George (no longer standing) on the Bullpasture River about 6 miles south of here on Route 678. It was never attacked by Indians, although a few arrows were shot in its direction.

As you enter McDowell, you'll see a red-brick Presbyterian church. Follow the Bullpasture River Road to the left of the church past an old school building that now houses the Stonewall Ruritan Club. The large field on your left is where the Battle of McDowell took place on May 8 and 9, 1862. After consulting with Robert E. Lee, General Stonewall Jackson received reinforcements to try to keep the Union forces of Generals Fremont and Banks from joining up and threatening the Valley.

This battle, the second in the Valley Campaign, came after Jackson's only battlefield defeat, at Kernstown (near Winchester) in late March. Jackson left General Ewell behind in Elkton (then called Conrad's Store) and took his men to Staunton on a roundabout route to try to fool Union spies. There, he joined up with Johnson's troops. They crossed the mountains on May 5 and headed to McDowell the next day. General Milroy and about 6,000 Union soldiers—a smaller force than the Confederates—took the offensive, but Jackson prevailed, ultimately chasing Milroy across the mountains toward Franklin, West Virginia.

Turn around, return to U.S. 250 West, and turn left to continue into McDowell. The town was named in 1860 for a governor of Virginia who often visited the area; its earlier names were Crab Run and Sugar Tree Grove. Early settlers were primarily Scotch-Irish, English, and German. Two places of interest to visitors, both located a block off the highway to the right, are the Sugar Tree Country Store (where you can buy maple syrup and other local products) and the Highland Museum and Heritage Center. The heritage center occupies an 1851 brick house that served as a stagecoach stop and a hotel. It also served as a hospital during the battle here. It is generally open afternoons from Thursday (Friday in winter months) to Sunday; call to confirm (see appendix). The heritage center contains a large exhibit and shows a documentary film about the Battle of McDowell. It displays local artifacts and antiques reflecting the area's past.

Highland Museum and Heritage Center

Continue about 9 miles down U.S. 250 to **Monterey**. There was only one cabin here when Monterey was named the county seat of newly created Highland County in 1847; that cabin was promptly made the temporary courthouse. The town was named after Monterrey, Mexico, the site of a famous victory by General Zachary Taylor in 1846. A popular hero of the Mexican War, Taylor was elected U.S. president in 1848. How the name lost an *r* is not known.

The town's population virtually exploded to 313 by 1861; today's citizens number fewer than 200. In the years after the Civil War, Monterey began to draw summer visitors seeking relief from city heat. By the early 1900s, it had three hotels.

One of those hotels is still popular with city people today—the Highland Inn, a two-story white frame Victorian structure with long porches on both levels.

The town of Monterey

Highland Inn

H&H Cash Store

You'll see it on your right as you enter town on Main Street. It was built in 1904 and has gone through a few renovations since. The inn offers a restaurant and 17 guest rooms.

Monterey is a great place to stop and have lunch in one of several cafes and to do a little shopping for high-quality local arts and crafts. Many of the shops carry a free walking-tour pamphlet that tells the history of the town's homes and buildings. The old Peterson's Store, still the town's general store but now called the H&H Cash Store (at the corner of Main and Spruce Streets) is a lingering reminder of how people used to shop.

The Landmark House—the cabin that served as the county's temporary courthouse—is still standing on Main Street. The building also served as the village tavern.

Across the street from the Landmark House is the county courthouse. The first courthouse here burned down in 1947.

From the flashing traffic light at the town's main intersection, turn south on to Route 220, heading toward Warm Springs. In 0.3 mile, look on the left for the old log cabin, which houses the Highland Maple Museum. This open-air structure explains how maple syrup is made.

Across the road from the museum is a large hill known as Trimble Knob, one of two extinct volcanoes in Virginia (the other is Mole Hill near Dayton, mentioned

Highland County Courthouse

Highland Maple Museum

in The Harrisonburg to Port Republic to Peales Crossroads Tour). Trimble Knob blew its top about 35 million years ago, making it one of the youngest volcanoes in eastern North America.

*It's about a 40-minute drive on a good road through pastoral countryside to **Warm Springs**, the next stop on the tour.* Warm Springs is the seat of Bath County, which was formed in 1790 by dividing Augusta, Greenbrier, and Botetourt Counties. Named for its numerous mineral springs baths—the major economic force here since the mid-1700s—Bath County has just 5,000 residents.

Today, only one of the many large-scale springs resort hotels that once prospered here still operates in a big way—the Homestead in Hot Springs, just 5 miles down the road from Warm Springs. (The other *grande dame* of area resorts, the Greenbrier—originally called White Sulphur Springs—is across the state line in West Virginia.)

Although many of the area's early residents played key roles in the Valley's beginnings and the nation's history, they fought their military battles elsewhere; no Revolutionary War or Civil War conflicts took place in Bath County. Even today, almost 90 percent of the county is forested; more than half its land lies within the George Washington National Forest.

The first person to own land here was John Lewis, who is considered the founder of Staunton. (See The Staunton to Steeles Tavern Tour, page 183.) It is thought that his grandfather was a French Protestant who fled to Ireland in the

Trimble Knob

A Bath County road

1600s to escape religious persecution. John Lewis came to America from Ireland in 1729, the story goes, not for religious freedom but to avoid arrest on a murder charge. Fifty years old at the time, he left Ireland in a hurry because he had killed his landlord in self-defense in a dispute about subleasing farmland. His tombstone reads that he murdered his "Irish lord."

Lewis's Scottish-born wife, Margaret Lynn, and their children joined him in Lancaster County, Pennsylvania, three years later. Lewis then heard about the promise of fertile land in the Shenandoah Valley. In 1732, the family began their journey south.

Blue Grass Valley Side Trip

Lovers of wildlife who have extra time to spend in this area's mountainous terrain might consider this scenic loop out of Monterey through the unspoiled landscape of the Blue Grass Valley. *Drive west on U.S. 250 out of Monterey and turn right at the intersection of Route 640 in Hightown. Follow Route 640 to Blue Grass, then take Route 642 to Forks of the Water. From there, follow U.S. 220 South to return to Monterey.*

Lewis bought about 2,000 acres in Augusta County and built his home, Bellefonte, near what is now Staunton. He was a leader in that county's affairs in the early days. After he died in 1761, his four sons—Thomas, Andrew, William, and Charles—continued to play important roles in shaping the history of the Shenandoah Valley.

Thomas Lewis, the oldest son, was a surveyor. With Peter Jefferson (the president's father), he created some of the early maps of Virginia. The two men surveyed the Fairfax Line, an important task because it determined the southern reaches of Lord Fairfax's massive landholdings. In the late 1730s, Thomas, his brother Andrew, and three men in eastern Virginia were granted 30,000 acres to survey and sell in the Cowpasture Valley, most of which lies in what is now Bath County. Thomas Lewis went on to become Augusta County's first official surveyor and one of its original magistrates. He later became an important figure in Rockingham County and built a home, Lynnwood, that still stands near Port Republic (see The Harrisonburg to Port Republic Tour, pages 160–61).

Andrew Lewis was also a surveyor. In the process of surveying Bath County, he selected for himself the land that included Hot Springs and Warm Springs. For a while, he served in the Virginia House of Burgesses, representing the newly created Botetourt County, but he soon became involved in fighting Indians. In 1774, he led the American forces to victory at the Battle of Point Pleasant, considered by

Laurel Fork Side Trip

Laurel Fork is a remote 10,000-acre special management area overseen by the U.S. Forest Service. It contains a variety of plants and wildlife not usually found in Virginia, including 25 species that occur in the state only in this preserve. The wildflowers here are especially beautiful and profuse.

To reach Laurel Fork, take U.S. 250 West from Monterey into West Virginia to its intersection with West Virginia Route 28. Turn north (right) on Route 28 and proceed about 6 miles to FDR 106 and the signs for the Locust Springs Recreation Area. Follow the signs for parking access.

One of the Laurel Fork's 13 blazed trails, Buck Run, features cranberry bogs similar to those seen in Canada, as well as several beaver ponds. Most of the 28 miles of hiking trails run along the railroad tramlines loggers once used.

This area was the scene of intensive logging operations until the Forest Service purchased the land in 1922. The hardwood forests at Laurel Fork reach elevations of 4,000 feet and consist primarily of birch, cherry, maple, and beech.

Camping and picnic areas are available at Locust Springs Recreation Area in the northern part of Laurel Fork. Contact the Warm Springs Ranger District for more information; see the appendix.

some historians to be the first battle of the American Revolution. Later, during the Revolution, he was credited with driving the despised Lord Dunmore—Virginia's royal governor—out to sea.

The third Lewis brother, William, developed a tract of land in the Sweet Springs area (south of Covington) beginning in 1792.

The fourth and youngest brother, Charles—the only Lewis son born in America—became a captain in the Virginia militia and gained a reputation as a brave and effective Indian fighter. In 1762, he and his wife built a home and farmed a large tract along the Cowpasture River, where a small stockaded fort that Charles had commanded in the 1750s stood. They called their home Fort Lewis. It was located about 7 miles east of U.S. 220, about halfway between Monterey and Warm Springs. In a family tragedy, Charles was killed during the opening shots of the Battle of Point Pleasant, while serving under the command of his older brother Andrew; he was 38 years old.

Williamsville Gorge Side Trip

Nature lovers may want to consider visiting Highland Wildlife Management Area south of McDowell. *From Route 250, turn left on Route 678 (Bullpasture River Road) as you enter McDowell. This 11.5-mile scenic road heads through Williamsville Gorge, passing Fort George along the way.*

Picnic areas are available at the wildlife management area; fishing and camping are also offered. A swinging suspension bridge lets visitors cross the Bullpasture River the old-fashioned way.

For other scenic drives in Highland County, pick up a free brochure, "Discover Highland County Scenic Driving Tour" available at area shops or from the Highland County Chamber of Commerce at www.highlandcounty.org.

In those dangerous early days, many Valley homes were designed as "forts" for area residents. A house could serve as a fort if, for example, it had few or no windows, had slits cut into its cellar walls through which rifles could be fired, had only one door, and was built near or over springs to guarantee a water supply in case of an extended attack. But stockaded forts were even more effective, since they allowed the settlers to defend themselves from all sides. Indians rarely attacked stockades. Instead, they camped around the fort and prevented supplies from reaching the occupants in an attempt to starve them out.

Slow down as you enter Warm Springs, just past the intersection with Route 39. On the right just beyond the intersection are the Warm Springs Baths, today called the Jefferson Pools. They are owned by the Homestead Resort, down the road in Hot Springs. The general public may "take the waters" here from noon to 5 P.M. daily for a fee. The pools are segregated by sex, and swimwear is optional during adult soaking hours.

It appears that the Indians who traveled through this area knew about these springs and used them for many years. Here is what one European visitor had to say about them in 1750: "We visited the hot springs and found six invalids there. The spring is very clear and warmer than new milk." By the 1760s, when the area was relatively safe from Indian attack, well-to-do families from eastern Virginia began spending the summer in the cool mountains of the Shenandoah Valley.

The bathhouses at Warm Springs are as old, if not older, than they look. The women's bathhouse was built in 1836. It's 50 feet across and can hold 60,000 gallons of 96-degree water. The men's building dates to 1761, making it one of the oldest spa buildings in existence anywhere; it is smaller, at 40 feet in diameter.

Thomas Jefferson wrote about Warm Springs and Hot Springs in his only book, *Notes on the State of Virginia*, published in 1787:

> The Warm spring issues with a very bold stream, sufficient to work a grist-mill, and to keep the waters of its bason . . . at the vital warmth, viz. 96 degrees of Fahrenheit's thermometer. . . . The Hot spring is about six miles from the Warm, is much smaller, and has been so hot as to have boiled an egg. Some believed its degree of heat to be lessened. It raises the mercury in Fahrenheit's thermometer to 112 degrees. . . . It sometimes relieves where the Warm spring fails. . . . These waters are very much resorted to in spite of a total want of accommodation for the sick.

Jefferson enjoyed coming here in his later years. In 1818, at the age of 75, he stayed for three weeks, taking three baths a day—much to his later regret. In a letter to General James Breckenridge that accompanied Jefferson's architectural drawings of the Botetourt County Courthouse, he mentioned that "the use of the waters of the Warm Springs began to affect me unfavorably. [My] sufferings, aggravated by the torment of the journey home over rocks and mountains I had to pass, had reduced me to the lowest state of exhaustion by the time I got back."

Across the street from the bathhouses is the Warm Springs Inn. The original Warm Springs resort buildings—a two-story hotel, cottages, and stables—stood

on these grounds. The main building of the present inn served as the county's first courthouse from 1792 until 1907; an annex to that building housed the jail and the sheriff's residence.

This area, dominated by the springs, was the center of social and political life in Bath County for more than a century. The original hotel, bought by the Homestead Resort in the 1890s, closed in 1924, but the springs remained open, and several smaller lodging places sprung up to accommodate summer guests.

To get to Warm Springs, visitors had to endure a long ride by stagecoach over rough, steep roads—imagine today's Routes 39 and 220 as unpaved nightmares, especially after a heavy rain. In *The Springs of Virginia, 1775–1900*, Perceval Reniers described the final leg of the journey: "Standing on his high-pillared portico, Colonel John Fry, the happy landlord of the Warm, could see each stagecoach as it appeared in the gap of the mountain up on the sky line. It stopped there to rest the horses, pay toll at the gate, and let the passengers get the view. Then it tipped its weight toward the valley, and with one wheel chain-locked raced down the dizzy, zig-zag mile until it pulled up at Colonel Fry's feet, every passenger dithering from fright."

Reniers wrote that Fry would see his guests off on their traditional tour of the other springs resorts with his favorite bad joke: "Go, said he, and get well charged at the White Sulphur, well salted at the Salt, well sweetened at the Sweet, well boiled at the Hot and then let them return to him and he would Fry them."

After the Civil War, General Robert E. Lee and his wife were frequent guests at the Warm Springs resort. At the time, the Lees lived in Lexington, where the general

Warm Springs Inn

served as president of Washington College (now Washington and Lee University). Their last surviving child, Mary Custis Lee, who was a great-granddaughter of Martha Washington, also came here but was a more frequent guest at the Homestead, where she died in 1918.

From the Jefferson Pools, continue on U.S. 220 past the green-and-white buildings of the Old Dairy on the left; then just past a sharp curve, look for a driveway to the left with a sign for Three Hills Inn. This inn began as the mansion of Mary Johnston, a well-known novelist in her day. It offers a beautiful view of the mountains from its front gardens. When Johnston's writing career began to falter—probably because of her outspoken views on women's rights—she had to start taking paying guests to pay the bills. After her death in 1936, one of her sisters ran the inn for several years.

Continue 0.1 mile past the Three Hills Inn and turn right on to Route 619, following the signs to the Warm Springs Courthouse. While the Warm Springs resort thrived in the 1800s, the nearby village of Germantown (thought to be settled by former Hessian prisoners of war who remained in America after fighting as mercenaries for the British during the Revolution) was becoming a sort of suburb to the springs. It had a mill, a tavern, stores, and a few log homes.

Old Dairy

Three Hills Inn

Bacova/Hidden Valley Side Trips

If time permits, you may want to take a short drive to see the old company town of Bacova and Hidden Valley Recreation Area, located along the Jackson River.

*From Route 39 west of Warm Springs, turn left on to Route 687 to reach **Bacova**, in about 1 mile.* This community began as a company town for a logging company in the early 1900s. The company ceased operations here in 1931. In the 1940s, the owners sold the town to private investors, giving its forestland (or what was left of it) to the U.S. Forest Service.

Malcolm Hirsh spent his childhood summers nearby. In 1957, he bought the town and began restoring the 42 employee cottages and other buildings. By 1965, he began a cottage industry called Bacova Guild, which produced household items—mailboxes in particular—made of laminated fiberglass and featuring wildlife scenes. (As you drive through Bath County, you may see these mailboxes at the ends of rural driveways.) Hirsh sold the company in 1981. The name Bacova, by the way, was derived from letters in BAth COunty VirginiA. Today, the Bacova Guild still makes rugs and floor mats at its

Warwickton Mansion

plant in Low Moor, near Covington.

*The road to **Hidden Valley Recreation Area**—Route 621—is to the right off Route 39 West just past the Route 687 cutoff to Bacova. After 1 mile, turn left at the sign for Hidden Valley, then drive another 1.5 miles. Turn right when you see the entrance sign to Hidden Valley Recreation Area and follow a dirt road to the picnic area. Then turn left and go over a bridge to see the mansion* where the 1992 film Sommersby, starring Jodie Foster and Richard Gere as a couple in the years after the Civil War, was filmed. This historic 1851 home, Warwickton Mansion, now operates as the Hidden Valley Bed and Breakfast. The house is owned by the Forest Service but is leased to the inn's operators on a long-term basis.

Today, that pretty mountain town is Warm Springs. The mill has been restored and is now a restaurant and inn, the classically designed old bank building is the town's library, and the "new" courthouse (built in 1913) sits in the center of town. Most of the old homes have been restored. The Bath County Historical Society Museum and Research Library is housed in an old cottage (with a modern extension) to the right of the courthouse. There is no admission fee and it is open to the public from May through September on Wednesdays through Saturdays, and on Fridays and Saturdays from October through April.

Drive past the courthouse and turn right on to Old Mill Road. The mill—restored and operated as the Inn at Gristmill Square—is on the right at the end of street. Turn right on to Route 692 beyond the mill. You'll pass Anderson Cottage and several other old homes, some of which once served as guesthouses (Anderson Cottage still does).

Route 692 intersects Route 39 East (Mountain Valley Road). Turn right, go to the stop sign, and turn on to U.S. 220 South (Sam Snead Highway), toward Covington. If

Bath County Library

Inn at Gristmill Square

this road looks familiar, it is; the tour has just completed a circle. In about 2.3 miles, the road passes the Garth Newel (Welsh for "new house") Music Center. The center was started by two musicians as a nonprofit organization offering weekend chamber music concerts.

U.S. 220 enters the Homestead Resort in less than 2 miles. One of the resort's well-known golf courses lines both sides of the road here. Continue on the road as it curves around the back of the main part of the resort, past the village of **Hot Springs***, through a neighborhood of lovely old homes, to Homestead's main entrance, on the left.*

For more than 100 years, the hotel at Hot Springs was the smallest of the three springs resorts in the area. It was popular among people who were seeking relief from physical ailments. The first hotel on what are now the grounds of the Homestead was erected in 1766 by Thomas Bullitt on 300 acres of land he owned with Andrew Lewis. Bullitt later died fighting in the American Revolution. The hotel operation hobbled along until the 1830s, when it was bought by a physician, Thomas Goode, who believed strongly in the healing powers of the springs. He built a larger and more modern hotel in 1846 but died eight years later. The next owner added a two-story structure that was 222 feet long and could accommodate 120 guests. During the Civil War, that hotel—like almost every other one in the Valley—was used as a hospital by both sides.

Anderson Cottage

The Homestead

As the economy slowly recovered after the Civil War, mineral springs resorts in Virginia gained in popularity, both as places of summer retreat and as social, business, and political gathering spots. Seeing an opportunity to increase traffic on the Chesapeake and Ohio Railroad, M. E. Ingalls, its president, brought together a group of investors in the early 1890s to buy several hundred acres that included Hot Springs, Warm Springs, and Healing Springs (an old resort a few miles south of Hot Springs, later called the Cascade Inn). Their plan was to modernize and enlarge the hotel at Hot Springs, which had been called the Homestead since Thomas Bullitt's time. It was then that today's Homestead was born, patterned after luxurious European spas. And Ingalls made sure the resort was easy to get to—in 1892, he extended the C&O Railroad from Covington to Hot Springs.

The Homestead's distinctive main building was built in 1902 after a fire the previous year destroyed the recently renovated and enlarged wooden hotel building. The tower portion was added in 1929 as part of an ongoing expansion. Some of the resort's earlier structures still stand. The old Virginia Hotel, located on the right as you wind past the town and toward the main entrance to the resort, houses

Falling Spring Side Trip

Falling Spring—described by Thomas Jefferson as "the only remarkable Cascade in this country"—is about 11 miles south of the Homestead on U.S. 220. The Falling Spring Gorge Scenic Lookout is on the right about 0.3 mile past the intersection with Route 640.

A small bronze plaque memorializing Mad Anne Bailey is mounted on a boulder across the street from the lookout (see The Staunton to Steeles Tavern Tour, page 186, for more about Mad Anne). Falling Spring is a 203-foot waterfall. As Jefferson noted, it can't compare with Niagara Falls in volume, but it is at least 50 to 80 feet higher.

On your way to Falling Spring, you'll pass the challenging Cascades golf course, which was developed by the Homestead Resort in the 1920s. Its grand clubhouse was the 1890s home of a former owner of Little Healing Springs. The white buildings of the Cascade Inn, built sometime before 1856 and originally operated as the Healing Springs resort, can be seen from the road. It is now owned by the Homestead.

You'll also pass a state historical marker for Fort Breckenridge, another of George Washington's forts erected along the frontier in the 1750s. Shawnee Indians led by Chief Cornstalk attacked the fort during Pontiac's War in 1763.

apartments today but was once an elegant turn-of-the-century hotel. The Homestead's shops and a children's activity center, now called Cottage Row, are on the left past the Virginia Hotel. Built as guest cottages in the 1800s, they survived the 1901 fire and were converted to their present use in 1984.

The Homestead's popularity continued even into the Depression years, but World War II caused some disruptions. For three months in 1942, 363 members of the Japanese diplomatic corps were detained here while an exchange for U.S. diplomats was negotiated. After the war, ski slopes and an airport were added. The resort was owned and operated by the Ingalls family until 1993. Today it is owned by a luxury resort management company.

From the Homestead, turn around and retrace your route 5 miles back to Warm Springs on U.S. 220. Just past the Jefferson Pools, turn right on to Route 39 East (Andrew Lewis and Charles Lewis Highway). After 7.8 miles, this road passes a turnoff for Douthat State Park, which offers a 30-acre lake, a restaurant, boating, swimming, picnic areas, and campgrounds.

Continue for 4.3 miles on Route 39 (which skirts the Cowpasture River) to Windy Cove Presbyterian Church, on the left. This still-active church was organized by Scotch-Irish settlers in 1749. The first church, about 1.5 miles from here, was made of logs and is said to have burned down during an Indian attack in the 1750s. A second church, also log, was built north of the present church in 1766. A third log building was erected in 1813, which was replaced in 1838 with this brick church, which was later expanded. It's known as the mother church for Presbyterians in Bath and Highland Counties.

*The next town is **Millboro Springs**. Continue straight on Route 39 East toward Goshen. About 3 miles southeast of Millboro Springs Fort Dickinson once stood.* It was one of the string of Indian forts George Washington was responsible for building in the 1750s. Named for one of the county's first settlers, Adam Dickinson, it was attacked twice by Indians, in 1756 and 1757. Washington thought this fort had particular importance because it was "directly in the Shawnee path to Ohio, and must be a place of rendezvous if an expedition is conducted against the Ohio Indians below Duquesne." He recommended that 250 men be posted here.

When Washington inspected this and other area forts in 1756, he noted that both settlers and soldiers seemed to be vigilant only when the threat of Indian attack was present. He wrote: "The militia keep no guard, but just when the enemy is about." On one occasion, several children playing outside the walls of Fort Dickinson were snatched by a group of Indians; somehow they were later rescued.

Douthat State Park

Douthat State Park was one of the first six Virginia state parks. It was built with the help of the Civilian Conservation Corps (C.C.C.), created by President Franklin Roosevelt to provide jobs to unemployed young men in the 1930s. Some 600 men lived in nearby camps while building the park's structures and dam, clearing hiking trails, and creating campsites and picnic areas. Douthat Lake is a trout-stocked 50-acre lake that features a beach and bathhouse. A visitor center tells the story of the park. During the summer, a restaurant—housed in one of the original C.C.C. facilities—and a camp store are open to the public (closed Monday and Tuesday in summer; open weekends only from Labor Day through October). A family travel publication has named it one of the top ten state parks in the nation.

Goshen Pass

Goshen is the next stop on Route 39. You have your choice of two right turns to stay on Route 39; you can take either one. Route 39 is designated a Virginia Byway as it enters Rockbridge County.

About 4 miles down the road (now called Maury River Road), you'll enter Goshen Pass, a 3-mile-long scenic delight. This gorge, carved out millions of years ago by the Maury River, is one of the most unusual sights in Virginia. The road twists past forests thick with rhododendron, dramatic rock formations, and the rocky river below. There are a few scenic overlooks along the way. In the summer, area swimming holes, hiking trails, and picnic spots make the river a family playground.

The Goshen Wayside, which has picnic tables, a covered picnic pavilion, and restrooms, is a popular weekend swimming spot in the summer. On the same side of the road just past the wayside is a plaque commemorating Commodore Matthew Fontaine Maury (1806–73), whose last job in a distinguished career was as a professor of meteorology at Virginia Military Institute in Lexington. Maury is considered one of the fathers of oceanography.

Maury began his career as a navy officer, but his seafaring days ended when his legs were injured in a stagecoach accident. He later compiled information on maritime winds and currents that made it possible for ship captains to plan shorter routes. This and other work led to the first international marine conference, held in 1853. He also made charts of the sea beds of the Atlantic, Pacific, and Indian Oceans, which made it possible for a transatlantic telegraph cable to be laid. During the Civil War, he became the head of coast, harbor, and river defenses for the Confederate navy.

He loved the Goshen Pass area so much that he directed that upon his death, his casket be carried through the pass when the rhododendrons were in bloom. He died in Lexington in February 1873, so his burial in Richmond was delayed until May. In later years, the North River was renamed the Maury River in his honor.

As you leave Goshen Pass, look to the right for a white frame residence with a double porch. This home was once part of the Wilson Springs Hotel, which dated to 1775. Visitors came to partake of the sulphur springs here. This was not a fancy resort; in fact, the owner let anyone who wanted to build a cabin on the property. During the Civil War, Confederate soldiers camped here while guarding Goshen Pass.

*Continue on Route 39 to **Rockbridge Baths**.* People first came here in the 1800s to take the magnesia springs baths—actually two pools that remain a constant 72 degrees Fahrenheit. Now part of a private residence, the pools were located behind a wall on the left side of the road beyond the creek.

This community was originally called Jordan's Springs. In 1857, developers built a hotel here and renamed the place Rockbridge Baths. Robert E. Lee often came here while he was president of Washington College in the late 1860s. Beginning in 1874, a former Confederate army physician, Dr. Samuel Brown Morrison, operated the hotel as a sanitarium; ill health forced him to give up the operation in 1900. Virginia Military Institute used the facilities as a summer school beginning in 1921. The hotel burned down in 1926.

Continue on Route 39 for 1.5 miles, then turn left on to Route 252 (Brownsburg Turnpike), following the sign toward Staunton. The first town on this old pike, which curves through woods and past farms and charming old homes, is **Bustleburg***. The town's name supposedly derives from the time "a fashionable young lady lost her composure while trying to ride a horse while wearing a bustle," according to one (possibly questionable) source.*

The next town is **Brownsburg***.* Designated a historic district by the Virginia Historic Landmarks Commission, this village has changed little over the past century. It was founded in 1783 and named for John Brown, the first pastor of New Providence Presbyterian Church, located just north of town. The Brownsburg Museum has been recently established in a lovely old house in town.

After passing through Brownsburg, follow the signs for I-81, turning right on to Sterrett Road. Stay on this road to get to I-81. As you turn, be sure to note Sleepy Hollow, the restored stone-and-brick home on the right; it dates to 1800. The Blue Ridge will come into view as you head east toward I-81.

The tour ends at I-81's Exit 200, which is between Staunton (22 miles north) and Lexington (14 miles south).

The Natural Bridge to Lexington Tour

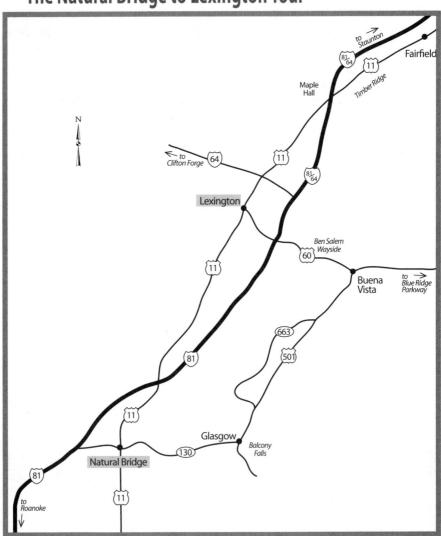

TOUR 12
The Natural Bridge to Lexington Tour

This tour begins at Natural Bridge, a geological wonder that Thomas Jefferson once owned. It then follows backroads to two 1890s boom towns, Glasgow and Buena Vista, both of which were stops along the North River Canal. The tour proceeds to Lexington, which has a well-preserved downtown area full of 19ᵗʰ-century buildings, two well-known universities, and the homes and graves of two Virginia Civil War heroes, Robert E. Lee and Stonewall Jackson. It then stops along U.S. 11 at Timber Ridge, an early Rockbridge County settlement and the birthplace of Sam Houston, the first governor of Texas. The tour ends in Fairfield after passing the historic McDowell family graveyard.

Total mileage: Approximately 50 miles

This tour explores much of Rockbridge County, which was formed in 1777 and named for its famous geological formation—the unusual rock "bridge" known as **Natural Bridge**. Most of the county was part of a 92,000-acre land grant made to Benjamin Borden, who came to Virginia from New Jersey in the 1730s. He brought in many Scotch-Irish settlers, who eventually formed much of the early population of the southern Shenandoah Valley.

There are two ways to get to Natural Bridge from I-81. If you are coming from the north, take Exit 180, then follow U.S. 11 South to the bridge. If you are coming from the south, take Exit 175 and drive U.S. 11 North, following the signs to Natural Bridge.

Natural Bridge really is a bridge. U.S. 11—the Valley Pike—runs on top of the 90-foot-wide, 215-foot-high stone formation, although drivers are not aware of it as they cross. In fact, "the bridge" makes it possible for the road to continue through this part of the Valley without having to make a considerable detour.

Natural Bridge was formed millions of years ago after the soft rocks that once formed the roof of a cavern collapsed around it, leaving the harder rocks standing to form the "bridge." The Monocan Indians are said to have worshiped Natural Bridge long before Europeans discovered it.

Natural Bridge

Perhaps the first person of European ancestry to see this amazing natural structure was Peter Jefferson, father of the third president and a surveyor who helped create an early map of Virginia around 1750.

Legend has it that Peter Jefferson had a young assistant named George Washington, who climbed straight up one side of the formation and carved his initials—which can still be seen today—in the rocks 23 feet above Cedar Creek. Some historians question the likelihood of that event, however. Although the time period seems correct, Washington spent most of his short career as a surveyor working for Lord Fairfax, whose five million acres of land were much farther north. Peter Jefferson never worked for Lord Fairfax, although while working for the Virginia colony in 1746, he did survey the disputed Fairfax Line, which in the Valley lies about 90 miles north of Natural Bridge. Washington did travel the entire length of the Virginia frontier from Winchester to North Carolina in the fall of 1756 while on an inspection tour of the forts he was responsible for building. However, no records exist to indicate that he came to Natural Bridge at that time. In fact, such a side trip seems unlikely, considering the seriousness of his mission.

In 1774, Thomas Jefferson—completely taken by this phenomenon of nature—asked the royal governor for, and was granted, a 157-acre tract that included Natural Bridge. He built a two-room cabin for himself and his friends to use when they visited the site. He called Natural Bridge "the most sublime of nature's works" in his *Notes on the State of Virginia.* He wrote, "It is impossible for the emotions, arising from the sublime, to be felt beyond what they are here: so beautiful an arch, so elevated, so light, and springing, as it were, up to heaven, the rapture of the Spectator is really indescribable!"

The bridge had practical value later on. It was used as a "shot drop" during the Revolutionary War; molten lead was dropped from the top into Cedar Creek below, an action that resulted in the rounded balls used for bullets. During the War of 1812, a nearby cave, visible today along the walking trail beyond the bridge, was mined for saltpeter, an ingredient in gunpowder and other explosives.

By the early 1800s, Natural Bridge had become a well-known tourist attraction. Artists' renditions of it became popular as framed prints both here and in Europe. Later in that century, the railroad made a stop here, and the popularity of Natural Bridge continued to grow.

The property has remained privately owned ever since Thomas Jefferson's heirs sold it after his death.

From the Natural Bridge parking lot, turn right to drive east on Route 130, following the signs toward Glasgow, about 4 miles away. This road is a Virginia Byway.

The natural advantages in this area—the James River and the nearby mountains' supply of iron ore and timber—supported numerous local mills, furnaces, and foundries. In 1851, the North River Navigation Company began building a series of locks and dams on the North River (later renamed the Maury River, after a well-known V.M.I. professor; see The Monterey to Hot Springs to Goshen Pass Tour, page 218, for more about Maury).

Completed in 1860, the North River Canal connected Lexington with the James River and Kanawha Canal at Balcony Falls, near Glasgow. Heading west from Richmond, the James River and Kanawha Canal project was a continuation of earlier canal efforts dating to the mid-1780s. Its ultimate goal (never achieved) was to reach the Ohio River, via the Kanawha River. The canal was nevertheless an impressive engineering achievement, running for nearly 200 miles to Buchanan, where construction ceased (see The Fincastle to Buchanan Tour, pages 260–61).

For the 15 or so years of its operation, the North River Canal brought prosperity to Rockbridge County, giving farmers and manufacturers a more efficient way to ship products to lucrative markets in the east. The canal continued operation during the Civil War, but the coming of the railroads to the area by the 1880s soon put it—and other canals—out of business. In many places, the railroad companies followed the channels of the canals, filling them in with dirt and often using the towpaths as foundations for the rail beds.

Glasgow was one of the many Shenandoah Valley boom-to-bust towns of the early 1890s. Its founders were optimistic: with two rivers and two railroads

A lock on the North River Canal

running through the area, they were sure it would become the "City of the South." It was founded in March 1890, with only 20 residents. Less than a year later, Glasgow had about 800 residents and 12 factories and other industries either under construction or up and running. In those days, land developers swept through the area with grand visions for business and industrial development, often creating planned towns out of the smallest of settlements. But their hopes for Glasgow failed to materialize when the national economy took a dive in 1893, and railroad failures led to bank failures and finally a nationwide depression.

Hints of Glasgow's former promise are hard to spot today. Nothing is left of the grand 200-room Glasgow Inn, built here in the early 1890s. The inn had the latest in modern conveniences, including electric lights and elevators. The story goes that the economic bubble burst before the first guest could be tucked in. The grand structure was torn down in the years that followed.

A century earlier, this area was the site of a brutal battle between Indians and settlers in 1742. According to the story, Iroquois Indians were traveling through the Valley when they began to frighten women and children and shoot at horses. A captain in the local militia, John McDowell, led a group of men who intended to "escort" the Indians away from the settlements. The two groups met at the river near here, and the resulting fight left eight Virginians—including McDowell—and 17 Indians dead. The Virginians were buried in the graveyard next to McDowell's home. The graveyard is still there today; see page 238 of this tour.

Continue on Route 130 out of Glasgow, heading east toward the mountains. At the intersection with U.S. 501, turn left.

If you were to turn right (instead of left) at the intersection, in about 0.2 mile on the right, you would see the Echols Farm, listed on the Virginia Landmarks Register because of its connection to canal history. The Echols Farm was built by Edward Echols around 1855 and is still owned by the Echols family. Here, Edward Echols operated the canal locks and ran a warehouse and a trading post. His mines in the mountains nearby provided the Confederates with a supply of iron ore during the Civil War. Past the Echols Farm on Route 501 are the remains of Balcony Falls Lock and Dam, which are difficult to see from the road. After passing through Balcony Falls, flatboats carrying cargo to Lynchburg had to negotiate 25 locks and eight dams. To continue on the James River and Kanawha Canal to Richmond, they had to go through 63 more locks and pass six dams and 10 aqueducts.

Shortly after you turn left on to Route 501, you may see a pair of brick gateposts on the left. The inscription reads, "Willow Grove 1780," suggesting that a historic mansion lies at the end of the drive. Unfortunately, the house there burned to the ground in 1958.

What is now U.S. 501 was built as the Blue Ridge Turnpike by the James River and Kanawha Canal Company. The North River Canal ran alongside the turnpike until curving west at what is now Route 663 (River Road); it then generally followed that road for several miles until it joined back up with the river. The tour will detour slightly to follow that old route.

In 1.2 miles, turn left on to Route 663, which is a Virginia Byway. Stay on Route

663 until it rejoins U.S. 501 in almost 7 miles. In about 3.5 miles, look to the left to see the ruins of canal locks; another lock can be seen on the river a little more than a mile from here. (These are a fair distance off the road, through private property; you'll be able to see other lock ruins close-up at Ben Salem Wayside later in the tour.)

*Route 663 ends at a stop sign at U.S. 501. Turn left to reach **Buena Vista**.* This was another developer-created boom town of the 1890s, although it had been settled for many years before that and had long been supported by its mills and furnaces.

As you enter Buena Vista (pronounced "Byoona Vista"), you'll see a sign at 10th Street for Glen Maury Park. This well-maintained city park lies next to railroad tracks that follow the path of the old North River Canal. The park offers picnic shelters, restrooms, a campground, a swimming pool, tennis courts, hiking trails, and other amenities. The old brick home on the grounds is Paxton Place, built by Elisha Paxton in the 1830s. During the Civil War, Paxton served as a commander of the Stonewall Brigade; he was killed in the Battle of Chancellorsville in 1863.

Continue through town on U.S. 501 (Magnolia Avenue). Several interesting old buildings still stand, including the former courthouse (now the city offices), which was built in 1890 as the headquarters of the local land development company. As you leave the town, you'll see Buena Vista's stunning 1890s resort hotel (it seems that every Virginia boom town had one) high on a hill at the north end of town.

Paxton Place

*The former courthouse
in Buena Vista*

Southern Virginia University

It's now the Main Hall for Southern Virginia University, which is affiliated with the Latter-Day Saints.

After passing through Buena Vista on Route 501, follow the signs to U.S. 60 West. The historical marker on the left as you leave town notes that in May 1863, a bateaux carrying the casket of General Stonewall Jackson traveled past Moomaw's Landing, on the North River Canal. Jackson's funeral took place in Richmond, after which the body was sent to Lexington for burial, as Jackson had specified in his will.

After about 2 miles on U.S. 60 West, you'll see a sign for the Ben Salem Wayside, on the Maury River. This park is the site of the well-preserved ruins of another lock once owned by the North River Navigation Company.

The 7-mile Chessie Nature Trail runs through the park; the trail travels from Buena Vista to Jordan's Point Park in Lexington. The trail is the unintended but fortunate result of a devastating 1969 flood in which C&O (now CSX) railroad tracks were destroyed and never re-laid here.

When the North River Canal was operational, a stone dam located about a

Ruins of a well-preserved lock at Ben Salem Wayside

mile downstream raised the water level here to nine and a half feet. (The dam no longer exists; people carried away its rocks in later years to build mills in Buena Vista.) The lock allowed operators to raise or lower the water level, permitting boats to go upstream or downstream. The stones of the lock rested on a wooden foundation, which sufficed as long as it could be kept continuously underwater to prevent it from rotting. Today, in an attempt to preserve those timbers, a stream has been diverted to the lock to keep its foundation wet.

During the 1800s, most goods that left or came into Lexington were shipped by way of flat-bottomed boats called bateaux (in this neck of the woods) along the river and this canal. Like the vessels called gundalows farther north in the Valley, these boats were about 90 feet long and often featured a canvas awning. They were guided by men who pushed against the canal bottom with poles.

Even before the canal was built in the 1850s, the North River had been improved for navigation by the addition of sluices, which allowed boats to pass through if the water level was not high enough, a frequent condition. Once the canal to Lexington was completed in 1860, the boats were pulled by mules or horses that walked along a towpath next to the water. In those days, it took 18 hours to make the trip from Lexington to Lynchburg. From Lynchburg, the James River Canal was used to carry goods to Richmond. From there, products were shipped down the James River to Norfolk and then out to sea.

U.S. 60 enters **Lexington** *on the town's eastern edge; continue straight, following the signs for the tourist information center and the downtown historic district. Turn right on Lewis Street and follow the signs to the Lexington Visitor Center, located at 106 East Washington Street at the corner of Randolph Street. Park in the lot at the visitor center to take the brief walking tour that follows.*

The visitor center is open daily. Inviting and well staffed, it offers maps, brochures, a map for the Chessie Nature Trail, a self-guided downtown walking tour (more comprehensive than the one we offer here), and information about area attractions and history. Free guided walking tours are given on Fridays at 3 P.M.; commercial horse-drawn carriage tours are available daily from April through October.

The downtown area is an enjoyable place to walk, shop, and have lunch or dinner. There are very few 20th-century buildings in the historic area, making it a good filming location for period movies such as *Sommersby* (*1993*) and *Gods and Generals* (2003). A few scenes in the more contemporary Spielberg movie *War of the Worlds* (2005) were filmed in the area.

Geography determined that Lexington, located in the center of Rockbridge County, would serve as the county seat. In the mid-1770s, the settlement here was so small that it barely qualified as a village. The new county was almost completely rural; its largest settlement was Timber Ridge, a few miles north, visited later in this tour.

Lexington was named after the first battle of the Revolutionary War, and the streets were named to honor its heroes. The town that began to grow here consisted mostly of log structures, which were destroyed by a fire in 1796. The town was soon rebuilt, this time using brick and stone.

Campbell House

Across the street from the visitor center is the Campbell House, home of the Rockbridge County Historical Society Museum. The museum contains several interesting exhibits of early Lexington history.

From the visitor center, turn right and walk to Randolph Street. Turn left and walk one block, crossing Nelson Street. Your destination is the stone structure on the left at 6 Randolph Street, one of the oldest structures in Lexington. Known as "The Castle," it was probably built in the 1790s.

Retrace your steps to East Washington Street and turn left. On the right at 8 East Washington is the Stonewall Jackson House, the only home the general ever owned. He moved here in 1859, two years after marrying his second wife, Mary Anna Morrison. They had one daughter, Julia. The house, which later was a hospital for many years, is open daily for guided tours.

"The Castle"

Stonewall Jackson House

DOWNTOWN
LEXINGTON

1 Visitor Center
2 The Castle
3 Rockbridge Historical
   Society Museum
4 Stonewall Jackson
   House
5 Alexander-Withrow
   House
6 Rockbridge County
   Courthouse
7 Lee Chapel

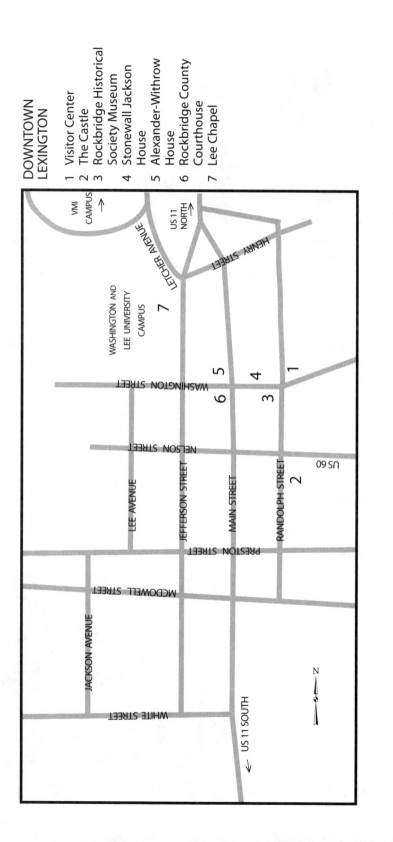

Continue walking up East Washington to Main Street. On the left is the old Rockbridge County Courthouse, constructed in 1897; this was the fourth county courthouse in Lexington. Behind the courthouse stands the old Rockbridge County Jail, built in 1841 and designed by Philadelphia architect Thomas U. Walter. Walter went on to design the United States Capitol's 1851 Senate and House extensions, as well as its cast-iron dome.

One of the most interesting downtown buildings is on the corner at 1 West Washington. The Alexander-Withrow House is now home to an art gallery on the ground floor and an inn on the upper floors. Jodie Foster and Richard Gere stayed here when filming *Sommersby*. The exterior features distinctive diamond-pattern brickwork and a hanging roof supported by carved wooden brackets, which is unusual for the Valley. The home was built around 1789, and its brick construction allowed it to survive the fire of 1796. Over the next 150 years, it housed a post office, printing presses, retail shops, a doctor's office, and a school.

During the 1850s, Main Street was lowered 10 feet as part of a project to remove some of the steep grades in the downtown area. At that time, stone underpinning was installed in the Alexander-Withrow House to create a new lower story—today's ground floor—so that what was once the front door of the building is now surrounded by an iron balcony on the second story.

Alexander-Withrow House

From the Alexander-Withrow House, cross Main Street and continue one block west on West Washington to Jefferson Street. Turn right and walk one block to the campus of Washington and Lee University, on the left.

Lexington has been a college town since 1785, when Liberty Hall Academy, a Presbyterian boys' school, moved here from Timber Ridge after a fire destroyed the school's building there.

Liberty Hall was founded as Augusta Academy in 1749 by Robert Alexander, who was educated at Trinity College in Dublin, Ireland. It occupied several Augusta County locations before it moved to Timber Ridge in 1776. A large log cabin was the school's main building. It was located on land donated by two local residents, one of whom was Samuel Houston, a Revolutionary War officer and the father of Sam Houston, who became governor of Tennessee, the first president of the Republic of Texas, and later governor of Texas.

With the move to Timber Ridge, the school's name was changed to Liberty Hall, a patriotic and daring statement in 1776. It struggled along for many years during and after the Revolution and was in dire financial condition by the 1790s. Around that time, George Washington was looking for a deserving school to which he could donate his 100 shares of stock in the James River and Kanawha Canal Company; the stock was worth about $20,000, a huge sum in those days. He chose Liberty Hall partly because it was already well established and well respected. In a show of gratitude, the school, which had about 40 students at the time, renamed itself Washington Academy in 1798.

The school became Washington College in 1813. In 1871, it was renamed Washington and Lee University to honor another famous general—the man who helped put the school on more secure financial footing after the Civil War—Robert E. Lee. General Lee served as president of the university for five years, from 1865 until his death in the Lee House on campus in 1870. He started its school of law, as well as classes in business and journalism, and instituted an honor code that is still in force. Today, Washington and Lee, the ninth-oldest college in the nation, has about 1,800

Washington Hall, Washington and Lee University

students, more than 300 of whom are in the law school. Interestingly, only about 14 percent of the students are from Virginia.

Over the past two centuries, George Washington's gift has been used to help pay the tuition of some 45,000 students. In a fitting gesture of appreciation, the university repaid the gift in 1999—the 200th anniversary of Washington's death— by donating $59,000 to support educational projects at Mount Vernon.

The university's main building—Washington Hall—is an impressive Greek Revival colonnaded structure built in 1824. It was designed by Lexington builder John Jordan, who constructed many other Lexington homes and buildings over a 50-year period. He built his own impressive mansion, Stono, in 1818; it is located on a hill next to the Virginia Military Institute.

Directly across from Washington Hall is Lee Chapel, which was built under General Lee's supervision while he was president of the university; this building also houses a museum. The focal point of the chapel is a marble sculpture portraying Lee on the battlefield, carved by 19th-century sculptor Edward Valentine. The museum contains a room displaying Lee's office, Lee family artifacts, and several oil portraits of the Lee, Custis, and Washington families, including a Charles Wilson Peale portrait of George Washington. (General Lee's wife, Mary Anne Randolph Custis, was a great-granddaughter of Martha Washington.) Many members of the Lee family, including Robert E. Lee and his father, Revolutionary War patriot Henry "Lighthorse Harry" Lee, are buried in a vault behind the museum. The remains of Lee's favorite horse, Traveller, rest in a grave just outside the door. The

Three Side Trips from Lexington

Lake Robertson is a 581-acre park located 12 miles west of Lexington. It offers camping, a 31-acre fishing lake, a swimming pool, hiking trails, and picnic grounds. It was named for A. Willis Robertson, a U.S. senator from Lexington and the father of television evangelist Pat Robertson. *To get there, take West Nelson Street to U.S. 60, then turn left at Beatty Hollow and travel southwest from Lexington to Collierstown. Then follow Route 770 (Turnpike Road) to the lake.*

Closer to town—about 2 miles away—is the Theater at Lime Kiln. Since 1983, concerts, plays, and musicals have been performed in this outdoor theater, which is situated on the grounds of an 1896 lime kiln. Every summer the theater puts on a popular musical called *Stonewall Country*, which tells the story of General Stonewall Jackson. *From downtown Lexington, follow U.S. 60 West (West Nelson Street) through town and go under the bridge at Washington and Lee University. Drive 0.4 mile past the bridge and make a left onto Borden Road across from the athletic fields. Borden Road will bear right through a residential neighborhood. The entrance to Lime Kiln is 0.2 mile on the left.*

Goshen Pass is 12 miles north of Lexington on U.S. 39, which is off U.S. 11 just past the I-64 interchange north of the city. This picturesque and striking mountain gorge is described in The Monterey to Hot Springs to Gosh Pass Tour, page 218. On the way to Goshen Pass, you'll pass the Virginia Horse Center, which was built by the state in 1985 to provide facilities for horse shows and competitions.

Lee Chapel,
Washington and Lee University

museum and chapel are usually open daily year-round; call to verify days and times (see the appendix).

Also on the campus is the earlier college president's house, now called the Lee-Jackson House, built in 1842; it is not open to the public. This is where Thomas J. Jackson (later known as "Stonewall") married Elinor Junkin in 1853. She was the daughter of Washington College's president. At the time of his marriage, Jackson was a professor at the other well-known school in Lexington, Virginia Military Institute (V.M.I), located next door to Washington and Lee.

The V.M.I. campus is just north of Washington and Lee. To see it, walk up Letcher Avenue (which is what Jefferson Street becomes after the Washington and Lee campus). If you prefer, you can reach Letcher Avenue and the V.M.I. campus by car from U.S. 11, which is called Main Street in town.

Established as one of several state arsenals in 1816, V.M.I. became a military academy thanks to the suggestion and efforts of one of the town's attorneys in 1839. It is the oldest state-supported military school in the nation.

The school's early academic programs were influenced by the first president of its board of visitors, Claudius Crozet, Virginia's chief engineer at the time. (For more about Crozet, see The Monterey to Hot Springs Tour, page 202.)

General Jackson began teaching here in 1851. A West Point graduate, he had served in the army during the war with Mexico. But he was not happy in the peacetime military, so he left the service.

The statue of Jackson that stands in front of the castle-like Barracks Building, built in 1850 and severely damaged during the Civil War, shows him inspecting the battlefield at Chancellorsville, where he was mortally (and accidentally) wounded by one of

Pendleton-Coles House

The white Gothic-style cottage with a peaked gable on Letcher Avenue as you enter the V.M.I. campus is the Pendleton-Coles House. The home now serves as the school's admissions office. It was built in 1876 and was once the residence of Colonel Edmund Pendleton, member of the V.M.I. class of 1842. In this house in 1902, Pendleton's granddaughter, Elizabeth Coles, married George C. Marshall—perhaps the most famous V.M.I. graduate ever.

Virginia Military Institute

The statue called Virginia
Mourning Her Dead

his own men in 1863, at the age of 39. He reportedly used the two cannons that sit on either side of the statue when teaching his artillery class. Jackson was buried in what is now called Stonewall Jackson Memorial Cemetery, on South Main Street in Lexington. A statue of Jackson by Edward Valentine stands above his grave.

Six of the 10 V.M.I. cadets who died in the Battle of New Market were buried on campus behind the statue called *Virginia Mourning Her Dead* at Nichols Engineering Hall.

That building is next door to Jackson Memorial Hall, which houses the V.M.I. Museum, open daily except during late December and early January. The museum completed a large expansion and renovation in 2009. It has several artifacts of Jackson's, including some of his classroom materials and the raincoat he was wearing the night he was shot. It also displays his favorite horse, Little Sorrel, whose remains have been preserved since the animal's death in 1886. Other exhibits include an antique firearms collection and displays of the achievements of the school's graduates.

A second museum on campus honors distinguished graduate George C. Marshall (class of 1901), who attained the U.S. Army's highest rank during World War II. He also served as U.S. secretary of state and won the Nobel Peace Prize for the Marshall Plan, his vision for European economic recovery after the war. The exhibits highlight aspects of 20th-century military and diplomatic history. The George C. Marshall Museum is open daily from 9 A.M. to 5 P.M. and on Sundays from 1 to 5 P.M.

To continue the tour, retrace your steps to the visitor center parking lot. From there, drive up East Washington Street to Main Street (U.S. 11) and turn right. This road will take you past the Washington and Lee and V.M.I. campuses. Follow the signs for U.S. 11 North. After crossing the bridge over the Maury River, continue on U.S. 11 for about 5 miles. The highway passes under I-64/I-81 twice. Just after it passes under the interstate the second time, look on the left to see the brick mansion known as Maple Hall. Its builder and first owner supposedly designed this impressive Greek Revival home in 1850 in an attempt to outdo his neighbors. It is now operated as an inn.

Less than 0.2 mile down the road from Maple Hall is the Sam Houston Wayside,

George C. Marshall Museum

Maple Hall

on the right at Route 716. Turn right into the wayside. The future hero of Texas independence was born in a cabin near here on March 2, 1793. A pink granite boulder brought here from Texas displays a bronze plaque describing Sam Houston's accomplishments.

Liberty Hall Academy (described earlier in this tour) was located here in **Timber Ridge.**

Continue through the wayside and look right to see Timber Ridge Presbyterian Church, which was founded in 1746. The original part of the present church was built in 1756. Expanded and renovated since then, it is considered the only pre–Revolutionary War Presbyterian church still in use in Rockbridge County.

Behind the church is a house called Church Hill, built in 1866. Historians believe that this house rests partially on the foundation of the log home in which Sam Houston was born.

Sam Houston's father had served with General Daniel Morgan during the American Revolution. After the elder Houston's death, the family moved to Tennessee. Sam

Sam Houston Wayside

Another Feisty Frontier Woman

Mary Elizabeth McDowell Greenlee, daughter of early settler Ephraim McDowell, was widowed at an early age. She supported herself by operating a tavern near Timber Ridge.

In the early days, Alice Lewis, daughter of John Lewis, the founder of Staunton, was kidnapped by Indians. Mary Greenlee offered John Lewis a deal. She would attempt to rescue the girl if he would provide a horse, saddle, and bridle—but only if she could keep the horse if her mission was successful. The story goes that Mary tracked down the girl at an Indian camp and brought her safely home.

Years later, when she was 95, Mrs. Greenlee was called to testify in court. When asked to state her age, she reportedly replied, "Why do you ask my age? Do you think I am in my dotage?" She lived another seven years.

Her grandson also lived to a remarkable age, dying in 1915 at age 99.

was about 13. One of his uncles said of him at the time, "I have no hope for Sam. He is so wild." At the age of 16, he tired of his job in the family's general store and went to live with some Cherokee Indian friends for nearly three years. He joined the army when he was 19 and served in the Creek War in Alabama under General Andrew Jackson. Sam was eventually stationed in Nashville. In 1817, Jackson appointed him to manage the removal of the Tennessee Cherokees to a reservation in Arkansas. The following year, Houston showed up in Indian clothing at a Washington, D.C., reception for the Cherokees. His senior officers reprimanded him, and he left the army shortly afterward.

Timber Ridge Presbyterian Church

In the years that followed, Houston was elected to Congress and became governor of Tennessee. In 1832, Andrew Jackson sent him to Texas, which then belonged to Mexico, to negotiate treaties with the Indians. Houston soon found himself in the middle of a rebellion of settlers against Mexico. He led the strategic defeat of Mexican general Santa Anna at the Battle of San Jacinto, near what became the city of Houston, resulting in an independent Texas republic. He became its first president.

When Texas became a state in 1845, Houston served as one of its United States senators. But his opposition to secession in the years before the Civil War cost him that office. He was elected Texas governor in 1859, but in 1861 he was deposed because he wouldn't swear allegiance to the Confederacy. He died two years later.

Return to U.S. 11 and turn right. In 3 miles, look on the left side of the highway for a state historical marker and a walled graveyard a few hundred feet beyond. The marker notes that the cemetery contains the graves of militia captain John McDowell and seven of his companions, who were killed by Indians in 1742 near Balcony Falls (the event described earlier in this tour).

John McDowell's father, Ephraim McDowell, was one of the first settlers in the Lexington area and the patriarch of one of its most distinguished families. Of Scottish descent, he came to America after years of fighting for civil and religious liberty in Ireland. He was in his 60s when he arrived here. He died in 1775 at the age of 104, outliving both his sons.

John McDowell received 1,000 acres of the original Borden land grant in exchange for his services in surveying the grant. In 1737, he built a house here using peeled logs stained to appear red, which gave the structure its name—the Red House. The house was torn down in 1783 by a later owner and replaced with a structure that became an inn and stagecoach stop.

John McDowell's son, Samuel, fought in the American Revolution and later became a judge in Kentucky. Samuel's son—named Ephraim, after his grandfather—was born in the Red House in 1771 and later became known as "the Father of Abdominal Surgery." In 1809, while practicing medicine in Danville, Virginia, he performed the first successful removal of an ovarian tumor in the United States.

Hull's Drive-In Theater

A piece of 1950s history still stands on U.S. 11, north of Lexington. Hull's Drive-In Theater is one of perhaps eight remaining drive-in theaters in Virginia and fewer than 400 nationwide. It opened as the Lee Drive-In in 1950; the name was changed when Sebert Hull bought it in 1957. When Hull died in 1998, a local group calling themselves the Hull's Angels formed a non-profit organization and began raising money to save the theater. Successful, they were able to re-open in 2000 and are today the only non-profit drive-in in America. Double-feature movies run on weekend nights from April to October.

Ephraim's cousin, James McDowell, was born near Lexington and was elected Virginia's governor in 1843. He built a grand home, Col Alto, in Lexington. That home is now part of a Hampton Inn, at 401 East Nelson Street.

Continue on U.S. 11 to **Fairfield**, *where the tour ends. Follow the signs to return to Exit 200 off I-64/I-81, about 25 miles north of where the tour began.*

The Fincastle to Buchanan Tour

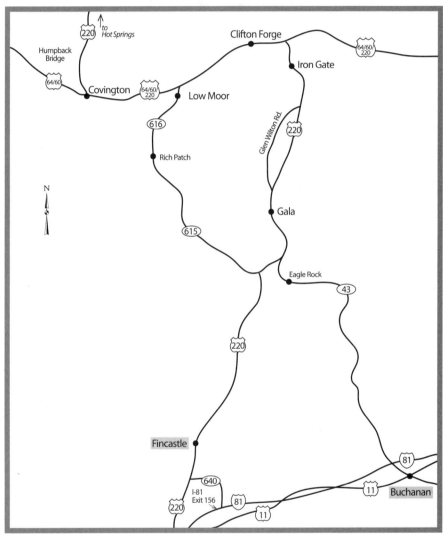

TOUR **13**
The Fincastle to Buchanan Tour

This tour explores the southernmost portion of the Shenandoah Valley, beginning in the historic village of Fincastle, one of the upper Valley's busiest places in the 1700s. From there, it winds through hilly farmland and across the Rich Patch Mountains into the Alleghany County towns of Covington and Clifton Forge, both important industrial and rail centers in the 1800s and early 1900s. Just outside Covington, it visits the famous Humpback Bridge, the only covered bridge of its kind in the United States. From Clifton Forge, the tour passes through rocky Rainbow Gorge and the villages of Iron Gate, Gala, and Eagle Rock as it heads southeast to Buchanan, once a thriving port town on the James River and the Kanawha Canal.

Total mileage: Approximately 98 miles

The tour begins in **Fincastle**, *the county seat of Botetourt County. To get there, take Exit 156 off I-81, marked "Troutville/640." Turn right at the stop sign at the bottom of the ramp; don't go to Troutville. This road is now called Brugh's Mill Road. In 1.4 miles, the road veers sharply to the left.*

Historians generally consider the Fincastle area to be the southern boundary of the Shenandoah Valley, while geologists put the southern edge at the James River. The Valley's tourist bureaus put the southern edge at Roanoke, 20 miles southeast of Fincastle. Roanoke, although an interesting city with plenty to see and do, is not covered in this book; however, it makes a good base from which to explore this part of the Valley. Roanoke was a late bloomer, developing from the small community of Big Lick to an important railroad hub beginning in the 1880s. But at least a century before Roanoke was on the map, Fincastle was the area's most important commercial, governmental, and social center.

Route 640 meets U.S. 220 North in about 2 miles. Turn right to go to Fincastle. In 1.1 miles, look for a state historical marker on the left side of U.S. 220 just before you enter the main part of town. It describes one of the most historically significant homes in the area, Santillane. The house, at present a bed-and-breakfast, is the red-brick

Fort William

About three miles west of Fincastle, on Catawba Creek, stood Fort William, one of the string of forts that the young George Washington was put in charge of building along the frontier. The purpose of the forts was to protect area settlers from random Indian raids during the French and Indian War. Constructed around 1756, Fort William was situated so its guards could see intruders coming across the pass through the Catawba Valley and two other mountain gaps. Washington specified that 75 men be stationed here.

In 1755, a group of Indians and their chief visited the fort. The settlers fed them, let them spend the night, and, according to a report by one settler, "endeavored to pay them all deference imaginable."

The mood was not as friendly a few years later, when area residents sought shelter at the fort in 1763 during Pontiac's War.

mansion at the end of Route 1211 (Housman Street), the road that runs next to the historical marker. It was built around 1830. This Greek Revival–style house is on the National Register of Historic Places and the Virginia Historic Landmarks Register.

Colonel George Hancock began building the original Santillane in 1795 when he was a member of Congress. Hancock had served as aide-de-camp to Count Pulaski during the Revolutionary War. His daughter, Judith (or Julia), married the explorer William Clark in that house in 1808, after Clark returned from his famous expedition west with Meriwether Lewis. Clark, who was from the Charlottesville area, met Judith in 1803 on his way to meet up with Meriwether Lewis in Indiana at the beginning of the expedition. The couple lived in the house for a time, and it was here that Clark worked on his report of that historic journey. That house burned down in 1820.

Henry Bowyer probably built the Santillane that stands here today. Bowyer fought in the Battle of Point Pleasant in 1774 at the age of 14. He then came to Fincastle to work in his uncle's store but left not long after to fight in the Revolutionary War. Bowyer returned to Fincastle after the war and served as county clerk—an important position in those days—for 43 years. The patriot Patrick Henry is said to have visited his niece, who was Bowyer's wife, at Santillane on several occasions.

To enter Fincastle's historic district, turn right on to Main Street just before the state historical marker for the town. The courthouse is just ahead on Main Street.

The surrounding area long served as hunting grounds for several Indian tribes, including the Catawbas, the Iroquois, the Delawares, the Tuscaroras, the Cherokees, and the Shawnees.

Fincastle is the county seat of Botetourt (pronounced "Bot-e-tot") County, which was formed from Augusta County in 1770. The town was laid out on 45 acres of land donated by a local merchant, Israel Christian, an immigrant who came to the area from Ireland around 1740. It was chartered as a town in 1772. At the time,

Botetourt County was huge—it extended to the Mississippi River, encompassing all or parts of what became Kentucky, West Virginia, Ohio, Indiana, Illinois, and Wisconsin. It was named after Norborne Berkeley, Lord Botetourt, who was the first royal governor of Virginia to actually live in the colony since 1698; he served from 1768 to 1770. Berkeley County, West Virginia, was also named for him. He was well-liked by the early Virginians, for reasons explained in The Clearbrook to Martinsburg Tour, page 12.

In 1774, the Battle of Point Pleasant took place in Botetourt County near what is now the town of Lewisburg, West Virginia. There, colonial troops fought the Shawnee Indians, led by Chief Cornstalk, in a successful attempt to open up Kentucky for settlement. That conflict was called "Dunmore's War" by some because they believed it was instigated by Lord Dunmore, Virginia's royal governor at the time. Dunmore supposedly stirred up the fight with the Indians in an attempt to divert Virginians' attention from their growing problems with the royal government. Some historians consider the battle to be the first of the American Revolution.

Most of the county's original settlers were Scotch-Irish Presbyterians, known as Ulster Scots, who began arriving in the Shenandoah Valley in the 1740s. They became strong supporters of the revolutionary cause, thanks in no small part to their dislike of the English government. It wasn't long, though, before German and Swiss immigrants from the northern part of the Shenandoah Valley and Pennsylvania began to move south. A few English and French families from eastern Virginia also moved to the area. Most of these settlers were farmers. Their most profitable crop was hemp, which was used to make rope for British shipping companies. They also grew wheat and corn.

After the Revolution, the movement of settlers to the south and west picked up considerably. Fincastle became the last place to buy supplies before crossing the nearby gap through the mountains.

Many of Fincastle's men fought for the Confederacy in the Civil War, but no battles took place in or near the town. Less than a decade after the war, however, two fires destroyed parts of the central and western sections of town.

In the 1870s, the townspeople began lobbying to bring the railroad to Fincastle, but Roanoke was chosen instead. As a result, by the 1920s, the town's importance as a commercial and resort center began to decline. Since then, its citizens have done a beautiful job of preserving the 19th-century look of the town as a tribute to Fincastle's historic significance.

Fincastle, a virtual museum of American architecture from the late 1700s to the 1900s, is on the National Register of Historic Places. Most of its early houses were of log construction; in later years, they were covered with weatherboarding and painted white. Many old buildings and houses have survived, making this small town a perfect place to get out of the car and walk around. Only 450 people live here today, about half the number who resided here in 1860. When viewed from the local hilltops, the town has a distinctive "skyline" of five white steeples—one on the courthouse and the others on four of Fincastle's historic churches.

The neighborhood around the courthouse appears to be locked in the past— the cars parked at the county office building next to the courthouse seem out of place. All the buildings retain a 19th-century appearance, and signs of commercialism are few.

The handsome brick courthouse is the fourth on this spot. The first was a log building completed in 1773. By 1818, a new structure designed by Thomas Jefferson was under construction. More than two decades later, a third courthouse was built to keep up with growing needs. Apparently, it looked much like the second one, but with a steeple instead of a Jeffersonian dome. Completed in 1848, that building burned down in 1970, and a new courthouse was built to look like the second building, at least on the exterior. A fireproof vault protected all the old county records during the 1970 fire, which was fortunate; they included the land grants made to George Washington and Thomas Jefferson for property that now lies in West Virginia and Kentucky.

Directly in back of the courthouse is the Botetourt County Museum, the oldest part of which was built around 1806 as a county office building. It contains furniture and artifacts dating back to the 1770s. The museum is open 10 A.M. to 2 P.M. daily except Sunday, when it is open from 2 to 4 P.M. Historic Fincastle, Inc., offers guided tours of the village by appointment; see the listing in the appendix.

The brick building to the left of the museum houses county court offices today, but it was once the Western Hotel. It was built to house visiting lawyers, and during the late 1800s it also served visitors to Fincastle Springs, a popular mineral springs resort just a mile from town. Visitors could also stay in another hotel, Hayth's House, which had a ballroom; that hotel was located on Roanoke Street near the courthouse. The springs here attracted people from New Orleans, Houston, Galveston, St. Louis, Vicksburg, and Mobile.

Next to the courthouse complex is the building that served as the county jail from 1897 to 1966. Its unusual (for Virginia) decorative ironwork has led many to suggest that the town's Southern summer guests—especially those from New Orleans—may have influenced its design. The jail's interior layout was interesting. The first floor served as living quarters for the jailer and his family, the second floor (with room for six) was reserved for women offenders, and the third floor (with room for 16) was for men.

Botetourt County Museum

To take a short walking tour of the town, park near the courthouse and head down Main Street to Church Street; turn right at the corner. Just behind the church is an old log structure beautifully restored by Historic Fincastle, Inc. It's now a coffee shop. Known as the Crowder House, it was built around 1791. Like so many other log structures in the Valley, it was covered with clapboards for many years. Note the careful notching of the logs at the corners of the building.

Return to Main Street and turn right. Continue to the end of the next block; turn left at Water Street. On the right at the end of the block is a home with brick garden walls known as Godwin Cottage. Some think that this unusual-looking house was based on a design of Thomas Jefferson's. It was built sometime before 1880.

Turn right on to Back Street, then left on to Jefferson Street. The house on the corner of Jefferson and Carper Streets at 119 Jefferson Street is one of the oldest in the area. This is the Peck Cottage, thought to have been built as slave quarters by town founder Israel Christian around 1784. Christian was a member of the Virginia House of Burgesses from 1756 to 1761 and served as one of the county's first justices. The house is log underneath clapboard; two of its rooms were added later.

Crowder House

Return to Back Street and turn right. This section of Back Street was once known as Jockey Alley. In the 1800s, "Court Day" was held once a month. People from the surrounding area would come to Fincastle to shop, gossip, discuss politics, and conduct business. Horse trading was one of the more popular events of Court Day, so much so that the sheriff was often called in to restore order. Jockey Alley was the official place for buying and selling horses and other animals. A local history book tells about a man who proudly claimed that he made seven trades in one day here and went home with 37 dollars, a watch, and a pocketknife—and the same horse he started trading with.

Walk past Big Spring Park on Back Street to the Fincastle Presbyterian Church. Originally the site of a Church of England church before the Revolution, the structure here today either evolved from the original building or from a newer structure. It was taken over by the Presbyterians after that war. The Greek columns and the steeple were added during an enlargement of the church in the 1840s; it underwent another renovation in the 1940s. The unmarked graves on the left side of the church are thought to be those of Revolutionary War soldiers.

Four other churches in town have contributed to Fincastle's history. The congregation of Fincastle Methodist Church was formed in 1789. The well-known traveling Methodist bishop Francis Asbury came to preach here on several occasions in the late 1700s. The current church was built in 1840; the cemetery on the hill above it offers a lovely view of the town and the surrounding countryside. St. Mark's Episcopal Church was built in the 1830s for a congregation that was formed in 1770. First Baptist Church started as First African Baptist Church in 1831. Fin-

Godwin Cottage

Peck Cottage

Fincastle Presbyterian Church

castle Baptist Church is the only church in town with stained-glass windows; it was built in 1896.

Continue past Fincastle Presbyterian Church for two blocks to Roanoke Street and turn left to return to the courthouse. To continue the tour, drive back to U.S. 220 (Botetourt Road) and turn right (north). After 12.2 miles, turn left on to Route 615 (Craig Creek Road) toward Roaring Run just after passing over the Craig Creek bridge. In 5.3 miles, turn right at Route 621 (Roaring Run Road); a general store sits at this corner. Follow the U.S. Forest Service sign to Roaring Run Park, which is on the left about 1 mile down Route 621. This road was once part of the old Fincastle and Covington Pike, which ran along what was probably once an Indian trail. Roaring Run Park is the site of an 1838 iron furnace. Picnic tables, restrooms, and several easy hiking trails are available. One of the trails goes to the furnace, which is in nearly perfect condition; another goes to a waterfall.

From the park, return to Route 621 and turn left. Drive 3.2 miles to the stop sign at the intersection with Route 616 (Rich Patch Road); turn right. You'll pass the white-frame Rich

Roaring Run

An 1838 iron furnace at Roaring Run Park

*Patch Union Church on the right before the turn. In 5 miles, you'll enter the community of **Low Moor**.* The name Rich Patch almost certainly didn't refer to the wealth of the area's residents; legend has it that the name came from the smell of rotting vegetation in a field near Low Moor.

At the next stop sign, turn left on to Route 696. Go under the railroad bridge, following the signs for I-64 West to Covington. Turn left on to I-64 West.

The Low Moor Iron Company stood not far from this spot. Built in 1873, the ovens here produced coke, a much more efficient fuel for blast furnaces than charcoal. The company was a large employer in the area by the 1920s, with 1,600 workers. Low Moor was the last of the county's many ironworks to survive. It shut down in 1926.

Today's I-64 runs conjunctively with U.S. 60, which had its origins as the Midland Trail, one of the first roads to connect the eastern part of Virginia with the lands across the Alleghenies. Settlers and their wagons traversed this route by the thousands in the 1800s as they headed west. By 1919, the road began to carry automobiles. A travel guide from that era claimed that the Midland Trail was the shortest coast-to-coast motor route.

West of Covington, U.S. 60 crosses the Allegheny divide. In the late 1700s, George Washington envisioned a canal in this area that would connect the eastern United States with the Ohio River. Its path would follow the James River and Dunlap Creek. From that point, goods would have to be loaded into wagons and carried across the mountains until the canal could resume along the Greenbrier and finally the Kanawha and Ohio Rivers, in today's western West Virginia and southern Ohio. Washington's dream of canal navigation eventually became a reality, except that the canal reached only as far west as Buchanan, a stop later in this tour.

Stay on I-64 past the three exits for Covington; at Exit 10 make a right turn to follow U.S. 60 East. The Humpback Bridge—the only bridge of its kind in the United States, and the oldest of the eight remaining covered bridges in Virginia—is less than 1 mile down the road.

Anne Royall, the Feistiest Frontier Woman of Them All

It was an unlikely match—a well-educated and prosperous, if hermit-like, Revolutionary War patriot, Major William Royall, married Anne Newport, an uneducated young woman born into a poor family in Baltimore.

Royall met Anne in the late 1700s, when she and her mother were taking the waters for health reasons at Sweet Springs, near Royall's home south of Covington. They were married for 16 years, until Royall's death in 1813. He left Anne almost all of his property, which prompted his nephews to begin a 10-year battle contesting the will. To take her mind off the lawsuit, she left the western Virginia mountains and began to travel throughout the South. She was in Alabama when the lawsuit was decided against her, leaving her penniless.

As a widow of a war officer, Anne figured she was entitled to a pension, so she went to Washington, D.C., in 1824 to collect it. But the wheels of government turned slowly even then. To support herself, she decided to write a book about her observations of everyday life in America. She managed to convince John Quincy Adams to make a five-dollar advance payment for a copy of the book; Adams took pity on her and tried to help her get her pension. After several weeks of selling advance copies, she had enough money to travel to New England to begin collecting material. The book, *Sketches of History, Life, and Manners in the United States*, was later published in Hartford, Connecticut.

Anne continued her travels. She wrote nine more volumes of sketches of American life. She spoke her mind in those volumes, which earned her many enemies.

In 1831, her funds exhausted, she returned to Washington, where she began to publish a weekly newspaper that she typeset and printed in her rented house near what is now the Library of Congress. She wrote about political corruption, graft, religious groups she viewed as hypocritical, and, last but not least, the bureaucrats who took 36 years to finally give her a widow's pension. By then, she was 80 years old. Sometimes called the first American woman journalist, she published her newspaper, *The Huntress*, until just before her death at age 85 in 1854.

This picturesque bridge crosses Dunlap Creek at a roadside park, a popular wading and picnic area. The bridge was built of oak timbers in 1857, held together by pins made of locust wood. The humpback shape allowed the load to be spread evenly over its 100-foot span without the need for a center support. At the center of the bridge, the floor is four feet higher than it is at the ends. It survived the Civil

Humpback Bridge

War and numerous floods. The bridge was used to carry traffic until 1929, after which it fell into disrepair until local organizations restored it in 1954. It retains its original timbers and decking, but the roof and walls have been replaced a few times since 1857.

Three earlier bridges stood here, the first of which was built in the 1820s as part of the James River and Kanawha Turnpike. Bridges were covered in the 1800s to protect the decking and trusses from the elements, allowing them to last much longer than uncovered bridges.

From the parking lot at Humpback Bridge, turn right on to U.S. 60 East toward Covington. U.S. 60 is known here as Midland Trail Road and then is renamed Monroe Avenue after it crosses the bridge over the Jackson River into Covington. Turn right at the second traffic light on to Main Street. You'll soon see the distant smokestacks of the bleached board division of Mead/Westvaco Corporation, a New York–based paper and pulp company that has been here since 1898. The plant is important to the local economy, and the unpleasant aroma that sometimes wafts into downtown Covington is a reminder of its presence.

Covington is the county seat of Alleghany County, which borders West Virginia. Half the county lies within George Washington National Forest.

In 1743, the royal governor of the Virginia colony granted 30,000 acres in the James River basin to Colonel James Wood, James and Henry Robinson, and Thomas and Andrew Lewis. Part of the tract was in what is now Alleghany County.

Two men from New York, Peter Wright and Joseph Carpenter, were the area's first settlers. They arrived in 1745 or 1746, bought land here from the original grant holders, and began farming. Other settlers, primarily Scotch-Irish, followed in the next several years.

Beginning in 1754, the settlers, like those in other parts of the Valley, had to deal with the constant fear of surprise Indian attacks. The reason for the attacks was political. The French, during their battle with the British over rights to land in the upper Ohio River Valley, found they had a friend in the Indians, who after years of mistreatment were not fond of the British. The French and Indian War began in 1754 and ended with the signing of the Treaty of Paris in 1763, in which the French gave up to Great Britain their claim on land east of the Mississippi River.

Fort Young, one of the defensive forts George Washington built along the frontier to meet these threats, was erected here in 1756. Washington came to inspect this and nearby Fort Breckenridge in the fall of that year. Local residents took shelter, often for days or weeks at a time, behind the stockaded walls of these forts. Covington citizens once built a reconstruction of Fort Young, but it was torn down in the 1990s because of a lack of funds to maintain it.

Until 1819, this area was largely farmland, with just a few houses and a gristmill. That year, the town of Covington was laid out. It was named after General Leonard Covington, a hero of the War of 1812.

Alleghany County was formed from parts of Bath, Botetourt, and Monroe Counties in 1822, and Covington became the county seat. It remained largely rural until the 1880s, when the economic boom going on elsewhere came to town. Covington grew rapidly from the 1890s to the 1920s, attracting paper and pulp

A barn in Alleghany County

industries, iron furnaces, a silk-making plant, and a tannery.

Without the railroad—which reached Covington in 1867—the town may never have amounted to much. Because the James River and Kanawha Canal never made it this far west, local farmers and merchants had no easy way to get their products to market. But the railroad—which was later extended west from here to Kentucky, Ohio, and Illinois—put Covington directly on a major east-west route, making it a prime location for industrial development. What began as the Virginia Central Railroad eventually became the great line of the Chesapeake and Ohio by the late 1800s.

Drive south on Main Street to see some of Covington's historic buildings.

The brick house on Main Street next door to the post office dates back to 1825, when it was built for a man named William Scott. It is best known for an event that took place here during the Civil War. Scott's daughter lived in the house while her husband, a Dr. Hammond, was serving with the Confederate army. Union soldiers under General Averill's command were camped nearby on a cold winter day. One of them came into town, entered the house, and tried to pry Mrs. Hammond's rings from her fingers. Her female servant saw what was happening and grabbed a frozen mop from the outside porch. She then proceeded to beat the soldier about the head and shoulders with it. He ran, leaving Mrs. Hammond and her rings intact. When the soldier's superior officer heard about the incident, he reportedly gave the woman 200 pounds of sugar and 100 pounds of coffee to make amends.

Main Street, Covington

Alleghany County Courthouse

The Alleghany County Courthouse, on the right farther down Main Street, is the third courthouse on this spot. The first structure was built in 1823; this one dates to 1910. A statue honoring the men from Alleghany County who served in the Civil War stands on the grounds.

On the left at the corner of Main Street and Court Avenue (at 301–303 West Main) is an old house that now houses a business. Known as the Brugh Building or the Callaghan House, it has survived on this spot without major changes for more than 150 years.

On the right, on the corner at 386 Main Street, is a lovely white multi-story structure that was considered the town's skyscraper when People's Bank built it. The Skeen Hotel—the site of one of the county's eight voting places in 1856—formerly occupied the lot.

Turn left on to North Maple Street and pass through two traffic lights. Look straight and to the left to see the beautifully restored Chesapeake and Ohio (C&O) Railway Depot.

This is the old 1908 C&O passenger depot, which closed its doors when passenger service ceased in Covington in 1971. The red building to the right of the depot is the old Railway Express Agency building. Railway Express specialized in delivery of small packages, much like U.P.S. and Federal Express do today. Covington citizens

Callaghan House

People's Bank building

Chesapeake and Ohio Railroad Depot

and businesses, led by the Alleghany County Historical Society, worked for years to raise funds to restore this unusual old building. About two-thirds of the terra-cotta roof tiles are original; amazingly, the new tiles were made by the same company that made the old tiles. The depot is used for changing exhibits of local history and as a meeting place for area residents. The depot is open to the public year-round on Tuesdays, Thursdays, Saturdays, and Sundays from 2 to 4 P.M.

Leaving the depot, turn right on to West Prospect Street and go to the stop sign. Turn right on to South Lexington. Pass through the traffic light at Main Street, then turn right on to West Riverside Street (following the signs for U.S. 220).

The house on the right at 441 West Riverside, near the corner with Lexington Avenue, is probably the oldest home in Covington. It is now called Merry's Stand. Its two front rooms date to 1800 and were built by Dr. James Merry, the merchant who laid out the town. The walnut logs of the original house have been covered with stucco, a common practice in the 1800s.

Merry's Stand

James Burke House

Continue down West Riverside. The brick house on the left at 232 West Riverside is known as the James Burke House. It dates to 1823, when it was built by Burke, who operated a trading post nearby; the two side wings were later additions. A subsequent owner, John Baker, came to the area from Delaware and was with General Stonewall Jackson when he was mortally wounded in 1863. Baker bought this house in 1887. His daughter, Eula, is said to have been the first female justice of the peace in Virginia.

Almost next door to the Burke House, at 212 West Riverside, is the Jacob Bishop House, built in 1832. The style of this house was typical of those built by settlers coming into the Valley from Pennsylvania. The bricks for the house were made on the property.

These are just a few of the interesting old homes in Covington; many lovely residences dating back to the Victorian era line the town's other streets.

Turn right on to North Monroe Avenue and continue straight past Main Street. You are now on U.S. 220 South/U.S. 60 East. Stay on this road through several traffic lights. At the last light, turn right on to U.S. 220 South/60 East to I-64. Get on I-64 heading east. Take Exit 24 (U.S. 60 East Business/U.S. 220 Business) to enter Clifton Forge. Turn right at the stop sign at the end of the exit ramp. In 1 mile, you'll begin to enter the downtown area.

Clifton Forge began as a center of mining and forging activities in the early 1800s. The name came from a forge in nearby Rainbow Gorge, visited in this tour. Its owner named the operation after his father's estate, Clifton, in Rockbridge County.

Like Covington, Clifton Forge owes its existence to the railroad. The first company to reach here was the Virginia Central, which completed the line from Staunton to the Jackson River, about a mile from the present station, in 1857. After the Civil War, it was extended west, ultimately connecting with the Covington and Ohio Railroad. Those two lines merged in 1868 to form the Chesapeake and Ohio (C&O) Railroad.

In 1881, the Richmond and Allegheny Railroad came to town to connect with the C&O. This event put Clifton Forge on the map as an important junction. In its heyday in the 1920s, more than 100 trains a day rolled through the town. It's no coincidence that Clifton Forge is the headquarters of the Chesapeake and Ohio Historical Society, which maintains archives of records and equipment and is one of the largest railroad societies in the nation. Directions to its offices at 312 East Ridgeway are given

later in the tour. A brief account of the railroad's fascinating history is provided on the
society's website; see the appendix.

As you begin to enter the downtown on Ridgeway Street, you'll see the rail yards on the right. The main office building, a frame structure, was built in 1906. The depot building still houses offices, as well as an Amtrak passenger station.

Many visitors come to Clifton Forge to shop at the Alleghany Highlands Arts and Crafts Center, just down the street at 439 Ridgeway Street. It features changing exhibits and juried arts and crafts by regional artists. It is open daily except Sundays for most of the year; it is also closed on Mondays from January to April.

Continue through the traffic light after the arts center, where the street curves to the right and becomes Main Street, past the City Hall. Look back to the left as you turn to see the three-story Beaux-Arts brick building at 512 Main Street, the Masonic Theater, built in 1905. The town now owns the theater and is in the process of restoring it. Many well-known western performers once entertained here, including Gene Autry, Tex Ritter, Cowboy Bob Steele, Hopalong Cassidy, and Red Ryder. If for no other reason, the theater will be remembered for two animal acts: one when Roy Rogers appeared on stage with his horse, Trigger, and the other when movie star Lash LaRue rode his horse down the aisle. Live performances—presumably humans only—are offered today; it's the current home of the Virginia Opry.

Turn right at the next traffic light on to D Street to enter the parking lot for the C&O Railway Heritage Center at 705 Main Street. This interesting museum and visitor center is worth a stop. Opened in 2008, thanks to the efforts of the C&O Railway Historical Society, it does a good job of telling the story of one of America's most recognizable railroads (remember Chessie, the railroad kitten?). The C&O began in 1836 as the Louisa Railroad, of Louisa, Virginia; many mergers later, it was folded into the current CSX system.

Masonic Theater

C&O Railway Heritage Center

The museum is housed in the restored 1895 C&O freight depot, which handled packages and small freight shipments until the 1960s. A 96-foot O-gauge train layout is the centerpiece of the museum; above it hangs a large mural depicting American transportation history that was once part of a display at the 1939 World's Fair in New York. Interpretive displays and artifacts reveal the railroad's importance to the area and the nation.

Outside, visitors can explore two restored cabooses; a 1922 dining car (complete with kitchen); a 1950s passenger/freight car; and a replica signal tower. A 7½-inch gauge track circles the museum, allowing children and adults to hop a ride on a live-steam train. The yards here at Clifton Forge were a major maintenance facility for the C&O's steam locomotives that once climbed west over the mountains.

The society is hoping one day to create the C&O Railway Heritage Trail, or the Chessie Trail, to connect C&O rail sites from Newport News to Huntington, West Virginia (including the Valley towns of Waynesboro and Staunton) and beyond. The Heritage Center is open Mondays through Saturdays from 10 A.M. to 4 P.M. and on Sundays from 1 to 4 P.M.

Turn right on to Main Street from the heritage center. You'll pass over a bridge on U.S. 220; follow the signs for U.S. 220 South. At the next stop sign, turn right to continue on U.S. 220 South, heading toward Iron Gate and Eagle Rock.

As you turn, be sure to note the dramatic rock outcroppings in the mountains across the road. Here, the road enters the gap known as Rainbow Gorge, the site of the iron forge that gave Clifton Forge its name. The Jackson River flows below, on its way to meet up with the Cowpasture River. They merge to form the James River at the southern end of Iron Gate.

*Continue less than 1 mile to **Iron Gate**.* This town was the bustling center of the iron industry in western Virginia in the 1800s. (If you have time, consider taking the Locust Bottom side trip described in the sidebar on page 257. You will be turning right on to Glen Wilton Road just after the James River bridge a little over 6 miles past Iron Gate.)

*In about 7 miles, the road passes the village of **Gala**.* When the Richmond and Al-

Restored trains at C&O Railway Heritage Center

Locust Bottom Cemetery Side Trip

To visit this out-of-the-way rural church and cemetery, take a 15-minute detour off of U.S. 220 on your way to Eagle Rock. *Drive on U.S. 220 for 6.3 miles after leaving Clifton Forge. After you cross the James River Bridge, turn right on to Glen Wilton Road. Continue for 4.4 miles to the Locust Bottom Cemetery.*

The picturesque little brick church was built about 1786 by Presbyterians and Lutherans. It sits alone on a small hill, surrounded by farmland and with mountains in the distance. A beautiful old tree in the back shades the headstones. The village of Glen Wilton is a little way down the road. *To return to U.S.*

220, you can either go back the way you came or continue on Locust Bottom Road, which becomes unpaved but eventually re-connects with U.S. 220.

---

legheny Railway excavated the roadbed for the line through here, the workmen uncovered evidence of an Indian town.

Just a few miles east of Gala on Route 622 (which was once a busy road to Natural Bridge) is Daggers Springs, a popular mineral springs spa in the 1800s. A man named Dagger opened the springs to visitors in 1820. Later in the century, new owners built a hotel that could accommodate 200 people. The springs were the hub of the area's social activities for many years.

Less than 2 miles past Gala, turn left on to Route 43 South (Narrow Passage Road), a Virginia Byway. The road passes through an area of unusual and varied rock formations on its way to Eagle Rock. In 1.5 miles, look to the right for a sign noting the last lock of the James River and Kanawha Canal. You can park here and take a 0.25-mile walk down a path to the James River, but you won't see the lock ruins—they're visible only from the river. One of the face stones from the lock holds a bronze plaque marking the spot; most of the rocks used to build the lock were reused long ago to construct railroad bridges in the area. As you enter the town, look to the right for the ruins of three lime kilns.

Eagle Rock was another industrial town that came alive with the boom times of the 1880s. In addition to its iron furnaces, Eagle Rock was known for its lime kilns, which operated until the 1950s. Fires and floods have plagued the town through the years, causing much damage to homes and businesses.

Before 1878, the town went by the more colorful name of Rat Hole. In those days, hobos and peddlers, referred to as "rats," were a common sight in the Valley. Many of them took shelter in an opening in the side of a nearby mountain, giving the town its name. When a post office was established here in 1878, the town was named Breckenridge, but folks complained it was too long. The following year the

Mount Carmel Presbyterian Church   *James River near Eagle Rock*

town was renamed Sheets, after a Civil War veteran. Finally, the picturesque name of Eagle Rock was adopted in 1883, after a bald eagle was killed on nearby Crawford Mountain.

Follow the signs for Route 43 South through Eagle Rock; you'll make several turns. Continue about 5 miles to another old settlement, Mount Carmel. Mount Carmel Presbyterian Church, just off Salt Petre Cave Road, to the right, was built in 1843. Across the road stands what must have been a grand farmhouse for its day, now barely standing. Saltpetre Cave was mined during the Civil War; saltpeter is an ingredient in gunpowder.

Route 43 follows the James River for a while, then begins to climb through Jefferson National Forest. It passes under I-81 just before reaching the town of **Buchanan**. Turn right to follow Route 43 South/U.S. 11 South, which is Main Street in town. (If you were to continue straight on Route 43, you'd reach the Blue Ridge Parkway in about 3 miles.) This historic town makes an interesting stop, both for its history and its shops, which include a used book store and an old pharmacy—Ransone's Drugs, where you can get a bite to eat at the Fountain Sandwich Grill.

As you enter Buchanan, you'll cross a concrete bridge over the James River; look to the right to see a swinging bridge still used by pedestrians. In 1864, the Confederates, led by General McCausland, attempted to keep General Hunter's Union army at bay by burning an earlier wooden bridge here. The tactic worked in slowing the Yankee advance, but sparks from the fire spread to homes and businesses at this end of town and destroyed many of them.

The Buchanan area saw its first settlers around 1738. Here, the Blue Ridge and Allegheny Mountains are only 2 miles apart, geographically their closest point. The town was established in 1811 by Colonel John Buchanan, an early Valley surveyor who married into the Patton family, which had settled in the area in the 1740s. Colonel Buchanan formed a militia company here in 1775.

In the 1850s, the coming of the James River and Kanawha Canal made Buchanan an important transportation center. From here, merchants and farmers in western Virginia and beyond could ship products to Richmond and other points east. Before the days of railroads, moving goods over water was easier and cheaper than hauling them overland on poor dirt or gravel roads. Surely, no one in those days could have

Old house in Mount Carmel

imagined that a century later roads would be the transport method of choice.

The canal's arrival quickly turned Buchanan into a boom town. The official terminus of the canal was about 4 miles to the east, but the construction of a dam created a deep, wide lake that allowed the boats to enter the town. Since Buchanan was the major shipping point for the many coal mines and iron forges in the area, businesses and professions began to locate here. One letter writer reported in 1852, "Buchanan has got to be a lively place, [with] dancing every night except Sunday." A walking guide of the town is available in the town hall, at 19753 Main Street.

One busy spot was the 23-room Hotel Botetourt, built in 1851 and destroyed by fire in 1997. It stood to the left of the Community House, originally called the Wilson Warehouse, located at 421 Lowe Street, one block west of Main Street. The Hotel Botetourt claimed Generals Robert E. Lee and Jubal Early among its guests. It was burned once before, when Union troops thought the Confederates were still in town.

The Community House, once known as the Wilson Warehouse, was built in 1839 as a store, dwelling, and warehouse by John S. Wilson, who prospered when the

Ransone's Drugs, Buchanan

Buchanan Town Hall

canal came to town. It's now a private residence. It was restored in 1928.

George Washington pushed the idea of an extensive network of rivers and canals all over America in the years before the Revolution. Already involved in building the C&O Canal in northern Virginia, he proposed a plan to the Virginia General Assembly in 1784 to build a canal "from Tidewater up the James as far as practicable," with the ultimate goal of connecting the Atlantic seaboard with the growing settlements across the mountains.

The assembly supported Washington's plan and made him the James River Company's first president. It also gave him 100 shares of stock in the company, which he later gave to the struggling Liberty Hall Academy in Lexington. Officials at the grateful Liberty Hall repaid him by renaming the school for him—Washington College, today's Washington and Lee University (see The Natural Bridge to Lexington Tour, page 231).

The James River Company began constructing the James River and Kanawha Canal in 1786. The goal was to reach across the Alleghenies to the Kanawha and Ohio Rivers. After years of slow progress, the state of Virginia took over the project in 1820. Twenty years later, it completed the first leg, between Richmond and Lynchburg, a distance of more than 156 miles. After many more delays, the 50-mile section from Lynchburg to Buchanan was completed in 1851. But then the dream died. The canal stopped in Buchanan, never to be extended to Covington and then to Ohio, as planned. The last lock to be built was near Eagle Rock (described earlier), at an elevation of 1,000 feet above sea level.

Costing more than $8 million (in mid-1800s dollars), the canal was an engineering feat. It had 90 locks, for a total lift of 728 feet up the mountains. In all, it required 23 dams, 12 aqueducts, 129 culverts, 135 road bridges over it, 20 towpath bridges, and one 100-foot street bridge at Lynchburg. Many of the lock ruins survive. (See The Natural Bridge to Lexington Tour, page 226, for directions to one of the old locks along the North River—now the Maury River—branch of the canal.)

The canal was used for passenger transport as well. Various companies operated "packet" (or passenger) lines that offered a fairly civilized means of travel to points between Buchanan and Richmond. Often, the freight boats took on passengers as well. They measured 75 to 100 feet long and were guided by men wielding long poles; the

Wilson Warehouse

boats could also be pulled by horses or mules that walked along the towpath next to the canal. The trip from Buchanan to Richmond took one week for freight boats and three days and nights for packet boats.

One woman who traveled from Locust Bottom to Buchanan by freight boat in 1852 wrote an account of her pleasant experience: "Each end of the boat was equipped for cooking and splendid meals were served. We had three dinners on board: fresh fish, bacon, chicken, roast potatoes, biscuits, coffee, and pie. The last was carried in stock and warmed. There was no table; the cook served the plates and we sat on stools and ate."

During the Civil War, the Confederates made good use of the canal to ship iron ore to Richmond, where a large ironworks made heavy artillery for the South.

Although hurt by the war, Buchanan continued to prosper until a terrible flood in 1877 destroyed much of the canal. That tragedy led to the canal's being put up for sale in 1880. It was then abandoned once the railroads extended their lines into western Virginia. Conveniently for the railroad builders, much of the track could be laid on the 12-foot-wide canal towpaths.

The tour ends in Buchanan. To return to I-81, go back to U.S. 11 (Main Street) and drive either south or north, depending on your destination; it joins I-81 in either direction.

Buchanan's Favorite Daughter

A popular writer of her time, Mary Johnston was born in Buchanan in 1870 in a house that was torn down years ago to make way for a car dealership. The daughter of a former president of the James River and Kanawha Canal Company, Mary was considered a "delicate" child. As a result, she was schooled at home for all but a few months of her life.

She became a prolific writer of novels, some of which were based on aspects of Virginia history. She published 23 novels in all, the most famous of which was the 1899 bestseller *To Have and To Hold*. In 1911, flush with royalties from her book sales, she and her three sisters built a mountain mansion they called Three Hills in Warm Springs. (See The Monterey to Hot Springs to Goshen Pass Tour, page 201, for more about this home.) Her book sales declined when she made no secret of her support for the women's suffrage movement. She died at Three Hills in 1936.

Appendix

General
Shenandoah Valley Tourist Information Center
I-81, Exit 264
P.O. Box 1040
New Market, VA 22844
800-VISIT-SV (800-847-4878), 540-740-3132
www.visitshenandoah.org

Tour 1: The Clearbrook to Martinsburg Tour
Berkeley County Historical Society/Belle Boyd House
136 East Race Street
P.O. Box 1624
Martinsburg, WV 25402
304-267-4713
www.bchs.org

Martinsburg-Berkeley County Convention and Visitors Bureau
115 North Queen Street
Martinsburg, WV 25401
304-264-8801
www.travelwv.com

L. Norman Dillon Farm Museum
Route 9
Hedgesville, WV 25427
304-754-3704, 304-267-7519

Tour 2: The Charles Town to Harpers Ferry to Shepherdstown Tour
Historic Shepherdstown Commission/Entler Museum
129 East German Street
P.O. Box 1786
Shepherdstown, WV 25443
304-876-0910
www.historicshepherdstown.com

Shepherdstown Visitors Center
136½ East German Street
P.O. Box 329
Shepherdstown, WV 25443
304-876-2768
www.shepherdstownvisitorscenter.com

Jefferson County Museum
200 East Washington Street
Charles Town, WV 25414
304-725-8628
www.jeffctywvmuseum.org

Harpers Ferry National Historic Park
P.O. Box 65
Harpers Ferry, WV 25425
304-535-6298
www.nps.gov/archive/hafe/home.htm

Tour 3: The Middletown to Winchester Tour
Newtown History Center
5408 Main Street
Stephens City, VA 22655
540-869-1700, 540-869-7102
www.newtownhistorycenter.org

Winchester-Frederick County Convention & Visitors Bureau
400 South Pleasant Valley Road
Winchester, VA 22601
540-542-1326
www.visitwinchesterva.com

Winchester-Frederick County Historical Society
Hollingsworth Mill
1340 South Pleasant Valley Road
Winchester, VA 22601
877-871-1326, 540-662-6550
www.winchesterhistory.org

Old Court House Civil War Museum
20 North Loudoun Street
Winchester, VA 22601
540-542-1145
www.civilwarmuseum.org

Stonewall Jackson's Headquarters
415 North Braddock Street
Winchester, VA 22601
540-667-3242
www.winchesterhistory.org/stonewall_jackson.htm

George Washington's Office
32 West Cork Street
Winchester, VA 22601
540-662-4412
www.winchesterhistory.org/george_washington.htm

Museum of the Shenandoah Valley
901 Amherst Street
Winchester, VA 22601
888-556-5799, 540-662-1473
www.shenandoahmuseum.org

Celebrating Patsy Cline, Inc.
P.O. Box 3900
Winchester, VA 22601
888-608-2726
www.celebratingpatsycline.org

Cedar Creek and Bell Grove National Historical Park
P.O. Box 700
Middletown, VA 22645
540-868-9176
www.nps.gov/cebe

Preservation of Historic Winchester
The Hexagon House
530 Amherst Street
Winchester, VA 22601
540-667-3577
www.phwi.org

Tour 4: The White Post to Millwood to Berryville Tour
Blandy Experimental Farm/The State Arboretum of Virginia
400 Blandy Farm Lane
Boyce, VA 22620
540-837-1758
www.virginia.edu/blandy

The Clarke County Historical Association
Museum and Archives
32 East Main Street
P.O. Box 306
Berryville, VA 22611
540-955-2600
www.clarkehistory.org

Long Branch Historic Home and Farm
P.O. Box 241
Millwood, VA 22646
877-868-1811, 540-837-1856
www.historiclongbranch.com

Tour 5: The Strasburg to Fort Valley to Front Royal Tour

Strasburg Museum
440 East King Street
Strasburg, VA 22657
540-465-3175
www.csonner.net/museum.htm

Fort Valley Museum, Inc.
P.O. Box 32
Fort Valley, VA 22652
540-933-6036
www.fortvalleymuseum.org

Front Royal–Warren County Visitors' Center
414 East Main Street
Front Royal, VA 22630
800-338-2576, 540-635-5788
www.frontroyalva.com

Warren Heritage Society
Ivy Lodge
101 Chester Street
Front Royal, VA 22630
540-636-1446
http://warrenheritagesociety.org

Warren Rifles Confederate Museum
95 Chester Street
Front Royal, VA 22630
540-636-6982

Tour 6: The Woodstock to Lost City to Columbia Furnace Tour

The Woodstock Museum
104 South Muhlenburg Street
Woodstock, VA 22664
540-459-5518
www.thewoodstockmuseum.org

Zirkle Mill Foundation
P.O. Box 127
Quicksburg, VA 22847
http://zirklemillfoundation.org/index.html

Strasburg Museum
440 East King Street
Strasburg, VA 22657
540-465-3175
http://sonner.biz

Lost River State Park
321 Park Drive
Mathias, WV 26812
304-897-7384
www.lostriversp.com

Lost River Museum
Lost River Artisans Center
Route 259
P.O. Box 26
Lost River, WV 26810
304-897-7242
www.lostrivercraft.com/museum.html

Tour 7: The Edinburg to Singers Glen to Mount Jackson Tour
Plains District Memorial Museum
176 North Main Street
Timberville, VA 22853
540-896-7900

New Market Battlefield State Historical Park/
Hall of Valor Civil War Museum
P.O. Box 1864
New Market, VA 22844
866-515-1864
www2.vmi.edu/museum

Mount Jackson Museum
Mount Jackson Town Hall/Visitor Center
5901 Main Street
Mount Jackson, VA 22842
540-477-3320, 540-477-3951
http://mountjackson.com

Tour 8: The Harrisonburg to Mount Solon to Port Republic to Peales Crossroads Tour
Hardesty-Higgins House Visitor Center
212 South Main Street
Harrisonburg, VA 22801
540-432-8935
www.harrisonburgtourism.com

Virginia Quilt Museum
301 South Main Street
Harrisonburg, VA 22801
540-433-3818
www.vaquiltmuseum.org

Grand Caverns
5 Grand Caverns Drive
Grottoes, VA 24441
888-430-CAVE (2283)
www.ci.grottoes.va.us

The Port Republic Museum
The Society of Port Republic Preservationists
P.O. Box 82
Port Republic, VA 24471
540-249-3156/540-249-9226
www.heritagecenter.com/SPRP

CrossRoads: Valley Brethren-Mennonite Heritage Center
1921A Heritage Center Way (off Garbers Church Road)
Harrisonburg, VA 22801
P.O. Box 1563
Harrisonburg, VA 22803
540-438-1275
www.vbmhc.org

Harrisonburg-Rockingham Historical Society
P.O. Box 716
Dayton, VA 22821
540-879-2681, 540-879-2616
www.heritagecenter.com

Reuel B. Pritchett Museum
Box 147, Bridgewater College
Bridgewater, VA 22812
540-828-5462
www.bridgewater.edu

Natural Chimneys Park/Augusta County Parks and Recreation
94 Natural Chimneys Lane
Mt. Solon, VA 22843
P.O. Box 590
Verona, VA 24482
540-350-2510 (park phone, seasonal), 540-245-5727

Augusta Military Academy Museum
AMA Alumni House
Fort Defiance, VA 24437
540-248-3007
www.amaalumni.org/Museum/default.htm

Augusta Stone Presbyterian Church
P.O. Box 118
Fort Defiance, VA 24482
540-248-2634
www.augustastone.org

Tour 9: The Fort Valley to Page Valley Tour
Page County Heritage Museum
Route 766
Luray, VA 22835
540-743-3915
http://pagecountyheritage.com

Luray and Page County Visitor Information Center
18 Campbell Street
Luray, VA 22835
888-743-3915, 540-743-3915
www.luraypage.com

Lee Ranger District
George Washington National Forest
102 Koontz Street
Edinburg, VA 22824
95 Railroad Avenue
Edinburg, VA 22824 (mailing address)
540-984-4101
www.fs.fed.us/r8/gwj/lee/

Tour 10: The Staunton to Steeles Tavern Tour
Historic Staunton Foundation
R.R. Smith Center for History and Art
20-22 South New Street
Staunton, VA 24401
540-885-7676
www.historicstaunton.org

Staunton Convention and Visitors Bureau
City Hall, Third floor
P.O. Box 58
Staunton, VA 24402
800-342-7982, 540-332-3865
www.visitstaunton.com

Staunton City Visitors Center
35 South New Street
Staunton, VA 24401
540-332-3971

Woodrow Wilson Presidential Library & Museum
20 North Coalter Street
Staunton, VA 24401
540-885-0897
www.woodrowwilson.org

American Shakespeare Center
10 South Market Street
Staunton, VA 24401
1-877-MUCH-ADO
www.americanshakespearecenter.com

Museum of Frontier Culture
1290 Richmond Road
Staunton, VA 24401
540-332-7850
www.frontiermuseum.org

Wade's Mill
55 Kennedy Wade's Mill Road
Raphine, VA 24472
800-290-1400
www.wadesmill.com

Plumb House
1012 West Main Street
Waynesboro, VA 22980
540-943-3943
www.waynesboroheritagefoundation.com

Waynesboro Heritage Museum
West Main Street and Wayne Avenue
Waynesboro, VA 22980
540-943-3943
www.waynesboroheritagefoundation.com

Shenandoah Valley AREC
P.O. Box 100
128 McCormick Farm Circle
Steeles Tavern, VA 24476
540-377-2255
www.vaes.vt.edu/steeles/mccormick

Tour 11: The Monterey to Hot Springs to Goshen Pass Tour

Douthat State Park
14239 Douthat State Park Road
Millboro, VA 24460
540-862-8100
www.dcr.virginia.gov/state_parks/dou.shtml

Warm Springs Ranger District
Route 2, Box 30
Hot Springs, VA 24445
540-839-2521
www.fs.fed.us/r8/gwj/warmsprings/index.shtml

Highland County Museum and Heritage Center
161 Mansion House Road
McDowell, VA 24458
540-396-4478

Highland County Chamber of Commerce
P.O. Box 223
Monterey, VA 24465
www.highlandcounty.org

Bath County Historical Society
P.O. Box 212
Courthouse Hill Road
Warm Springs, VA 24484
540-839-2543
www.discoverbath.com/historic.htm

Bath County Chamber of Commerce
P.O. Box 718
2696 Main Street, Suite 4
Hot Springs, VA 24445
800-628-8092, 540-839-5409

Tour 12: The Natural Bridge to Lexington Tour

Lexington Visitor Center
106 East Washington Street
Lexington, VA 24450
540-463-3777
www.lexingtonvirginia.com

Campbell House
Rockbridge Historical Society
101 East Washington Street
Lexington, VA 24450
540-464-1058
www.rockhist.org

George C. Marshall Museum
1600 VMI Parade
Lexington, VA 24450
540-463-2083
www.marshallfoundation.org

Lee Chapel and Museum
11 University Place
Lexington, VA 24450
540-458-8768
http://chapelapps.wlu.edu

Museum of Military Memorabilia
122 South Main Street
Lexington, VA 24450
540-464-3041

Stonewall Jackson House
8 East Washington Street
Lexington, VA 24450
540-463-2552
www.stonewalljackson.org

Virginia Military Institute Museum
VMI Parade Ground
P.O. Box 1600
Lexington, VA 24450
540-464-7334
www.vmi.edu

Tour 13: The Fincastle to Buchanan Tour
Roanoke Valley Convention and Visitors Bureau
101 Shenandoah Avenue, NE
Roanoke, VA 24016
540-342-6025
www.visitroanokeva.com

Historic Fincastle, Inc.
P.O. Box 19
Fincastle, VA 24090
540-473-3077
www.hisfin.org

Botetourt County Historical Society
1 West Main Street
P.O. Box 468
Fincastle, VA 24090
540-473-8394
www.bothistsoc.org

Alleghany Highlands Chamber of Commerce
241 West Main Street
Covington, VA 24426
888-430-5786, 540-962-2178
www.ahchamber.com
www.covington.va.us/tourism.shtml

Chesapeake and Ohio Historical Society, Inc.
312 East Ridgeway Street
Clifton Forge, VA 24422
540-862-2210
www.cohs.org

C&O Railroad Heritage Center
705 Main Street
Clifton Forge, VA 24422
540-862-8653
www.candoheritage.org

Downtown Buchanan
19753 Main Street
Buchanan, VA 24066
540-254-1212
www.townofbuchanan.com

Bibliography

Adams, Charles S., ed. *Roadside Markers in West Virginia*. Self-published, 1997.

Adamson, John H. *A Pictorial History of Shenandoah County*. Shenandoah County Historical Society, 2007.

Bath County Historical Society. *The Bicentennial History of Bath County, Virginia, 1791–1991*. Marceline, Mo.: Heritage House Publishing, 1991.

Bly, Daniel. *From the Rhine to the Shenandoah*. Baltimore: Gateway Press, 1993.

Boley, Henry. *Lexington in Old Virginia*. 1936. Reprint, Natural Bridge Station, Va.: Rockbridge Publishing Company, 1990.

Botetourt County Historical Society. *Botetourt Bicentennial Souvenir Program and History*. Botetourt County Historical Society, 1970.

Branch, Michael P., and Daniel J. Philippon. *The Height of Our Mountains*. Baltimore: Johns Hopkins University Press, 1998.

Bruce, Thomas. *Southwest Virginia and Shenandoah Valley*. 1891. Reprint, Bowie. Md.: Heritage Books, 1997.

Cartmell, T. K. *Shenandoah Valley Pioneers and Their Descendants: A History of Frederick County, Virginia*. Winchester, Va.: Eddy Press, 1909.

Christian, Frances Archer, and Suzanne Massie. *Homes and Gardens in Old Virginia*. Richmond: Garrett and Massie, 1950.

Clem, Gladys Bauserman. *Stories of the Shenandoah*. Staunton, Va.: self-published, 1948.

Clower, J. B., ed. *Glimpses of the Past in Shenandoah County*. Woodstock, Va.: Woodstock Museum, 1984.

Cohen, Stan. *Historic Springs of the Virginias: A Pictorial History*. Charleston, W. Va.: Pictorial Histories Publishing Company, 1981.

Comstock, Jim. *Hardesty's West Virginia Counties*. Richwood, W. Va.: 1973.

Couper, William. *History of the Shenandoah Valley*. New York: Lewis Historical Publishing Company, 1952.

Cozzens, Peter. *Shenandoah 1862: Stonewall Jackson's Valley Campaign*. Chapel Hill: University of North Carolina Press, 2008.

Davis, Julia, and Lucian Niemeyer. *Shenandoah: Daughter of the Stars*. Baton Rouge: Louisiana State University Press, 1994.

Dohme, Alvin. *Shenandoah: The Valley Story*. Front Royal, Va.: Greatland Publishing Company, 1973.

Dolmetsch, Christopher L. *The German Press of the Shenandoah Valley*. Columbia, S.C.: Camden House, 1984.

Downs, Janet. *The Mills of Rockingham County*. Harrisonburg, Va.: Harrisonburg-Rockingham County Historical Society, 1997.

Egloff, Keith, and Deborah Woodward. *First People: The Early Indians of Virginia*. Charlottesville: University Press of Virginia, 1992.

Farrar, Emmie Ferguson, and Emilee Hines. *Old Virginia Houses—Shenandoah*. Charlotte, N.C.: Delmar Publishing Company, 1976.

Flexner, James Thomas. *Washington: The Indispensable Man*. New York: NAL Penguin, 1984.

Foreman, Michael. *Images of the Past: A Photographic Review of Winchester and Frederick County, Virginia*. Winchester, Va.: Winchester–Frederick County Historical Society, 1980.

Frye, Keith. *Roadside Geology of Virginia*. Missoula, Mont.: Mountain Press Publishing Company, 1986.

Funkhouser, Wendell E., and Nancy H. Powell. *Lost City: Its People and Their Heritage*. Lost City, W. Va.: Ivanhoe Presbyterian Church, 1999.

Fulwiler, Harry, Jr. *Buchanan, Virginia: Gateway to the Southwest*. Self-published, 1980.

Gardner, William M. *Lost Arrowheads and Broken Pottery*. Front Royal, Va.: Thunderbird Museum, 1986.

Gilbert, David T. *A Walker's Guide to Harpers Ferry, West Virginia*. 5th ed. Harpers Ferry, W. Va.: Harpers Ferry Historical Association, 1995.

Greene, Michael J.L. *Valley Churches: Churches in Shenandoah County and Adjacent Locales in the Valley of Virginia*. Shenandoah County Library, 1997.

Gurnee, Russell. *The Discovery of Luray Caverns*. Closter, N. J.: self-published, 1978.

Hale, Laura Virginia. *Belle Boyd: Southern Spy of the Shenandoah*. Front Royal, Va.: Warren Rifles Chapter, United Daughters of the Confederacy.

———. *On Chester Street: Presence of the Past Patterns the Future*. Stephens City, Va.: Commercial Press, 1985.

Hart, Freeman H. *The Valley of Virginia in the American Revolution, 1763–1789*. Chapel Hill: University of North Carolina Press, 1942.

Heatwole, John L. *The Burning: Sheridan in the Shenandoah Valley*. Charlottesville, Va.: Rockbridge Publishing, 2008.

Heatwole, John L. *Shenandoah Voices: Folklore, Legends and Traditions of the Valley*. Berryville, Va.: Rockbridge Publishing Company, 1995.

Hildebrand, John R. *Iron Horses in the Valley: The Valley and Shenandoah Valley Railroads, 1866-1882*.

Historical Fincastle, Inc. *Around Town: A Pictorial Review of Old Fincastle, Virginia*. Fincastle, Va.: Historical Fincastle, 1989.

Hofstra, Warren R., and Karl Raitz, eds. *The Great Valley Road of Virginia: Shenandoah Landscapes from Prehistory to the Present*. Charlottesville, Va.: University of Virginia Press, 2010.

Hofstra, Warren R. *The Planting of New Virginia: Settlement and Landscape in the Shenandoah Valley*. Baltimore: Johns Hopkins University Press, 2004.

Ingalls, Fay. *The Valley Road*. New York: World Publishing Company, 1949.

James River Project Committee and the Virginia Academy of Science. *The James River Basin: Past, Present, and Future*. Richmond: Virginia Academy of Science, 1950.

Jefferson, Thomas. *Notes on the State of Virginia*. 1788. Reprint, New York: W. W. Norton and Company, 1954.

Johnston, Wilbur S. *Weaving a Common Thread: A History of the Woolen Industry in the Top of the Shenandoah Valley*. Winchester, Va.: Winchester–Frederick County Historical Society, 1990.

Keister, E. E. *Strasburg, Virginia, and the Keister Family*. Self-published, 1972.

Kercheval, Samuel. *A History of the Valley of Virginia.* 1833. Reprint, Harrisonburg, Va.: C. J. Carrier Company, 1994.

Kerkhoff, Jennie Ann. *Old Homes of Page County, Virginia.* Luray, Va.: Lauck and Company, 1962.

Koons, Kenneth E., and Warren R. Hofstra, eds. *After the Backcountry: Rural Life in the Great Valley of Virginia, 1800-1900.* Knoxville: University of Tennessee Press, 2000.

Lambert, Darwin. *The Undying Past of Shenandoah National Park.* Boulder, Colo.: Roberts Rinehart, Publishers, 1989.

Lewis, Thomas A. *West from Shenandoah: A Scotch-Irish Family Fights for America, 1729-1781: A Journal of Discovery.* Hoboken, N.J.: John Wiley, 2004.

MacMaster, Richard K. *Augusta County History, 1865–1950.* Staunton, Va.: Augusta County Historical Society, 1987.

Magin, Irvin D. *Shenandoah County Gazetteer and Historical Geography.* Edinburg, Va.: Shenandoah County Library, 1991.

May, C. E. *Life under Four Flags in North River Basin of Virginia.* Verona, Va.: McClure Press, 1976.

———. *My Augusta, A Spot of Earth, Not a Woman.* Self-published, 1987.

McCary, Ben C. *Indians in Seventeenth-Century Virginia.* Charlottesville: University Press of Virginia, 1957.

McCue, Elizabeth B. *Staunton, Virginia: A Pictorial History.* Staunton, Va.: Historic Staunton Foundation, 1985.

Melson, William G. *Geology Explained: Virginia's Fort Valley and Massanutten Mountains.* Fort Valley, Va.: InterPress, U.S.A., 2004.

Moore, Robert H., II. *Tragedy in the Shenandoah Valley: The Story of the Summers-Koontz Execution.* Charleston, S.C.: History Press, 2006.

Morton, Oren F. *A Centennial History of Alleghany County.* 1923. Reprint, Harrisonburg, Va.: C. J. Carrier Company, 1986.

———. *A History of Highland County, Virginia.* Baltimore: Regional Publishing Company, 1979.

———. *A History of Rockbridge County, Virginia.* Staunton, Va.: McClure Company, 1920.

Mount Jackson Area Chamber of Commerce. *Mount Jackson, Va.: The Past of the Present and the Future.* 1989.

Munch, E.H. *The History of the Fort.* Fort Valley, Va.: The Fort Valley Museum, Inc., 1925.

National Park Service, Office of Publications. *John Brown's Raid.* Washington: GPO, 1974.

Niederer, Frances J. *The Town of Fincastle, Virginia.* Charlottesville: University Press of Virginia, 1965.

Norris, J. E. *History of the Lower Shenandoah Valley.* Chicago: A. Warner and Company, Publishers, 1890.

Northern Virginia Daily. Standing Ground: The Civil War in the Shenandoah Valley. Strasburg, Va.: Shenandoah Publishing House, 1996.

Page: The County of Plenty. Luray, Va.: Page County Bicentennial Commission, 1976.

Patchan, Scott. *Shenandoah Summer: The 1864 Valley Campaign*. Lincoln: University of Nebraska Press, 2007.

Pierce, Leola B. *Covered Bridges in Virginia*. Glen Rose, Tex.: Upstream Press, 2002.

Reeder, Carolyn. *Shenandoah Heritage: The Story of the People before the Park*. Washington: Potomac Appalachian Trail Club, 1978.

Reniers, Perceval. *The Springs of the Virginias: Life, Love, and Death at the Waters*. Chapel Hill: University of North Carolina Press, 1941.

Rothery, Agnes. *New Roads in Old Virginia*. Boston: Houghton Mifflin Company, Riverside Press, 1929.

Rouse, Parker, Jr. *The Great Wagon Road: From Philadelphia to the South*. Richmond, Va.: Dietz Press, 1995.

Salmon, Emily J., and Edward D. C. Campbell, Jr. *Hornbook of Virginia History*. 4th ed. Richmond: Library of Virginia, 1994.

Salmon, John S. *A Guidebook to Virginia's Historical Markers*. Charlottesville: University Press of Virginia, 1994.

Shenandoah County Bicentennial Committee. *Dunmore 1772–1778, Shenandoah 1778–1972*. Woodstock, Va.: Shenandoah County Bicentennial Committee, 1972.

Stevens, William O. *The Shenandoah and Its Byways*. New York: Dodd, Mead, 1941.

Stoner, Robert Douthat. *A Seed-bed of the Republic: A Study of the Pioneers in the Upper (Southern) Valley of Virginia*. Roanoke, Va.: Roanoke Historical Society, 1962.

Strickler, Harry M. *A Short History of Page County, Virginia*. 1952. Reprint, Harrisonburg, Va.: C. J. Carrier Company, 1974.

Suter, Scott Hamilton. *Shenandoah Valley Folklife*. Oxford: University Press of Mississippi, 1999.

Tanner, Robert G. *Stonewall in the Valley: Thomas J. "Stonewall" Jackson's Shenandoah Valley Campaign, Spring 1862*. Mechanicsville, Penn.: Stackpole Books, 1996.

Tennery, Katherine, and Shirley Scott. *Country Roads: Rockbridge County, Virginia*. 2nd ed. Berryville, Va.: Rockbridge Publishing Company, 1995.

Terrell, Isaac Long. *Old Houses in Rockingham County*. Verona, Va.: McClure Press, 1983.

Troubetzkoy, Sergei. *Images of America: Staunton*. Charleston, S.C.: Arcadia Publishing, 2004.

Trout, W. E., III. *The Maury River Atlas: Historic Sites on the North River Navigation*. Lexington, Va.: Virginia Canals and Navigations Society, 1992.

Vaughan, E. Dean. *The Orkney Springs of Virginia*. New York: Carleton Press, 1982.

Virginia Writers Project (Works Progress Administration). *Virginia: A Guide to the Old Dominion*. New York: Oxford University Press, 1940.

Waddell, Joseph A. *Annals of Augusta County, Virginia, from 1726 to 1871*. 2nd ed. Bridgewater, Va.: C. J. Carrier Company, 1958.

Wayland, John W. *Historic Harrisonburg*. 1949. Reprint, Harrisonburg, Va.: C. J. Carrier Company, 1990.

————. *Historic Homes of Northern Virginia and the Eastern Panhandle of West Virginia*. Staunton, Va.: McClure Publishing Company, 1937.

————. *History of Rockingham County, Virginia*. 1912. Reprint, Harrisonburg, Va.: C. J. Carrier Company, 1980.

————. *History of Shenandoah County, Virginia*. 1927. Reprint. Baltimore: Regional Publishing Company, 1998.

————. *Scenic and Historical Guide to the Shenandoah Valley*. Dayton, Va.: Ruebush, 1923.

————. *Stonewall Jackson's Way*. Staunton, Va.: McClure Company, 1940.

————. *Twenty-five Chapters on the Shenandoah Valley*. 1957. Reprint. Harrisonburg, Va.: C. J. Carrier Company, 1989.

————. *The Valley Turnpike, Winchester to Staunton, and Other Roads*. Winchester, Va.: Winchester–Frederick County Historical Society, 1967.

Williamson, Mary Ann, and Jean Allen Davis. *The History of Edinburg, Virginia*. Stephens City, Va.: Edinburg Heritage Foundation, 1995.

Willis, Carrie Hunter, and Etta Belle Walker. *Legends of the Skyline Drive and the Great Valley of Virginia*. Richmond: Dietz Press, 1937.

Wilson, Howard K. *Great Valley Patriots: Western Virginia in the Struggle for Liberty*. Verona, Va.: McClure Press, 1976.

Wine, J. Floyd. *Life along Holman's Creek*. Self-published, 1982.

Wise, William Harvey. *From the Rhineland to the Promised Land of the Shenandoah*. Lynchburg, Va.: Warwick House Publishers, 2009.

Woodhead, Henry, and Paul Mathless, eds. *Shenandoah 1862: Voices of the Civil War*. Alexandria, Va.: Time-Life Books, 1997.

Wust, Klaus. *The Virginia Germans*. Charlottesville: University Press of Virginia, 1969.

Zapton, Steve. *Singers Glen: Portrait of a Village*. Harrisonburg, Va.: Harrisonburg–Rockingham County Historical Society, 1979.